Narratives of Learning and Teaching EFL

Narratives of Learning and Teaching EFL

Edited by

Paula Kalaja
Vera Menezes
Ana Maria F. Barcelos

palgrave
macmillan

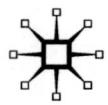

Editorial matter and selection © Paula Kalaja, Vera Menezes and
Ana Maria F. Barcelos 2008
Chapters © their individual authors 2008

All rights reserved. No reproduction, copy or transmission of this
publication may be made without written permission.

No portion of this publication may be reproduced, copied or transmitted
save with written permission or in accordance with the provisions of the
Copyright, Designs and Patents Act 1988, or under the terms of any licence
permitting limited copying issued by the Copyright Licensing Agency,
Saffron House, 6-10 Kirby Street, London EC1N 8TS.

Any person who does any unauthorized act in relation to this publication
may be liable to criminal prosecution and civil claims for damages.

The authors have asserted their rights to be identified as the authors of this
work in accordance with the Copyright, Designs and Patents Act 1988.

First published 2008 by
PALGRAVE MACMILLAN

Palgrave Macmillan in the UK is an imprint of Macmillan Publishers Limited,
registered in England, company number 785998, of Houndmills,
Basingstoke, Hampshire RG21 6XS.

Palgrave Macmillan in the US is a division of St Martin's Press LLC,
175 Fifth Avenue, New York, NY 10010.

Palgrave Macmillan is the global academic imprint of the above companies
and has companies and representatives throughout the world.

Palgrave® and Macmillan® are registered trademarks in the United States,
the United Kingdom, Europe and other countries.

ISBN-13: 978–0–230–54543–4 hardback
ISBN-10: 0–230–54543–2 hardback

This book is printed on paper suitable for recycling and made from fully
managed and sustained forest sources. Logging, pulping and manufacturing
processes are expected to conform to the environmental regulations of
the country of origin.

A catalogue record for this book is available from the British Library.

Library of Congress Cataloging-in-Publication Data

    Narratives of learning and teaching EFL / edited by Paula Kalaja, Vera
Menezes, Ana Maria F. Barcelos.
      p. cm.
    Includes bibliographical references and index.
    ISBN 0–230–54543–2 (alk. paper)
      1. English language – Study and teaching – Foreign speakers.
I. Kalaja, Paula. II. Paiva, Vera Lúcia Menezes de Oliveira e. III. Ferreira,
Ana Maria (Ana Maria Barcelos)

PE1128.A2.N326 2008
428.0071—dc22   2008016163

10 9 8 7 6 5 4 3 2 1
17 16 15 14 13 12 11 10 09 08

Printed and bound in Great Britain by
CPI Antony Rowe, Chippenham and Eastbourne

Contents

List of Tables	vii
List of Figures	viii
Acknowledgements	ix
Notes on Contributors	x

Part I Introduction

1. Narrativising Learning and Teaching EFL: The Beginnings — 3
   Paula Kalaja, Vera Menezes and Ana Maria F. Barcelos

Part II Written Narratives

2. The Seeds of Agency in Language Learning Histories — 17
   Tim Murphey and Christopher Carpenter

3. Learning English: Students' Beliefs and Experiences in Brazil — 35
   Ana Maria F. Barcelos

4. Self-Observation and Reconceptualisation through Narratives and Reflective Practice — 49
   Deise P. Dutra and Heliana Mello

5. Brazilian EFL Teachers' Experiences in Public and Private Schools: Different Contexts with Similar Challenges — 64
   Laura Miccoli

Part III Self-Narratives

6. Turning the Kaleidoscope – EFL Research as Auto/Biography — 83
   Leena Karlsson

7. 'To Speak English Is Tedious': Student Resistance in Japanese University Classrooms — 98
   Keiko Sakui and Neil Cowie

Part IV Oral Narratives

8. Passion and Persistence: Learning English in Akita — 113
   Sara Cotterall

9. Communities of Practice: Stories of Japanese EFL Learners 128
   Garold Murray

10. EFL Narratives and English-Mediated Identities: Two Ships Passing in the Night? 141
    David Block

11. Frequent Flyer: A Narrative of Overseas Study in English 155
    Alice Chik and Phil Benson

Part V Multimodal Narratives

12. Using Photographs to Access Stories of Learning English 171
    Tarja Nikula and Anne Pitkänen-Huhta

13. Self-Portraits of EFL Learners: Finnish Students Draw and Tell 186
    Paula Kalaja, Riikka Alanen and Hannele Dufva

14. Multimedia Language Learning Histories 199
    Vera Menezes

Part VI Conclusion

15. Narrativising Learning and Teaching EFL: Concluding Remarks 217
    Vera Menezes, Ana Maria F. Barcelos and Paula Kalaja

References 233

Index 251

List of Tables

1.1	Summary of Chapters 2 to 14	6
2.1	Negatively and positively coded context factors for all items	23
2.2	Negatively and positively coded common factors for all items	25
13.1	EFL learning: mediational means in the self-portraits	193
13.2	EFL learning: mediational means in the verbal interpretations on the reverse side of the self-portraits	196

List of Figures

2.1	Positive and negative in-school factors	24
2.2	Positive and negative out-of-school factors	24
2.3	Positive and negative general factors	25
2.4	Positive and negative relationship factors	26
2.5	Positive and negative activity factors	26
2.6	Positive and negative 'Q' factors	27
2.7	Proportion of agency coded items	28
2.8	Agency associated context factors	28
2.9	Agency associated common factors	29
12.1	Photographs of school textbooks and a dictionary 'English-Finnish dictionary'	176
12.2	Photographs of skateboarding and snowboarding	181
13.1	An EFL learner without others (originally hair coloured brown)	192
13.2	An EFL learner with others (in black-and-white)	193
13.3	An EFL learner without books (originally in blue-and-white)	194
13.4	An EFL learner with books (originally in bright colours)	194
14.1	Close-up	205
14.2	Manga	205
14.3	In a conference	205
14.4	Boredom	207
14.5	English teacher	207
14.6	The verb *to be*	208

Acknowledgements

This volume has grown out of shared professional interest and cooperation of a number of applied linguists in Finland and Brazil by us jointly attending or organising conferences or seminars in our home countries and elsewhere and compiling and editing another volume (on beliefs about SLA). Importantly, *Narratives of Learning and Teaching EFL* has grown out of other contacts with researchers all over the world sharing our interest in life stories (or self-narratives) as data in doing research on issues related to foreign language learning and teaching (or more specifically, to English as a Foreign Language). As editors, we would like to thank the contributors for their enthusiasm, patience and cooperation in dealing with our questions and suggestions in the editing process over the past two years, and trust in us getting this volume completed. A special thanks goes to Tim Murphey for his constant support and suggestions during this period and to Phil Benson for his idea of inviting the contributors to be the first members of an online forum – http://groups.yahoo.com/group/llh/ – for 'discussion and information exchange on language learning histories and narrative research in language teaching and research'.

We would also like to express our gratitude to all learners and teachers who allowed us to tell their stories. We are also grateful to Vanessa Bohn, Federal University of Minas Gerais, Brazil, for taking care of the AMFALE site, an international narrative databank http://www.veramenezes.com/amfale.htm, where some of the stories mentioned in this volume can be accessed. In addition, we acknowledge the essential support of our own universities – the University of Jyväskylä, Finland, Federal University of Minas Gerais and that of Viçosa, Brazil, and Brazilian research agencies – CNPq and FAPEMIG – in getting this project accomplished.

We would also like to thank Jill Lake of Palgrave Macmillan for her encouragement and experience (wishing her many happy years after her retirement in June 2007) and Melanie Blair and all others involved in the production of this volume. In addition, we are grateful to Terhi Ikonen (at the University of Jyväskylä) for minding some editorial details.

Finally, we are grateful to the anonymous outside reader of the chapters, who turned out to be Dr. Jean-Marc Dewaele. His feedback was indeed valuable in compiling the final version of *Narratives of Learning and Teaching EFL*.

Notes on Contributors

Riikka Alanen is Adjunct Professor in Applied Linguistics at the Centre for Applied Language Studies and Lecturer in Language Pedagogy in the Department of Teacher Education of the University of Jyväskylä, Finland. Her research interests include second/foreign language learning and teaching as mediated activity and metalinguistic awareness. She has written articles in Finnish and English about children's learning of English as a Foreign Language, being also co-editor (with Sari Pöyhönen) of *Language in Action: Vygotsky and Leontievian Legacy Today* (Cambridge Scholars Publishers, (Cambridge Scholars Publishers 2007)).

Ana Maria F. Barcelos (PhD, University of Alabama, Tuscaloosa) is Assistant Professor in the Department of Languages at the Federal University of Viçosa, Brazil, where she teaches English as a Foreign Language and Language Teaching Methods to student teachers. Her research interests are beliefs about language learning and how they relate to the social context of language learning and teaching. She is also co-editor of *Beliefs about SLA: New Research Approaches* (Kluwer 2003), among others.

Phil Benson is Professor in the Department of English at the Hong Kong Institute of Education. He has published widely on the subject of autonomy, including the book *Teaching and Researching Autonomy in Language Learning* (Pearson 2001). His current research interests also include narratives of language learning and teaching, and he is co-editor of the recent collection *Learners' Stories: Difference and Diversity in Language Learning* (Cambridge University Press 2005).

David Block is Reader in Education in the Faculty of Culture and Pedagogy at the Institute of Education, University of London. He has published articles and chapters in a range of applied linguistics and educational journals and books. He is co-editor (with Deborah Cameron) of *Globalization and Language Teaching* (Routledge 2002) and author of *The Social Turn in Second Language Acquisition* (Edinburgh University Press 2003), *Multilingual Identities in a Global City: London Stories* (Palgrave 2006) and *Second Language Identities* (Continuum 2007). His main interests are the impact of globalisation on language practices of all kinds, migration and migrant identities, and the interface between identity and second language learning.

Christopher Carpenter (MA, Georgia State University) teaches at Dokkyo University, Japan, and is co-editor of the semesterly publication *Languaging!*, a newsletter of exploratory learning and teaching. His interests include the support and development of dynamic communities of practice that nurture and sustain autonomous growth and development, whether in the classroom or professional contexts.

Alice Chik is Assistant Professor in the Department of English at the City University of Hong Kong. Her research interests include language learning histories, second language learner identities, language testing policies and popular culture in education.

Sara Cotterall is Associate Professor at Akita International University in Japan. She is an experienced language teacher and teacher educator, and her research interests include language advising, individual differences in second language acquisition and learner strategies.

Neil Cowie teaches English in the Foreign Language Education Centre at Okayama University, Japan. He is especially interested in emotional aspects of studying and teaching foreign languages, and classroom applications of socio-cultural theories of language learning.

Hannele Dufva is Full Professor of Language Education in the Department of Languages at the University of Jyväskylä, Finland. She has explored issues in second and foreign language learning and teaching using a socio-cognitive approach that is based on dialogical thinking. Her work includes papers, edited volumes and textbooks in these areas – both in English and in Finnish. She has co-authored a textbook with Paula Kalaja and worked extensively with Riikka Alanen in examining children's metalinguistic awareness and foreign language learning.

Deise P. Dutra is Associate Professor at the Federal University of Minas Gerais, Brazil. She works as a professor in the English major undergraduate course and also in the Linguistics Studies Program. Her research interests are teacher education and grammar teaching.

Paula Kalaja is Full Professor of English in the Department of Languages at the University of Jyväskylä, Finland. She is an expert on second/foreign language learning and teaching and her research interests include learner identities, beliefs about SLA, motivation, and attributions or explanations that students provide for success or failure in learning foreign languages. She is co-editor of *Beliefs about SLA: New Research Approaches* (Kluwer 2003), among others, and co-author (with Hannele Dufva) of a textbook on language awareness.

Leena Karlsson is Lecturer in English at the University of Helsinki Language Centre, Finland. Her research interests include learner autonomy, autobiographical and experiential foreign language education, and teacher development.

Heliana Mello is Associate Professor of English and Linguistics at the Federal University of Minas Gerais, Brazil. Her research focuses on teacher education, second language acquisition and cognitive linguistics.

Vera Menezes (http://www.veramenezes.com), former president of ALAB (Brazilian Association of Applied Linguistics), is Full Professor at the Federal University of Minas Gerais, Brazil, where she teaches and carries out research on second language acquisition and computer assisted language learning, sponsored by CNPq and FAPEMIG. She is also the editor of *Revista Brasileira de Lingüística Aplicada* (http://www.letras.ufmg.br/rbla/english_version.html).

Laura Miccoli (PhD, OISE, University of Toronto, Canada) is Associate Professor of English and Applied Linguistics at the Federal University of Minas Gerais, Brazil, where she teaches undergraduate and graduate level courses. Her research interests revolve around the concept of experience in EFL classrooms with a focus on the meaning of social and affective events in the teaching and learning processes as well as on particular experiences with evaluation, motivation and autonomy.

Tim Murphey (PhD, Universite de Neuchatel, Switzerland) teaches and learns at Kanda University of International Studies, Japan, and has co-authored, with Zoltan Dörnyei, *Group Dynamics in the Language Classroom* (Cambridge University Press 2003). He explores sociocultural theory, identity issues, and psychological models and their applications to language learning, teaching, and life.

Garold Murray is Professor at Akita International University, Japan. His research interests in the field of language education centre on employing narrative inquiry to explore learner autonomy in classroom, out-of-class, and self-access learning contexts. He is also interested in the development of self-access centres and programmes. In his current position, he has developed two self-access centres, one of which is open to the general public.

Tarja Nikula is Full Professor in the Centre for Applied Language Studies at the University of Jyväskylä, Finland. Her research interests include interpersonal aspects of language use, pragmatics in language learning and teaching, classroom discourse analysis, English-Finnish language contacts, and the role of English in Finnish teenagers' everyday lives.

Anne Pitkänen-Huhta is Senior Lecturer in English in the Department of Languages at the University of Jyväskylä, Finland. Her research interests include literacy practices in formal and informal contexts, multimodal literacies, classroom discourse, and English as a global language, especially in the everyday lives of Finnish teenagers.

Keiko Sakui is Associate Professor at Kobe Shoin Women's University, Japan. Her research interests include learner and teacher beliefs about language learning. She is particularly interested in student resistance, learner motivation and classroom management from the perspective of language teachers.

Part I
Introduction

1
Narrativising Learning and Teaching EFL: The Beginnings

Paula Kalaja, Vera Menezes and Ana Maria F. Barcelos

1 Rationale of *Narratives of Learning and Teaching EFL*

This introductory chapter provides background to the volume at hand, explaining its rationale, describing some specific contexts of learning English to give an idea of their great variety, and finally, providing an overview of its contents.

Mainstream literature has tended to view learning second or foreign languages in terms of the *acquisition* metaphor. Thus, the learner is considered a processor of input and negotiator of meaning with those around him/her, leading ultimately to output (the Input-Interaction-Output or IIO model, for a critical review, see e.g., Block 2003). The teacher, in turn, is one involved in providing input and negotiating meanings. With the acquisition metaphor gradually being replaced by (or complemented with) another one, that is, the *participation* metaphor, learning becomes a matter of the learner actively seeking learning opportunities and being eventually socialised into the practices of a specific group or community and accepted as its member. The active role of the learner also means that learning – and using the second or foreign language – turn(s) into *subjective* experiences, not universal ones, with his/her body, identities and emotions involved, and so the language and its learning get very *personal* meanings. In addition, the teacher becomes a provider of learning opportunities and a guide in the socialisation process. Context opportunities and constraints are also factors to be considered in the complexity of language learning and teaching.

Being aware of these developments, *Narratives of Learning and Teaching EFL* is a compiled collection of articles on *lived experiences of the English* language – with a focus on the subjective meanings (including attitudes and beliefs) and emotions invoked – in English as a Foreign Language (EFL)[1] contexts of learning and/or teaching it or being its learner and/or teacher. In approaching these issues the contributors to this volume make use of fresh theoretical frameworks and innovative methods of data collection and/or analysis, including narratives.[2] As pointed out for example by Benson (2005), narratives are indeed suitable for these purposes. Overall, the chapters make up a cohesive kaleidoscope[3] of different perspectives in research on EFL narratives.

Generally speaking, *Narratives of Learning and Teaching EFL* stands out from previous work on second or foreign language learning and teaching in its:

- unity in the research context: EFL (however, acknowledging diversity within this context, see Section 2), including both formal and informal contexts;
- diversity in focus within the chosen context: learners, teacher trainees and teachers. For example, the collection of articles on second language learning edited by Benson and Nunan (2005) focuses on students or that by Johnson and Golombek (2002) on teachers only;
- diversity in EFL learning and teaching experiences (with attention paid to emotional aspects of the experiences). There are a couple of collections of articles on affect, for example Arnold (1999) and Pavlenko (2006), but the focus of these is on second language learning (not foreign language learning);
- diversity in theoretical frameworks: instead of subscribing to one theoretical framework *Narratives of Learning and Teaching EFL* cherishes the idea of multiplicity in these (for details, see Table 1.1): there are, for example, a few collections of articles on second or foreign language learning conducted within a single framework, for example a Vygotskyan one, consider Lantolf (2000) or Kelly-Hall et al. (2005);
- unity and at the same time diversity in methodology not only in data collection but also in its analysis: the volume extends the types of data used in research on narratives in second and foreign language learning and teaching. Written and oral narratives are complemented with visual (e.g., drawings and photographs) and multimodal ones, thanks to modern information technology (including sounds and pictures). Furthermore, the chapters illustrate two distinct ways of doing research with narratives (however, within a variety of frameworks): *analysis of narratives*[4] in which case data consist of narratives, the analysis of these focusing on aspects of their content and/or form

or *narrative analysis* in which case sets of data are analysed, the outcome being an explanatory narrative. However, a classification into two types like this (with possible overlapping) does not do full justice to the individual chapters and their intricacies, so for details, see Table 1.1 (especially its last two columns).

Importantly, the use of English (and its learning and teaching) are rapidly increasing, and these days especially in the EFL contexts. There are millions and millions (the exact number is not easy to estimate) of citizens living on different continents and in countries ranging from China and Japan to countries in South America and Europe – wishing to learn English for their own specific purposes, and no longer just for international ones but also for national and local ones, including Lingua Franca situations, in which the language is nobody's first language. This is due to the globalisation of the English language and a consequent spread in its uses and users.

2 Contexts of EFL

We opted to use traditional terminology when referring to the contexts where learning and teaching English takes place in our studies (see Endnote 1) but at the same time we do acknowledge their diversity politically, economically, socially as well as culturally. Thus the contributions can only be viewed as illustrating this diversity and by no means exhausting it. However, as a number of the studies have been conducted in three specific countries (on three different continents), that is, Finland, Brazil and Japan, an attempt is made in the following to characterize these, concerning the status of English and its users and uses in these specific contexts of EFL – and in more practical terms, to avoid repetition from one chapter to another.

When comparing the contexts in Sections 2.1 to 2.3, there is huge variation to be noted in the users and uses of the English language and in its perceived importance (in comparison with other foreign languages, too); and furthermore in the challenges of organising teaching and providing learning opportunities for learners, considering, for example, the training of qualified EFL teachers and the production and provision of teaching materials in each country.

2.1 Finland (by Paula Kalaja)

Finland is a Scandinavian welfare state with some 5.2 million inhabitants. There is an established Swedish-speaking minority (5.5 per cent of

Table 1.1 Summary of Chapters 2 to 14

Chapter/author(s)	EFL Context(s): formal or informal	Type of analysis	Participant(s) (Numbers)	Data	Framework/focus
Chapter 2 Tim Murphey and Christopher Carpenter	Japan: (in)formal	Analysis of narratives	University students (20)	Written narratives	Attribution theory: analysis of experiences of EFL learning in terms of contexts, relationship and affective factors, and attributions of hope and agency
Chapter 3 Ana Maria F. Barcelos	Brazil: formal	Analysis of narratives	University students (75)	Written narratives	Content analysis of experiences of and beliefs about EFL learning
Chapter 4 Deise P. Dutra and Heliana Mello	Brazil: formal	Analysis of narratives	Pre- and in-service teachers (2 + 2)	Written narratives, journals	Dewey's educational theory: analysis of experiences of EFL teaching in terms of open-mindedness, responsibility and wholeheartedness
Chapter 5 Laura Miccoli	Brazil: formal	Analysis of narratives	Teachers in public and private schools (14 + 20)	Written narratives	Thematic analysis of experiences of EFL teaching in two types of schools

Chapter 6 Leena Karlsson	Finland: formal	Narrative analysis	University student and teacher/counsellor/scholar	Written narratives, email, interviews, counselling sessions	Reflexive analysis of learning experiences of an EFL learner and (emotional) responses to these by the teacher
Chapter 7 Keiko Sakui and Neil Cowie	Japan: formal	Narrative analysis	University teachers/scholars (2)	Notes/reflections, student evaluations, journals, interviews	(Reflexive) Analysis of resistance patterns by students in EFL classrooms and (emotional) responses to these by teachers
Chapter 8 Sara Cotterall	Japan: formal	Analysis of narratives	Adult learners (3)	Interviews over time (within advising sessions), informal conversations, email	Analysis of EFL learning experiences, incl. beliefs, motives, goals and strategies
Chapter 9 Garold Murray	Japan: (in)formal	Analysis of narratives	Adult learners (3)	Interviews (turned into stories)	Content analysis of the role of (EFL) communities of practice inside the home country (and learner/user identity)
Chapter 10 David Block	Spain: formal	Analysis of narratives	Adult learner	Interviews over time	Analysis of learner identity in an EFL classroom
Chapter 11 Alice Chik and Phil Benson	Hong Kong and the UK: (in)formal	Narrative analysis	Post-graduate student	Interviews over time (turned into a story)	Analysis of overseas experiences, incl. learner/user identity,

Continued

Table 1.1 Continued

Chapter/author(s)	EFL Context(s): formal or informal	Type of analysis	Participant(s) (Numbers)	Data	Framework/focus
					being mistaken for an EFL learner from Mainland China
Chapter 12 Tarja Nikula and Anne Pitkänen-Huhta	Finland: (in)formal	Analysis of narratives	Secondary-school students (5)	Visual narratives: photographs of occasions of using EFL and discussions based on them	(Discursive) Analysis of the role of EFL in the everyday lives of young people (and learner/user identity)
Chapter 13 Paula Kalaja, Riikka Alanen and Hannele Dufva	Finland: (in)formal	Analysis of narratives	University students (110)	Visual narratives: self-portraits (or drawings) of EFL learners and written interpretations of these	Sociocultural theory: analysis of mediational means (e.g., books) resorted to in EFL learning and what their depiction tells of the nature of learning the language (or beliefs about SLA)
Chapter 14 Vera Menezes	Brazil: (in)formal	Analysis of narratives	University students (38)	Multimodal narratives, making use of modern IT (pictures, sounds)	Chaos/complexity theory: analysis of experiences of EFL learning in terms of two distinct but interacting phases of a complex system

the population). Three Sami languages (spoken in the northern most parts of the country) and the Finnish sign language are other minority languages.

Finnish and Swedish are the two official languages of the country, while the Sami languages have a regionally recognised status, and the rights of users of the Finnish sign language have been legally recognized to some extent. Finnish and Swedish have a mandatory status at school: Finnish first-language speakers study Swedish and Swedish first-language speakers Finnish. In addition, there is an increasing number of Russian (0.8 per cent) and Estonian (0.3 per cent) speakers and a number of people speaking other foreign languages, the largest group being speakers of English.

In Finland, English has had the status of EFL, to use the traditional term. However, in the past few decades the uses and users of English have been on the increase because of political, economic and social changes, and thanks to technological innovations. As a result, Finns use English not only when abroad on business or leisure to interact (presumably) with first-language speakers of the language, but also in various domains for example business, education and leisure time in their home country.[5] Besides, most TV programmes of Anglo-American origin are broadcast with subtitles (in Finnish and Swedish), as are films in cinemas. In other words, they are not dubbed. Furthermore, English functions frequently as a Lingua Franca, especially now that Finland has become a member of the European Union (with some 460 million people) and the commercial markets ever more global, with increased mobility of labour and commodities across borders.

Finns start studying the first foreign language in Grade 3 (at the age of nine). In 2005, almost 90 per cent opted for English. Additional foreign languages can be studied from Grade 5 or 7 onwards and in upper secondary school[6] (Grades 10 to 12). In upper secondary school, English is still the most widely studied language, followed by other languages spoken in Europe: German, French, Spanish, Russian and Italian. Before graduating from upper secondary school, students have to pass the Matriculation Examination, a nationally organised set of tests in a number of subjects, some compulsory, others optional. A student is tested on his or her knowledge of Finnish or Swedish as the first language, and up to four foreign languages. In other words, within the Finnish school system there is a great emphasis on learning and teaching foreign languages, with considerable investment of resources by the Government. This is in accordance with the European Union language policy: every citizen is expected to know at least two languages spoken in the area, in addition to their first language. While in the past knowledge of English used to be a privilege of the well-educated few, or of the Elite, as an editorial in *Helsingin Sanomat*, the leading national newspaper, put it in 2003; nowadays (some) use of English can be expected of all Finns.

2.2 Brazil (by Vera Menezes and Ana Maria F. Barcelos)

Brazil is a continental country, the biggest country in South America, with an area of 8,511,965 km2, and estimated population of around 186 million inhabitants, the fifth largest population in the world. Brazil is the only Portuguese-speaking country in South America, but there are around 180 indigenous languages still spoken in reservations. Portuguese is the official language in Brazil, except for the Indian tribes living in remote reservations and their languages. Besides, a sign language called LIBRAS has just gained a mandatory status in Portuguese teacher education. Brazil has received a large number of immigrants and bilingual communities speak varieties of Italian, German, Polish or Japanese languages, but Portuguese is the only language of daily life. It has a mandatory status in schools, and these are supposed to teach at least one foreign language, too.

English has had the status of EFL in Brazil, although in some circles it can be used as a Lingua Franca for business, tourism, education, etc. It is worth mentioning that English pervades the entertainment industry and that Channel TV functions as a kind of an immersion context for the Elite with programmes broadcast with subtitles – in contrast to Open TV where films are dubbed.

According to Brazilian educational laws, foreign languages should be taught to children from around the age of ten until they graduate from high school. English is taught all over the country from Grade 5 (from the age of 10 or 11) until secondary school (up to Grade 8) or high school (Grades 9 to 12), students being 17 years of age by that time. Few schools offer other foreign languages, although teaching Spanish is growing as it has recently become mandatory in high school. In fact, students usually do not have much of a choice in regular schools: most offer only English.

In the majority of regular schools, English is taught from Grade 5 onwards with at most two classes a week of 50 minutes each. As salaries tend to be low, Brazilian teachers teach many classes per day and most of them complain that their classrooms are rather crowded (with around 30 to 40 students).

However, middle-class Brazilians usually start to study English at the age of seven by attending private schools or taking private courses.

Private schools are commercial institutions (some of these are bi-national centres financed by the American or British Government) and they offer classes in English as well as other languages such as German, French, Spanish and Italian for people who can pay for courses. Some of these institutions may offer scholarships for people who cannot afford them otherwise.

2.3 Japan (by Tim Murphey and his colleague Charles Browne, both with long academic careers in the country as occasional teacher trainers for the Ministry of Education and various prefectures)[7]

Japan, an Eastern Asian island chain between the North Pacific Ocean and the Sea of Japan, east of the Korean Peninsula, is officially a constitutional monarchy with a parliamentary government. Slightly smaller than California, Japan is mostly rugged and mountainous. Since the end of World War Two, the basic structure of the Japanese educational system has been very similar to America's with its six years of elementary school (*shougakkou*), three years of junior high school (*chugakkou*), three years of high school (*koukou*) and either two years of junior college (*tankadaigaku* or *karejji*) or four years of university (*daigaku*). Education is compulsory until 15, but about 90 per cent of the people complete high school and 40 per cent graduate from university or college.

Reiko Hatori (2005) usefully describes the linguistic environment in Japan:

> Japan is sometimes misconceived as a homogeneous country, even by politicians. In reality 127.5 million 'Japanese' (Foreign Press Center Japan, n.d.) include two indigenous groups, Ainus and Okinawans. Because the census does not include ethnicity, the population and the numbers of the speakers of indigenous languages are unknown, leaving them categorized as 'Japanese'.

In addition to the indigenous population, in 2002 there were nearly two million foreign residents, 33.8 per cent of whom are South and North Korean nationals and 22 per cent Chinese nationals (Foreign Press Center Japan, n.d.). These statistics do not include people who have been naturalised as Japanese citizens, and the number of people from Korean and Chinese heritage backgrounds is also quite considerable. In 2002, nearly six million foreign visitors came to Japan, and the number of foreign students 'reached a record high of 109,508' in 2003 (Foreign Press Center Japan, n.d.). The majority of the foreign residents, visitors and students are from Asian countries. While junior and senior high schools can choose to teach a variety of foreign languages the vast majority teach only English with a select few teaching Korean, Chinese, French, German, or Spanish.

English education has benefited from a certain priority status for quite some time in Japan. Yet it is still not seen as being very efficient due to (1) the influence of traditional university entrance exams, which until recently did not test listening comprehension skills (and still does not assess speaking ability), (2) the dominance of grammar-translation teaching methods and (3) the severe lack of pre-service and in-service training for English teachers. Another contributing factor is that classes in regular schools are large, with junior high schools averaging 34.3 students, about 30 per cent more students than in other Organisation for Economic Co-operation and Development (OECD) countries (MEXT 2005, p. 23). This has led to a thriving cram school and conversation school industry to supplement the official school system. The conversation schools also often offer courses in other foreign languages as well, and there are regular TV programmes for learning the six major foreign languages. While CNN and cable movie channels are available, there are no foreign language TV channels in Japan.

In reaction to this lack of efficiency with regard to English education, in 2003, the Ministry of Education proclaimed the 'Action Plan to Cultivate Japanese with English Abilities' which funded a variety of educational initiatives including a call to send at least 10,000 high school students to study English abroad annually, giving primary schools the right to begin English lessons in the third grade as part of their Integrated Study curriculum, including for the first time criterion-based assessment of student ability via such measures as the STEP and TOEIC tests, short term funding for in-service training in EFL methodology for junior and senior high school teachers, and the creation of more than 100 accredited high schools throughout Japan known as 'Super English Language High Schools' (SelHi), for the purpose of creating and researching new and more effective ways of teaching English as a foreign language. Though ambitious-sounding, independent research has shown decidedly mixed results. In 2006, MEXT finally included a listening portion on their national Center Exam, which many universities use as part of their entrance procedures, something that Korea and China did decades ago.

Thus, while English enjoys a high status in part due to its necessity for globalisation, traditional teaching methods, high-stakes testing, and large class sizes have kept much of the population in the dark ages of language learning. Things do appear to be changing slowly, however, and the host of recent initiatives may be evidence that enlightenment and a desire for more practical and communicative English instruction is finally dawning.

3 Organisation of *Narratives of Learning and Teaching EFL*

The volume consists of an Introduction (Chapter 1), laying out the rationale of the collection and providing an overview of its contents. This is followed by a number of chapters (Chapters 2 to 14) by individual contributors, divided into four sections based on what type of data was made use of and who produced and analysed the stories: (1) written narratives, or more specifically, language learning histories (LLHs), (2) self-narratives, (3) oral narratives, and (4) multimodal narratives. Each chapter has either theoretically and/or methodologically something new and innovative to contribute to the existing knowledge concerning the issues addressed. As far as possible, the 13 Chapters follow the same overall organisation of an empirical research report, starting off with Introduction, Background, Data collection and analysis, Findings, and closing with Discussion, including Implications, and Conclusion. *Narratives of Learning and Teaching EFL* closes with a Conclusion (Chapter 15) that comments on the preceding chapters, pointing out similarities and differences in the studies reported, evaluating the work done so far, and suggesting directions for further research.

Table 1.1 is a summary of the contributions by the authors: by context of study, type of analysis, data, participants and framework and/or focus.

Organised in this way it is easy to see how the chapters are similar or different, or how they complement one another. However, at this point we wish to stress that the volume is far from exhausting, rather it illustrates ways of conducting research that could be carried out in yet other contexts of EFL or even beyond (say in ESL contexts), or applied to other second or foreign languages and their learning and teaching.

As editors, we acknowledge the kaleidoscope of contexts, experiences and theoretical lenses in portraying the complexity of learning and teaching EFL. We do not advocate in favour of this or that approach, but of a multidisciplinary perspective which can show the different images at each turn of the kaleidoscope.

Notes

1. We decided to stick to traditional terminology (i.e., *EFL* as opposed to English as a Second Language, ESL) instead of making use of some more recent terminology such as that of Braj Kachru (Expanding Circle as opposed to Inner Circle and Outer Circle) or more novel terms such as Type B macro-acquisition as opposed to Type A (Brutt-Griffler 2002), or English as a Lingua Franca (ELF) (e.g., Jenkins 2007).
2. As for key terminology, we opted for the term *narrative*, however, being aware of alternatives, such as (auto)biography, (self-)narrative, life stories, and a more specific term, that is, language learning histories or LLHs; for a nice summary in the context of second language learning, see Benson (2005).
3. Inspired by Chapter 6 written by Leena Karlsson, we extended the metaphor of kaleidoscope to cover all types of narrative research on learning and teaching EFL.
4. As mentioned, Polkinghorne (1995) divides ways of doing narrative research into two types; Lieblich et al. (1998) into four types: holistic-content vs. holistic-form; categorical-content vs. categorical-form; and most recently; Pavlenko (2007) into three types: analysis of subject reality (as a rule, making use of content or thematic analysis), life reality, and text reality.
5. A research project *English Voices in Finnish Society* addresses these issues. It is a project funded by the Academy of Finland and part of a Centre of Excellence in Research *The Study of Variation, Contact and Change in English*, or VARIENG, a joint venture of the University of Helsinki and University of Jyväskylä, Finland.
6. School terminology is problematic, so please note that it varies from one section to another of this chapter and later on from one chapter to another.
7. We wish to thank Dr Tim Murphey and Professor Charles Browne (Meiji Gakuin University) for providing us with this description.

Part II
Written Narratives

2
The Seeds of Agency in Language Learning Histories*

Tim Murphey and Christopher Carpenter

1 Introduction

Studies of attribution theory (for a short review from the perspective of Second Language Acquisition (SLA), see Kalaja 2004) have demonstrated the relationship between the causes to which people attribute their successes and failures and their subsequent behaviours. If people's beliefs form the basis of their behaviour, there is much to be learned in an investigation of those beliefs. Thus it is pertinent for teachers to ask: To what factors do learners attribute their successes? And by what variables and in what contexts are learners more likely to attribute their successes, and failures, to factors within their own control? One rich source of data on student beliefs and perceptions can be found in their own narratives of their learning experiences recorded in the form of language learning histories (LLHs).

Our analysis is also informed by recent meta-analytic reviews of 40 years of psychotherapy research highlighting the 'common factors' which lead to psychological improvements in clients regardless of the particular techniques involved (Hubble et al. 1999). Once dismissed as 'placebo effect,' factors such as setting, relationship, beliefs and expectancy were found to be much more important than methodology. Murphy (1999, p. 365), investigating the efficacy of therapy in educational settings, finds some compelling parallels between the fields and notes that, 'just as effective psychotherapy requires the client's active participation, the success of teaching rests largely on the student's involvement in the learning process.' Indeed, *empowering individual agency* may be the most important step for success in both disciplines. Consistent with attribution theory, this research supports teachers confirming useful behaviours so that learners might recognise their own agency in their learning and engage in such behaviours more robustly, helping them learn more effectively in and out of the classroom.

From the perspective of socio-cultural theory and learner subjectivities, a discourse of agency attribution (i.e., blaming students for their successes) within a social group may also be a 'social capital' generator. Identity is closely tied to the communities in which we imagine ourselves as actors and agents. The degree to which we can avail ourselves of the resources of these communities, whether material or symbolic, can be defined as social capital (Portes 1998). A discussion of the beliefs of students should also consider the social contexts in which the learner perceives their actions, and the communities to which they claim membership.

This exploratory study investigates such questions through the analysis of LLHs written by students studying English at a medium sized university in Japan. Similar to the attribution analysis or Discursive Action Model (DAM) of Kalaja (2004), in this chapter we investigate our students' LLHs for the prevalence of a range of factors in and out-of-school as well as to what degree they attribute the outcome of their experiences to external factors or to their own agency. We look especially at instances of agency and how they interact with other elements in the composition of a student's LLH.

2 Background

2.1 Agency and hope

People, who are able to pursue their goals and create various pathways, experience a feeling of empowerment that may in itself be one of the keys to their progress. Snyder et al. (1999) explain these modes of thinking as *agency thinking*, the determination to meet certain goals, and *pathways thinking*, the ability to imagine and find possible routes to these goals. On the other hand, when people find their pathways blocked, or when they cannot think of how to begin and execute a plan toward their goal, they often become demoralised. Their feeling of powerlessness is caused by their modes of thinking, which may in turn be caused by both psychological and actual barriers. Therefore, the therapist does well to both confirm their client's acts of agency and to model hopefulness, producing, in our terms, an empowering discourse of agency attribution.

In education, a look at motivation from the perspective of hope, agency, and expectancy, shifts the discourse away from the methodological approach of the teacher to the evolving identity of the learner.

Like a self-fulfilling prophecy, if students expect to learn, they are more likely to do so, and if they recognise the effects of their own agency, they are more likely to exercise agency and pathways thinking in the future.

In psychotherapy, expectancies were also supported when clients had confidence in the 'therapeutic myth' of the therapists' methodologies, but this held constant across methodologies. As Snyder et al. (1999, p. 188) suggest, 'the more important issue is the degree to which given therapeutic approaches derive their effectiveness through teaching people to have productive pathways to reach their goals and fostering the determination to use those pathways.' Applied to the field of language teaching, these ideas suggest again that teachers should think more in terms of how they are scaffolding the *agency* and *pathways thinking* of their students, and whether they are confirming the agency that students demonstrate. Such a discourse initiated within a learning community could be called *a discourse of attribution*, a discourse which holds students accountable for their own learning and attributes progress to factors within their own control, in other words, a discourse that 'blames' a student for their successes (Murphy 1999). Seeing themselves as active agents, who can make learning happen with their peers (as might be brought to their attention by their teachers, see Johnston 2004), may further reinforce learner agency by validating the social networks and cultural information they have around them.

2.2 The social capital of interaction

The term *social capital* was first introduced by Bourdieu (1985). Sociologists have come to define social capital as 'The ability of actors to secure benefits by virtue of membership in social networks or other social structures' (Portes 1998, p. 6). Hooker et al. (2003, pp. 231–2) propose that, 'we can use social capital to mean the social resources and relationships that assist an individual in the developing vocational and career opportunities that would otherwise not exist.'

From this perspective, the positive interactive relationships among classmates and the teacher create social capital for students, and perhaps is one of the most important and under-emphasised aspects of good classroom dynamics (Murphey 1998a; Dörnyei and Murphey 2003). When a student finds others in the class with similar interests, or is able to identify with a group working toward common goals, she is networking and her social and cultural capital become greater. Because she begins to recognise a *community of practice* (Wenger 1998) that welcomes and values her and her knowledge, she starts identifying more with the class and finds it's a place she enjoys going to – both she and her knowledge are worth something. Agency interacts with social and cultural capital in a catalytic manner and they can mutually increase each other. Nevertheless, we have also seen how some people can show lots of agency thinking but lack the social skills to build their social networks or the cultural knowledge to become a part of a group (e.g., lawyers, doctors, etc.). Thus, while these three help to construct each other, the lack of any one can impinge upon the development of the others (see also Block this volume).

When people in a group can help each other increase social capital and agency intensively for an extended period, they have formed an effective ecology for learning (Hawkins 2005), an affinity space (Gee 2004) in which collaboration, acceptance, and empowerment happen naturally. One indication of an effective ecology in an English as a Foreign Language (EFL) class is when students say that the best thing about their classes is that, 'I made many friends, and I did it in English.' Teachers may then know the atmosphere is appropriately stimulating and students are acquiring the cultural capital of another language through the social capital of supportive relationships. In the present study, we were interested to see to what degree students recognised the interaction of social and cultural capital with their individual agency as facilitators of their success in language learning.

2.3 Exploring language learning histories qualitatively

Personal narratives of language learning have been given attention for the insight that they might provide concerning personal investments in language learning (see, Block this volume; Pavlenko and Lantolf 2000). Learners' stories can also provide researchers with data concerning the typical psychological differences concerning motivation, affect, age, learning strategies and identity, as well as the typical settings for learning: classroom, distant learning, and self-instruction (Benson and Nunan 2005). Research is showing that the social construction in action of learners' imagined communities (Norton 2001) nourishes investments in learning (Norton 2000) and the building of new identities as L2 users (Cook 1999). Most of this research has been done in ESL contexts and thus the need for more EFL research.

LLHs, while perhaps problematic to code, are more emic than questionnaires, in other words, they offer more insight into the meaningful aspects of learning from the perspective of the students themselves. Writing about beliefs elicited by standard Likert scaled questionnaires, Dufva (2003, p. 148) argues that 'positivist experimental and quantitative approaches (such as surveys) are slightly problematic in the sense that they do not measure beliefs but, rather responses to the researcher's formulation of a belief.' The LLHs in our sample are also certainly influenced by our prompt questions used to help students generate ideas, but we believe the freedom that the students had in crafting their narratives gives room for more genuine interpretation of their experiences.

The beneficial aspects of asking students to reflect on their own experiences of language learning has been explored for over a decade now (Murphey et al. 2005). Most students report periods of progressive learning spurred by particular social encounters involving *language use*. These are mixed with other periods of frustration with *educational abuse*, in which language is often taught just for exams. Barcelos and Kalaja's (2003, pp. 232–3) depiction of student and teacher beliefs could also be used to describe LLHs. For them, beliefs are 'dynamic and emergent', 'socially constructed and contextually situated,' 'experiential,' 'mediated', and 'contradictory.' In this continual flux, we scaffold student agency and appropriation of social voices and cultural knowledge through eliciting our student voices in LLHs. In other words, by collaboratively *asking* in supportive groups we display and create agency and manoeuvre our way into social-capital-generating environments, hothouses of SLA. Or in Dufva's (2003, p. 148) ventriloquation of Bakhtin, 'Being in the world is fundamentally a dialogue with the world, a process of asking questions.'

In summary, the discourse in LLHs is particularly suitable for analysing the attributions students make regarding causes of their learning as they relate to the construction of learner subjectivities and communities. These narratives can reveal contexts in which students recognise and value their own agency and in which they perceive their learning as an investment in social capital. How students explain their learning and display agency are the questions under investigation in this study.

3 Methods

3.1 Participants, context, and instructions

The present data set comes from 20 students (4 males and 16 females) from a university English Department in Japan. Students were enrolled in an elective English communication course in which the main pedagogical emphasis was on developing communicative competence and confidence. They were asked to write their LLHs in the fall of 2006 (see http://www.veramenezes.com/nar_tim.htm for complete instructions). The average length of each LLH was 680 words. Below we sketch out our coding procedure and then proceed to provide data from the histories.

3.2 Exploratory coding procedure and rationale

Taking our cues from research in the field of psychotherapy, we analysed the 20 LLHs for 'what works' for language learners. The LLHs are subjectively constructed narratives that have much to reveal about the learner's thoughts and attitudes, and our quantitative analysis is meant to elucidate certain aspects and general trends within this group of learners. We gave particular attention to factors that learners reported as useful, helpful, or encouraging, and instances in which learner agency was evident. Each LLH was coded for a matrix of such factors through three periods: 'early childhood and junior high school', 'high school,' and 'university.'

The factors analysed quantitatively include the following:

- *Positive or Negative*: Each item of analysis (from a phrase to several phrases in length) in the context of students' narratives was coded as positive (i.e., useful, helpful, or encouraging) or negative (not useful, not helpful, or not encouraging);
- *Learning context*: 'In School,' 'Out-of-School,' or 'General.' Each item was coded for context (i.e., the environment of a reported experience, where an activity was initiated, where a relationship was formed, as well as the context of other more qualitative expressions);
- *Active Factors*: 'Relationships,' 'Activities,' 'Qualitative Aspects.' All relationships that students reported as relevant to their learning were coded, not simply relationships with teachers. Techniques and methods of learning were most clearly expressed as activities, whether in formal educational settings or outside of such settings. 'Qualitative aspects' was a default category that included very general affective statements about learning;
- *Agency*: Each item showing evidence of agency was also coded. Using the framework of 'hope' or expectancy as outlined by Snyder et al. (1999), examples of both 'agency thinking' and 'pathways thinking' were coded.

After the coding protocol was formalised, the inter-rater reliability of the two researchers was calculated to be around 90 per cent. When coding of the LLHs was completed, the data was sorted into the three time periods. It was then compiled, and analysed for strong trends and correlations.

4 Results of quantitative analysis

Although there were only 20 LLHs, a total of 586 items were coded and analysed. Below we report on the results of analysis of each of the axis of our coding matrix (the context factors and active factors) and the pattern of distribution for items coded with agency. Discussion of these results will follow in a separate section.

4.1 Context factors

In Table 2.1 we can see the whole number totals for negatively and positively coded context factors with a combined total of 586 items (IS = 'In-School'; OS = 'Out-of-School'; G = 'General').

While there were very few items that were negatively coded out-of-school or in the general category (in which students could express their agency more freely), the in-school (IS) category had about a third of the items negatively coded.

In Figures 2.1–2.3 we can see this same data as it was distributed across the three educational time frames discussed in the LLHs (from childhood to junior high school (Ch/JHS), senior high school (HS) and university (U)), looking at the three context factors separately (expressed as percentages of the total items in the respective time frame). In each graph, the solid line represents the trend of change for positively coded items and the dashed line that of the negatively coded items, with the three points along each line marking the percentage of total items within a given time frame. Figure 2.1 indicates positive and negative *in-school* factors, Figure 2.2, positive and negative *out-of-school* factors, and Figure 2.3, positive and negative inter-contextual or *general* factors.

Positively coded items during the *high-school* time frame in both *in-school* and *out-of-school* contexts drop remarkably (n.b. given the small sample size these changes could not be called statistically significant). In the *in-school* context this is accompanied with an almost equal rise in the number of negatively coded items. Positively coded *general*

Table 2.1 Negatively and positively coded context factors for all items

	IS	OS	G	Totals
Positive (+)	208	154	90	452
Negative (−)	107	8	19	134
Totals	315	162	109	586

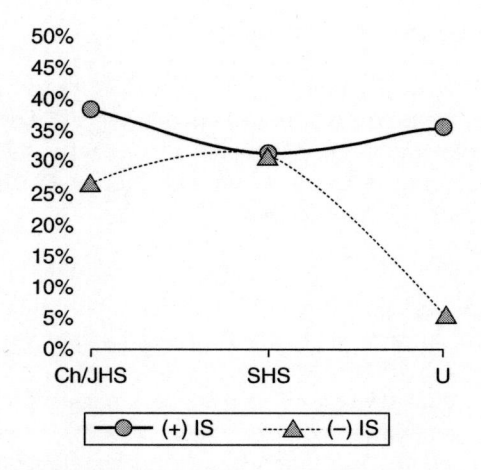

Figure 2.1 Positive and negative in-school factors

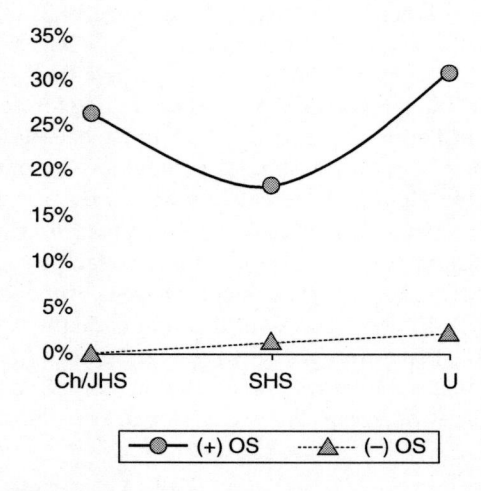

Figure 2.2 Positive and negative out-of-school factors

context factors, however, show a steady increase, with negatives rising slightly during high school. In all contexts, positive factors go up during the *university* time frame, with only *in-school* factors failing to exceed the standard set in the *childhood-to-junior-high-school* timeframe.

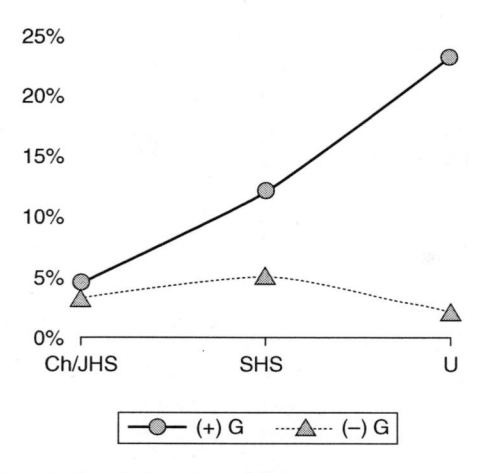

Figure 2.3 Positive and negative general factors

Table 2.2 Negatively and positively coded common factors for all items

	R	A	Q	Totals
Positive (+)	89	195	168	452
Negative (−)	4	75	55	134
Totals	93	270	223	586

4.2 Active factors

In Table 2.2 below we can see the whole number totals for negatively and positively coded active factors. The active factors again include items coded for relationships (R), activities (A), and quality (Q), a category we will discuss in more detail.

4.2.1 Common factors for all items

In Figures 2.4–2.6 we can see this same data as it was distributed across the three educational time frames discussed in the LLHs (from childhood to junior high school (Ch/JHS), senior high school (SHS) and university (U)), looking at the three active factors separately (expressed as percentages of the total items in the respective time frame). In each graph, the solid line represents the trend of change for positively coded

26 *Narratives of Learning and Teaching EFL*

items and the dashed line that of the negatively coded items, with the three points along each line marking the percentage of total items within a given time frame coded positive or negative for the variable in question. Figure 2.4 indicates positive and negative *relationship* factors, Figure 2.5, positive and negative *activity* factors, and Figure 2.6, positive and negative Q factors.

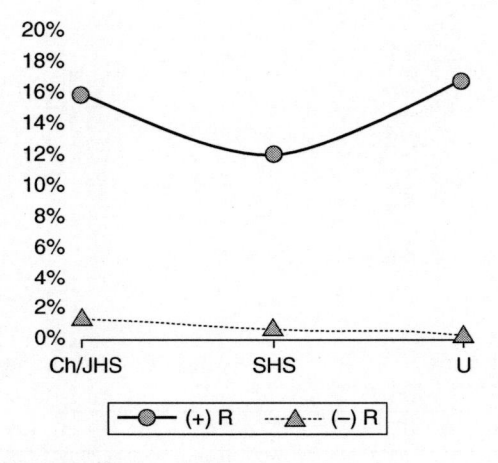

Figure 2.4 Positive and negative relationship factors

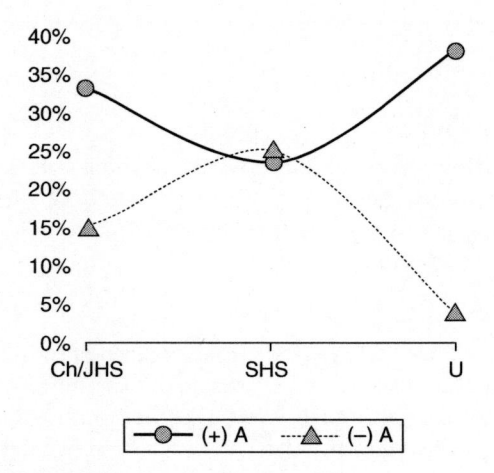

Figure 2.5 Positive and negative activity factors

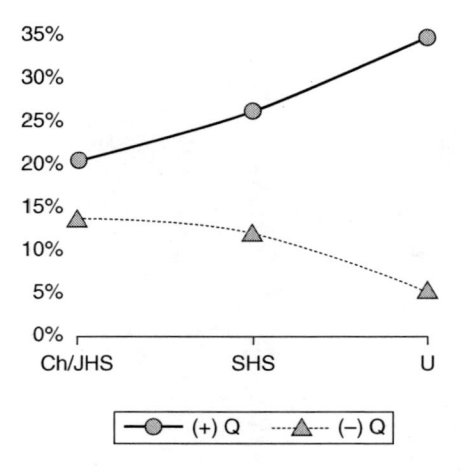

Figure 2.6 Positive and negative 'Q' factors

Again we see a drop in the positively coded items for both *relationship* and *activity* factors during the *high-school* time frame in Figures 2.4 and 2.5. In the case of *activity* factors, this is accompanied by a sharp increase in negatively coded items, actually rising higher than positively coded items (25 per cent negative; 24 per cent positive). Among the Q factors seen in Figure 2.6, often representing simple qualitative statements, we see a steady rise in positive factors from the childhood/junior high school time period, with an almost equal drop in negative factors.

4.3 Agency

Out of 586 items, 120, or 20 per cent, were coded as showing agency (decision making, hope, expectancy). The diagrams below show the proportion of agency-coded items in each time frame (Figure 2.7), the trend of agency associated context factors (Figure 2.8) and that of agency associated active factors (Figure 2.9).

Figure 2.7 shows a steady and continual rise in agency-coded items through time frames. Figure 2.8 shows us that agency-coded items associated with *out-of-school* factors remain steady from junior high school to high school, but then double in university. Curiously, on the other hand, agency-coded items associated with *in-school* factors drop slightly in university, after having increased in high school. Figure 2.9 shows us a steady increase in the number of agency-coded items

28 *Narratives of Learning and Teaching EFL*

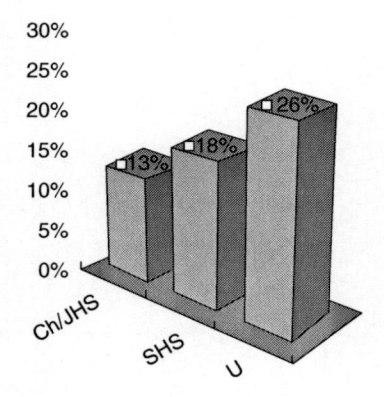

Figure 2.7 Proportion of agency coded items

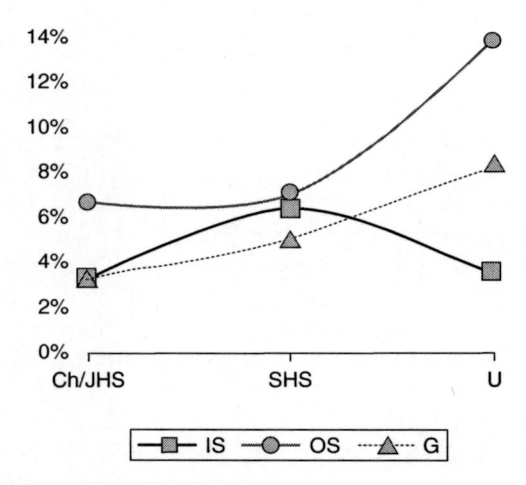

Figure 2.8 Agency associated context factors

associated with *activity*s through university. On the other hand, there is a drop in such items associated with *relationships* after high school.

5 Discussion

5.1 Trends and tendencies of attribution

Reading these narratives, one is struck by the intensely personalised nature of the learning experience for these students despite the many

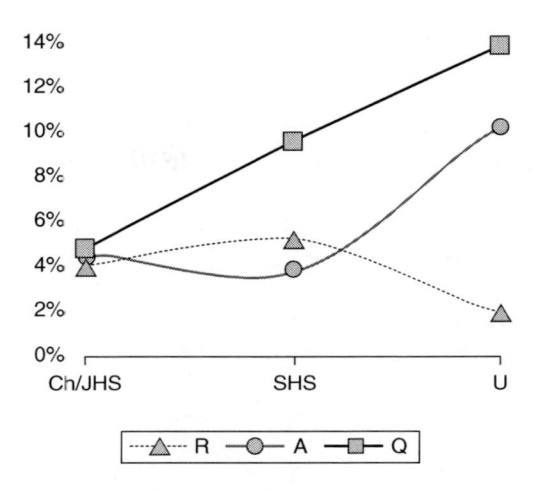

Figure 2.9 Agency associated common factors

experiences they have shared in the Japanese educational system and as moderately successful English learners (who are now majoring in the language in university). Predictably, students report a much higher rate of negative associations *in-school* than *out-of-school*. After all, English is a school subject and experiences outside of this context are generally fortuitous. On the other hand, negative associations with the *in-school* context seem to drop sharply after high school where they peaked. At the same time, both *in-school* and *out-of-school* contexts show a drop in positive associations in the high-school time frame.

It is important to remember that this study was done in Japan, a context in which English represents a major obstacle to be overcome during high school while preparing for university entrance exams. Despite this role for English in general education, it is interesting to note that while *in-school* factors accounted for 46 per cent of the positively coded items, 54 per cent of these items (34 per cent out-of-school + 20 per cent general) were not specifically *in-school*. In other words, in recounting their learning histories, more than half of what students attributed to their learning was not directly associated with learning in an academic context. This would seem to parallel studies in the field of psychotherapy which found extra-therapeutic factors accounting for 40 per cent of what 'works' (Assay and Lambert 1999).

Looking at the active factors, 46 per cent of all items were associated with *activities*. Students were influenced by examples and prompt questions which they referred to while writing their LLHs. Thus it may be even more surprising that among positively coded active factors, 57 per cent were not specifically activity factors; that is, they were items reporting on relationships (20 per cent) or Q factors (37 per cent). The relationship category included all relationships that students reported as relevant to their learning experiences and did not differentiate between relationships with teachers, classmates, or others. However, our impression was that the majority of relationship-coded items were associated with classmates and near peers. Often students talked about relationships in their community of learners that were influential in their learning. As one student recalls of her junior high school experience, *'Some of my friends had already studied [English] when they were elementary school students. So, they could understand what English teachers said. But I couldn't.'* It is also important to note that this group of learners reports a strong relationship influence in the initial period of their learning (the childhood to junior high-school time frame). This may indicate an early learning variable that correlates with future success.

The qualitative category presented us with some difficulty and became somewhat of a default category for items that were not specifically limited to the categories of activities or relationships. The label 'qualitative' was at first meant to denote items that were more of an affective quality: *I started studying English when I was 12 years old. I really liked studying English, because English was totally new to me.* Such statements, however, often were related to with a number of other factors. A re-examination of Q coded items reveals that these items often seem to address the environment of learning (not to be confused with the context): *When I entered JHS, I started to study English. Fortunately, my English teachers in my JHS were good, it was easy to understand, and I enjoyed classes.* The learning environment is of course influenced by a number of factors, including relationships, activities and context. Perhaps there is a parallel to the concept of 'therapeutic setting' discussed in the psychotherapy context (Hubble et al. 1999). Further analysis would be necessary to untangle the various factors surfacing within the category of Q. Still, it is interesting to note that, as found in psychotherapy, students attribute a great part of their learning to non-methodological factors.

5.2 Emergent agency in social capital

Of all coded items in the LLHs, 20 per cent were associated with agency thinking. We can again note a resonance with studies in psychotherapy finding that at least 15 per cent of client progress could be linked to such thinking (Assay and Lambert 1999). Furthermore, there is an increase in agency-linked items through the time frames, with the most marked jump seen in university. One aspect of the attributions that the coded data does not reveal, however, is the complexity of the relationship between agency and other people. In fact, we have seen that there is a small drop in the association of agency with *relationship* factors in university, something we need to think about more.

While students begin applying more agency thinking in university to help themselves progress in their language learning, meeting new friends becomes easier. This is in sharp contrast to, say, the Japanese high school environment where students are marched through their years in set groups, with rigid guidelines for interaction and almost no interaction with students outside of their immediate group. The LLHs reveals a much more complex picture in university:

> Fortunately I could get over [depression] helped by one of my friend...His motivation to improve his English is really incredible!...he had great influence on me, and I was inspired. Then I tried to study hard and at last I could get good grades in the second year's spring semester.

Here we see the direct effects of a near peer role model (Murphey and Arao 2001) on the agency thinking of a classmate. One of the recurring patterns in many of the LLHs is how agency often originates through social capital, that is, the networking with peers and others. It is through such interactions that we are able to find new pathways and new models of persistence. Attributions associated with agency seem to be sadly missing from many of these narratives until university. Indeed, previous research has shown that there is not much interaction at all in the target language before university (Murphey 2002, 2004), thus, the social and cultural capital in which SLA agency grows simply is not there. We ask ourselves how we as teachers can engender more agency and social capital for students. Understanding the power of creating a good group dynamic (Dörnyei and Murphey 2003), that is, a supportive and interactive group climate gets us part way there, but we suspect there is more to it.

We find that students who show agency seem to construct identities and communities at the same time and develop their abilities more quickly through increasing social capital. For example, one student who made an effort to meet foreign students in Japan and go to parties with them said quite explicitly: *'I could make good circumstances to study*

English with fun. I think that kind of circumstances don't appear if you are just waiting, but if you try to make it with great effort, then that attitude will naturally attract the good circumstance'.

At the same time, other students seem to be at a loss with vague pathways that seem to have little attraction to them. It is interesting to note that even successful students may feel unfulfilled in environments that don't encourage agency, as seems to be the case with this student reflecting on her high school experience: *'When I entered HS, I liked English as well as in JHS. And my motivation for learning English was high, but I did nothing special except prepare for classes and test. My scores of English tests were high, so maybe I was satisfied'.*

5.3 Future research

Through attribution analyses of student narratives, we can uncover valuable insights into how students perceive their learning processes and how to positively empower our students with greater agency. There are still many limitations to this exploratory study; we analysed only 20 LLHs, all by Japanese university students, too few and homogeneous to generalise; there were many factors influencing the data, such as context of writing, structure of the assignment and instructions. Still, we believe that such analyses have the potential to elucidate the learning process.

Conducting attribution research with a greater number of LLHs could of course tell us even more and give more weight to our conclusions. Kalaja (2004) and other researchers have already started us off in this direction. Projects such as Vera Menezes's LLH E-Collection in Brazil are developing rich databases of student narratives for more extensive research in the future.

6 Conclusion

In this attribution analysis of 20 university students' LLHs, we investigated a wide range of factors common to learning in most contexts and looked closely at the part agency played. Our data shows a drop in high school in terms of enjoyment and agency with a marked rise in university, due most probably to the extreme pressure of university entrance exams. We think that teachers might improve the situation by fostering agency through 'blaming' the students for their successes and improvements, and thus stimulate the emergence of social capital and learner autonomy.

At another level, we have learned from the psychotherapy common factors that the act of asking is itself a way of stimulating reflection and scaffolding agency, but as attribution theory suggests, the questions we ask and the way we ask must be carefully considered. We have learned that we can empower students to succeed by stimulating their agency thinking and their investment in communities in which their learning generates social and cultural capital. We think that teachers can increase student agency when they encourage students to notice their own part in their progress. When teachers openly attribute student success to their own efforts (e.g., through showcasing student agency in class newsletters, videos, and online), students learn to take more responsibility for their learning and to act with more agency and self-determination (Deci and Ryan 2002).

We have learned also that student-teacher relationships need more care and research so that they might become even more empowering and less de-motivating (Falout and Falout 2005). Furthermore, the importance of relationships with near peers and others played a crucial part in the LLHs (Murphey and Arao 2001). This suggests that teachers should focus on rapport building among all parties in the learning context.

At still another level, we, ourselves, are 'asking our way to agency' for it is in asking 'What works?' that we, and researchers in any field, find pathways and construct socio-cultural capital. Asking, it seems, is a fractal pattern generating agency that replicates itself up from the single student struggling to understand a foreign language and asking how they might do it better, to a system wide search for better methods which finds that 'which method' is less important than the *asking about* and confirming of whatever methods learners use to engage with learning. We suspect that in most cases the asking will emically lead learners to a variety of methods, role models, and pathways, permitting them to ecologically and continually adjust the conditions in their environments, and construct social and cultural capital for each other in effective communities of practice (Wenger 1998). We find this parallels somewhat the Socratic method of asking students questions and is also one of the principal tools of psychotherapy. It also reminds us of Goethe's call for recognition of the dynamic capacity of active agency, 'Whatever you can do or dream you can, begin it. Boldness has genius, power and magic in it.' Asking is the door opening to 'whatever you can do or dream you can.'

As teachers, we hope to encourage communities of inquiry, *learning ecologies* (Hawkins 2005) and *affinity spaces* (Gee 2004), inviting the cultivation and consideration of student agency and voice (Thiessen 2006), rather than behaving as if we were mechanically producing goods or banking knowledge (Freire 2000). In such communities, ecologies, and spaces, we need to be open to learning ourselves and to letting go of our obsession with methods, as we begin to understand the power of asking about and confirming individual agency, relationship support, and the creation of students' social capital.

Note

* We would like to thank Jim Elwood, Mika Falout, and Joe Falout for some great advice in the number crunching phase of our study.

3
Learning English: Students' Beliefs and Experiences in Brazil*

Ana Maria F. Barcelos

1 Introduction

The use of narratives and stories as instruments of research for the analysis of aspects of the language learning and teaching processes has increased around the world. According to Telles (2002), narrative research is present in several fields such as history, theatre, linguistics, anthropology, theology, philosophy, psychology, and arts. It has been a part of the North American and European educational context since the 1970s and 1980s (Telles 2002), with the studies of Connelly and Clandinin (1990, 2000) serving as reference for several other fields, such as Linguistics and Applied Linguistics. According to Telles (2000), narrative research allows teachers to reconstruct their personal knowledge and representations, helping them to become more aware of their actions and more able to be agents in their own practice.

The interest in learners' and teachers' experiences and narratives is not new in Applied Linguistics. Several studies exemplify this interest (see e.g., Swain and Miccoli 1994; Oxford and Green 1996; Murphey 1997). Other studies, such as Pavlenko (2001, 2002), open space for a more detailed analysis of published narratives of language learners whereas Johnson and Golombek (2002) present language teachers' own narratives. More recently, Benson and Nunan (2002, 2005) analysed language learners' learning experiences through the analysis of narratives. In Brazil, a good number of studies have also investigated language learners' experiences and beliefs (see e.g., Barcelos 1995, 2000; Conceição 2004).

This chapter adds to these studies by reporting on the investigation of Language and Secretarial Science students' experiences and beliefs about learning English in Brazil. It is divided into four parts. In the first part, I present important background information on the cultural context of English learning and teaching in Brazil. In the second section, I explore the interrelationship between narratives, experiences and beliefs. In the third part, I present the methodology used, the context and information on the participants. In the fourth part, I present and discuss the results. In the last part of the chapter, I draw implications of this study and give suggestions for future research.

2 Background to the study

2.1 The socio-cultural context of learning English in Brazil

Based on the assumption that beliefs are contextual and are embedded in the cultural and discursive practices of a given context (Kalaja and Barcelos 2003), some background into the socio-cultural situation of English teaching in this country is necessary. Of interest here is the presence of Private English Courses[1] (hereafter PECs) in Brazil, since this is going to be one of the most prominent aspects in students' narratives.

According to Bohn (2003), English teaching in Brazil has been marked by the presence of PECs, some of which are bi-national centres while others are commercial enterprises, which started to flourish in Brazil in the 1970s along with visits of young privileged Brazilians to the United States to learn English. Bohn emphasises that the creation of the powerful business of language school franchise all over the country came from the elite's perception of the importance of English in a globalised world. As a result of their popularity and of the belief in their efficiency, some of these institutions nowadays have become responsible for teaching English in public or private schools.

Other authors in Brazil, such as Walker (2003), Paiva (2003) and Garcez (2003) make similar considerations to Bohn's. According to Walker (2003) the existence of these private language courses corroborates the pervasive belief in Brazilian society that it is not possible to learn English in the regular school and that you need extra classes to accomplish that. Paiva (2003) also acknowledges the presence of this belief in Brazilian society and explains that the prestige of PECs is related to economic and historical reasons. She recognises a paradox in English teaching in Brazil: although the importance of English is recognised in society, its quality insertion in schools has never been guaranteed, with the privileged class trying to guarantee their learning in these PECs, while the underprivileged continue on the margins of this knowledge. As we shall see in the narratives, students mention the sacrifices they had to make to attend a PEC. But before I talk about the results, it is necessary to explain the relationship between narratives, beliefs and experiences, which is the topic of the next section.

2.2 Beliefs, experiences and narratives

Narratives are an excellent method to capture the essence of human experience, and of human learning and change. According to Beattie (2000), narratives show the unique ways that each person deals with his/her dilemmas and challenges. To Bruner[2] (cited in Beattie 2000, p. 5), we construct ourselves and give meaning to our life through the stories that we tell and share with others. It is impossible to talk about narrative without talking about experiences and beliefs since experience is a key term in narrative research (Clandinin and Connelly 2000). According to these authors, education is a form of experience, and a narrative way of understanding it; thus, narrative is also the best way to represent experience. Their approach to narrative research is based on Dewey's concept of experience and the principles of interaction and continuity. For Dewey (1938, p. 111), teaching and learning are 'continuous processes of reconstruction of experience'. Experience is the human mode of being in the world. It is not a mental state, but the interaction, adaptation, and adjustment of individuals to the environment, through the principles of continuity and interaction. The first refers to the connection between past and future experiences. Everything that we experience takes up something from the past and modifies the quality of future experiences. The latter refers to the transaction between an individual and the environment. Both principles involve reciprocal influence of the elements, that is, in interacting with others and with the environment the individual both shapes and is shaped by the interaction (Eldridge 1998).

These principles of experience are in accordance with the latest developments in research on beliefs which views beliefs as a paradoxical, dynamic, social, experiential and mediated construct (Alanen 2003; Dufva 2003; Kalaja and Barcelos 2003). Thus, beliefs can be defined as a 'form of thought, as constructions of reality, ways of seeing and perceiving the world and its phenomena, co-constructed in our experiences and resulting from an interactive process of interpretation and (re)-signification' (Barcelos 2006a, p. 18). This definition shows the interrelationship between beliefs and experiences and suggests that narratives are an adequate method to investigate them.

According to Gudmundsdottir (1995), because beliefs are values, they are intrinsically related to narratives for they both constitute practical and selective tools we use to make sense of the world around us.

Although a number of studies have used interviews or questionnaires (closed or open-ended) to investigate beliefs (see e.g., Horwitz 1985; Cotterall 1995; Carvalho 2000 among others), more recently, narrative and life stories have been used in the investigation of teachers' beliefs in teacher education (see e.g., Vieira-Abrahão 2002; Coelho 2005; Lima 2005), language learners' experiences and identities (Leppänen and Kalaja 2002), learner's autonomous learning (Paiva 2005) and learners' constructions of identity and imagined communities (Murphey et al. 2005). Other studies have focused on learners' language learning experiences and beliefs (see e.g., Barcelos 1995, 2000; Malcolm 2005). Below, I discuss Leppänen and Kalaja's (2002), Paiva's (2005), and Malcolm's (2005) studies.

Through a discursive socio-psychological perspective, Leppänen and Kalaja (2002) asked students to write their language learning histories starting with their first contact with English. The analysis indicated that students made use of thematic sequences that the authors defined in terms of the roles they attributed to themselves and to others, such as: acquisition without effort, learning as struggle, as passion, suffering or by-product.

Paiva (2003, p. 142) used language students' narratives in Brazil for the purpose of ascertaining 'if autonomy in foreign language learning really behaves as a complex system'. Her analysis of the narratives has indicated that even in the face of difficulties and adverse conditions, students develop a sense of autonomy and search for ways to learn the language.

Malcolm's study (2005) presupposes that beliefs are not stable, but in constant fluctuation and can be changed and revised according to different contexts and experiences. Through a series of interviews, the author investigated the progress of a learner from Saudi Arabia and his development of effective learning strategies and his beliefs in the value of reading. The results suggest that the learner, influenced by his experiences, changed his beliefs as to: (a) the importance of reading; (b translation and (c) vocabulary.

3 Data collection and analysis

A total of 53 narratives of Brazilian students was collected in 2004 – 31 from Language students and 22 from Secretarial Science students, all in the third year of their courses.[3] The guide for the narratives followed Murphey's protocol (1997).

The research questions which guided this study were:

a. Which beliefs about the place to study English in Brazil underlie students' experiences?

b. How do these experiences shape their beliefs?
c. How do they characterise their language learning experiences in their narratives?

Narratives were analysed according to qualitative research parameters (Lincoln and Guba 1985). Thus, data was first reduced through notes in the form of short phrases, key words and ideas and concepts focusing on participants' words (Patton 1990; Creswell 1998). Then, the data was coded through the classification of significant units (Lincoln and Guba 1985) and verification of students' statements referring to their beliefs about the places to learn English. Finally, similar units were grouped into categories which were revised repeatedly for consistency.

4 Findings and discussion

4.1 Public school and private English courses: two worlds apart

In students' narratives, the public school[4] and the PEC are conceived of as distant worlds. In the former it is not possible to learn. In the latter, it is. Thus, they repeat the discourse present in Brazilian society in which English teaching in public schools is always seen *vis-à-vis* the 'quality of private language courses' (Oliveira and Mota 2003, p. 125).

4.1.1 Public school[5]

For most students, the experience of learning English in public schools is seen as bad and demotivating. The reasons allude to factors such as pedagogical problems, demotivation, use of L1 and teachers' lack of competence and proficiency in the language. Students rank their experience in public schools as negative because they *learned only the 'verb to be'* (a common phrase used in the Brazilian context to illustrate the repetitive aspect of many learning situations). Students refer to the repetition of a teaching situation which is generally devoted to grammar and to teachers' lack of competence to teach the language, as illustrated in excerpt 1:[6]

(1)
As many of my friends, I've always studied in public schools in my city and, unfortunately, the teachers couldn't give a good language class, because they weren't able to do this. So, I liked English, but I didn't have vocabulary and I couldn't talk to anybody in this language. (FCC)

To this student, learning English in schools is experienced as poor and he blames his teachers. However, the student says he likes English, would like to speak the language, but believes he does not have vocabulary for that. I would like to highlight two aspects in this excerpt: the first is the image of incompetence attributed to teachers, an aspect also mentioned by Oliveira and Mota (2003); second, his desire to speak the language, although he sees that the teaching he receives does not make him able to do that. This desire to speak the language is also present in the narratives in Paiva's study (2005) and in Coelho's (2005) with public school students. Other students believe that the reason for their problems in that context had to do with the focus on grammar only, excluding alternative ways of teaching, as this student explains: *At school, the teachers didn't motivate the students to learn and to like the language as I expected them to. No games, or other extra activity; It was a kind of mechanical learning: this is this and that is that.* (LFF). This student uses a structure in English to represent the sameness of the teaching he had: *this is this and that is that*. In other words, *this* cannot mean something else, like games or extra activities. The use of negative words such as *no, didn't* suggests a view of the public school as a place where students' expectations about teaching are not fulfilled. This excerpt shows, once again, the student's criticism of public school teachers, whose competence is usually questioned and compared to that of PEC teachers. In addition, English is seen as *only a subject* at school. According to one student, *the classes were much 'superficial' and everything was in Portuguese, the students weren't stimulated to read, to speak or to write* (AC). The *superficial teaching* contributes to students' lack of motivation and interest, an aspect illustrated in EP's narrative:

(2)
I started learning English in public school, where I studied this language for three years and in fact did not learn nothing. My school didn't have a book or any other material to teach, the students were not interested and the teachers only taught the verb *to be* and memorize vocabulary. (EP)

The explanation for not learning, for this student, has to do with lack of material, emphasis on rote memorisation and grammar teaching only. Because of these, public schools are characterised as the place where English learning does not happen. Only one student sees his experience in public school positively:

(3)
'When I was in 8th grade I started to have classes about English. It was (very) awesome because I had a good teacher and I knew

most of the vocabulary reading lyrics. Since then, everything worked out. I could perceive, by studying grammar, how words got connected' (R).

This student characterises his experience as good because his teacher taught vocabulary through songs and he believes this worked out because he could understand how the language worked. Yet, for most students, the best place to study English is the PEC, as we shall see in the next section.

4.1.2 The private English course

The PEC is seen by most students as an investment, as an ideal place to which the access is compared to winning the lottery:

(4)
In that time, I studied in a public school and I wouldn't really learn English there. So, I asked my father to pay an English course to me. He couldn't, but he did. In the English course, I really started learning. I wanted to go to class everyday. I was in love with English. (RFR)

This investment in the PEC is seen as necessary and good, because it motivates students. In the first excerpt, the student already held the belief that *she wouldn't learn English in public school*, which may have motivated her to learn in the PEC. This excerpt also illustrates that the PEC is seen as something better, a way of social access, as an investment in the future of one's child.

Contrasting with the language that was used to describe the public school, the PEC is described in a very positive light: *great, I really started learning, I wanted to go to class, I was in love* all related to *love* and *passion* (words commonly used by Brazilian students to justify the reason(s) for studying English). The PEC is thus characterised as a place that does not present learning problems to the students and where teachers' competence is not questioned or challenged. Much to the opposite, teachers in this context are seen as proficiency models for public school teachers, as mentioned by Oliveira and Mota (2003) as well as in the students' narratives. One student questions the teacher's linguistic knowledge and believes she is the only one who can detect this lack of linguistic competence for she is studying in a PEC: *Sometimes I had discussions with teachers because they used to teach wrong things and I was the only one who knew it was wrong. It was so different from the English course* (RFR). Another student compares her knowledge to the school teacher's:

(5)
I didn't have a good experience of English at school. My teacher used to speak Portuguese and she asked us only to translate texts and guess the grammar points. Of course this wasn't so terrible to me because I was studying English outside school. So I had feedback that many of my friends didn't have. (AT)

In this excerpt, AT believes she is knowledgeable about things her teacher and classmates were not because she studied at a PEC. This was mentioned by Oliveira and Mota (2003, p. 131), who state:

Students in public schools, in contact with statements which convey the meaning that public school teachers are not able to teach English, are constituted in a way as not to accept their actions, or even question their statements based on the explanations given by teachers in private English schools.[7]

One of the big allurements for PEC students are the teaching materials used in this place, characterised by students as *complete, beautiful, great* in opposition to the lack of any textbooks[8] in public schools and of classes whose focus is mainly on grammar structures and not on speaking skills.[9] Teachers' competence and the small number of students in PECs are also highlighted by participants, as illustrated below:

(6)
I started learning English at a private language school and I studied there for five years. I always thought that the classes at X school were better than at my public school, because at X there was a beautiful and great book and there weren't many students in class. Nowadays, I think that school isn't the most important thing when you're learning English, but the interest of each person. (NCM)

In this excerpt, the student mentions the few numbers of students in class as an advantage that the PEC offers in comparison to public schools. Yet, she recognises that students' interest is what really counts.

These students' language learning experiences and views will shape their beliefs about public school and PEC, the value attributed to the learning in each place, as well as their perceptions, judgments and evaluations of their future language learning experiences, illustrating the principles of interaction and continuity mentioned previously.

4.2   Experiences: interaction and continuity

Students' experiences and beliefs described above about the two most common places to learn English in Brazil shape their beliefs and experiences in college. In their narratives, it is possible to notice that what they have lived in the past affects how they perceive themselves as learners and colours their first language learning experiences in college. The excerpts below illustrate this aspect:

(7)
I remember my first class at university, it was terrible. I can't forget it...I discovered that I didn't know anything. I almost cried when I saw the teacher speaking everything in English, everybody understanding and I knew nothing. At first, I thought of giving up, but 'Thanks God' I met many friends who helped me to surpass this terrible moment. (AC)

(8)
'In the first classes here I thought it very difficult: most of the students were speaking with the teacher and I couldn't do the same. I would pass through a long and hard work. Even though, this became a challenge for me' (LFF).

Excerpt 7 shows how the student sees herself because of her previous experience in public school – as a survivor who conquered her dream through the help of friends. In excerpt 8, the student also believes that he can have problems at university because of his previous experience in public school. He describes his journey as long and hard, but which he sees as a challenge. None of them, despite the difficulties experienced, feels inferior or has given up learning because of that. This, however, is what happened to PD who explains: *When I came here, I started to talk with the other girls and then I realized that all of them had already studied English for a long time. I felt terrible with this, as if I were 'below' everybody.* Unlike her classmates in the previous excerpts, PD feels inferior and compares herself to those who had studied English for a long time. Actually, what she means is that her peers had studied English in other places, because everyone that studies English in public schools in Brazil studies it for a 'long time', at least four years.

This feeling of inferiority is not so explicit, but hidden in the narratives which portray learning as a difficult and painful journey, as seen before. Thus, these students see themselves as disadvantaged compared to others who had the opportunity to *speak* the language. In this sense, the advice one of the participants gives to classmates is a reflection of this disadvantage they believe they have, as LFF explains: *some advice for those who want to learn English or any other foreign language, is that the process, sometimes, is very difficult, mainly if you study (or studied) only in public schools*. To LFF, the experience of learning English in public school made the process more painful; thus he warns other students about this experience. This theme is recurrent in many of the narratives. Learning English in public schools is seen as difficult; thus, learning English in college for these students is seen as struggle and survival. This view is not necessarily related to the difficulties of the learning process itself. The participants of this study did not have any learning problems and seemed motivated. The difficulty refers to being positioned as someone who studied in a place which is viewed by society (and by themselves) as not having such competence. Then, the struggle is to study in a more prestigious or recognised place, as seen in the following excerpt:

(9)
However, I couldn't study English in a private school because I didn't work and my mother didn't have enough money for that. So, the *only* English classes that I had were in public school and they weren't so good. Therefore, for many years I studied English by myself, saving money to buy English books to study at home. Some years later I got my first job. That was the moment I could pay a private English school. (DCR, my italics)

For DCR, learning is seen as struggle and hardship, which is similar to the results by Leppänen and Kalaja (2002). Unlike the participants of that study however, to DCR, the constraint is not the material, the exams, methods or classmates, but not being able to pay for studying at a PEC. This fact ends up forcing this student to work even harder to pursue his dream and thus to develop autonomy, similar to some of Paiva's (2005) participants, who created the conditions for language exposure and practice with the resources they had.[10] To DCR, not being able to afford studying in a private English course is a problem, a flaw, a disadvantage that needs to be made up for with a lot of study.

The PEC is also seen as the place that will save students from some bad experiences they had in public school, a sort of *quality seal* that certifies the quality of English learning they have, as illustrated in the following excerpt:

(10)
My will of learning English started with a trauma: in my first English class, the teacher asked the students to say their names and ages. She wrote on the board the numbers – because nobody knew how to speak English – and my colleagues seemed very calm with the situation. Except for me. When it was my turn, I should have said 'thirteen', but I was very nervous and it sounds a 'tortin'. Everybody laughed at me, of course. After this, I had promised myself: I will learn English. In the second class, I was still trembling like a leaf, but I dared to risk. At home, I persuaded my father to pay a private English course. Some months later, I was laughing at my colleagues because they had stopped in their apprenticeship and I was just starting to increase. (IRO)

Leppänen and Kalaja (2002), within their characterisation, explain the student role as victim or martyr as suffering. In this respect, the learner is afraid of being misinterpreted, ridiculed or laughed at. By the same token, IRO places herself as the victim in a situation in which she felt ridiculed. To solve this incident, she seeks for the PEC as the place which will legitimise her knowledge, or which will help her be 'on top' since it is common sense that the knowledge of English acquired at a PEC is credited for in our society as surpassing the non-legitimised knowledge of English acquired in public school. This common belief in the efficiency of PEC is used by this student to deal with a difficult situation in which she had her knowledge questioned. IRO, in giving advice to other students, highlights her perseverance and determination, as a model to be followed by others and say: *For those who want to learn English I suggest follow my example and never, never give up!* Other students see themselves somewhat as heroes, for having survived this experience of learning in a public school and for, at present, being able to be at university and learn this language. This is transparent in the following excerpts:

(11)
'But try to discover if you REALLY want this, because if you do (as it happens to me) the problem can be overcome. Watch movies! Listen to music! Speak up! Read, read aloud. And last but not least: don't give up' (LFF).

(12)
'If you want something and fight for it, you get it. There are many people in the same situation as me and my advice to these people is to study hard and conquer your goals' (AC).

The students who studied in public schools want to tell others that, even though it is difficult, they should not give up and should persevere. They should want to reach their goals. On the other hand, students who studied at PECs advise their classmates to do exactly that: to study in a PEC, as GGMF explains: *If you don't know anything about English, I advise you to study a lot and if you can, to do one English course to help you in the University and for you to improve your English* (GGMF). For GGMF, the PEC is seen as a strategy that will help him with his difficulties at university.

For the participants of this study, learning does not seem to happen in public schools, but in PECs. There is no mention of learning strategies from these students or autonomous steps such as those mentioned by students who studied in public schools. Thus, we may speculate that, the participants of this study who studied in public schools, for having to struggle harder for their learning, ended up fighting more for their learning and developing more responsibility for this, searching for a force inside themselves and not outside.

5 Final considerations

What does the analysis of these students' narratives tells us about their language learning experiences and beliefs? First of all, they suggest that for these students, the public school is not the place where they learn English. Their experiences in their respective public schools are not described as good or as promoting language learning, although for some this was the propelling spring for them to become more responsible for their learning. The results of this study confirm the results of Grigoletto (2003) in which for her participants, English learning happens outside public school, perhaps because what students want – speaking – is not offered in public schools due to contextual constraints. However, for the participants of Coelho's (2005) study, the public school is the only place they have to learn English. At the same time, the desire of speaking English manifested by the participants of this study is similar to the results of Coelho (2005) and Paiva (2005). In short, the results of this analysis echo Paiva's (2005) about learners' frustration with school teaching and their autonomy in face of adverse situations.

Secondly, the students' narratives suggest their beliefs in the PEC as the best place to learn English, since their experiences in it are seen as good and as a promoter of language learning. The PEC is seen by students as the place many aspire to belong to, as a *guarantee* for learning and as an investment in their future. In a way, this view of the PEC is similar to how learning in the target-country is seen as the best place to learn as suggested by the participants in Barcelos' studies (1995, 2000).

Yet, we must ask – who is responsible for the investment in the future of students who study in public schools? The situation in Brazil so far has been that, in most cases, the lower classes go to public schools and do not have the chance to learn the language, whereas the more economically advantaged class pay for the PECs. The answers to these questions must come from a conscious effort of the whole Brazilian society who must be committed to quality public education. We live in a system that violates the rights of common citizens of free access to culture and education through foreign language learning.

What implications do these results bring to language teachers, researchers and students? First, teachers can benefit from using students' language learning histories to know better their beliefs and experiences. In addition, other students can also learn, exchange ideas and reflect on their own learning by reading their classmates' histories. This can be used to help students reflect on their own learning, their beliefs and experiences. However, it's important to point out that only telling and writing narratives or life stories is not enough. This is only the first step in teachers' and students' awareness of their own learning narratives – an important step, but which does not exclude other actions that must be taken such as the investment and political engagement with public school and within language teachers' associations to change the present state of devaluation of the English language as a subject in Brazilian schools. For researchers, it is important to say that although this study did not include students' views on the analysis of their narratives, this would be a positive step in the future.

In this study, I have used fragments of students' narratives. As suggestions for future studies, longitudinal investigations of the developments of the beliefs and experiences of only one participant could bring interesting insights about learning experiences and contributing factors to the change in their belief systems.[11]

Narratives have allowed the uncovering of students' experiences, beliefs about themselves and the places for language learning in Brazil, as well as a better understanding of the interaction between their previous, present and future experiences. According to Clandinin and Connelly (2000, p. 42), narrative research does not 'prescribe general applications and uses but rather creates texts that, when well done, offer readers a place to imagine their own uses and applications'. I hope that the reading of these narratives may help students, teachers and researchers to reflect on their own learning experiences and beliefs and imagine (and realise) possible English language learning and teaching experiences in Brazil and thus write different narratives from the ones reported here.

Notes

* A previous version of this article has been published in Portuguese in Brazil (Barcelos 2006c).

1. I use the term 'private English courses' to refer to language institutes supported (in part) by foreign governments and also commercially-operated institutions. These teach only languages while the 'official schools', which can be public or privately-owned, offer the full elementary and secondary curricula.
2. Bruner, J., 1986. *Actual Minds, Possible Worlds*. Cambridge, MA: Harvard University Press.
3. Written permission was obtained from the students.
4. Public schools refer to state and municipal schools for elementary, secondary and high school students in Brazil.
5. In their narratives, students referred to public schools and thus, this term was used here. However, it is important to point out that some of the problems mentioned by students as referring to public schools also happen in private schools in Brazil, as shown in Miccoli's chapter (this volume).
6. All excerpts were originally written in English and were minimally edited in cases where comprehension was hindered. The letters in parentheses after each excerpt refer to students' initials.
7. Private English schools here refer to private English courses.
8. In Brazil, the government donates the textbooks for all subjects in public schools, except for English.
9. See Miccolli's chapter for a view of the contextual factors of English teachers' work in Brazil.
10. See also Murphey and Carpenter's chapter on agency, this volume.
11. See Block, this volume for an example.

4
Self-Observation and Reconceptualisation through Narratives and Reflective Practice*

Deise P. Dutra and Heliana Mello

1 Introduction

By talking about past and present stories, teachers can envision their professional lives, having the possibility of understanding and recreating their pedagogical actions as they revisit their own history through the means of retelling and reconceptualising them. In an attempt to discuss how self-observation and reconceptualisation of theoretical issues can be encouraged by narrative production and reflective practice, our research with English as a foreign language (EFL) teachers presented in this chapter focuses on and connects three different axes: pre- and in-service education, discourse representation, and the theory and practice dichotomy.

In order to describe and discuss how pre-service and in-service English teachers, participating in a teacher education programme, are able to self-observe them so as to reconceptualise language teaching and learning theories and to better understand their practice, this chapter departs from the assumption that an important part of teacher development is sustained by the opportunities teachers have to become aware of what they do, who they are, where they come from, where they teach and who they teach. Many times, within the rush of daily life, fuelled by too many professional pressures, teachers might forget their very motivation to become teachers. This is the major reason why in the context of a teacher continuing education programme, stories past and present are sought and told as a means to bring back and reunite pieces that might have been left behind in teachers' paths. Therefore, here we present and discuss written and spoken data produced by teachers, in narratives about their learning and teaching experiences and about their personal and professional development, in reflective journals about the classes they taught and about feedback sessions of these classes, in collaborative sessions about classes they previously taught and about plans for future actions. The context of our research is a continuing teacher education programme, within one of the major public universities in Brazil. Our teacher-participants are two in-service teachers and two pre-service teachers, who have named themselves Amy, Sophie, Ann and Cherry for the purposes of the experience narrated here.

The aim of our research was to validate narrative inquiry and reflective teaching as tools for self-evaluation and reconceptualisation of teaching and to investigate how the connection between theory and practice is presented in the teachers' discourse. In order to present our research, we first introduce a brief discussion of the area and the theoretical perspectives we subscribe to, then we explore the methodology, data analysis and reach some conclusions.

2 Theoretical foundations

In this section we present the theoretical background that inspired our research. First, we give a general background of teacher research and, then, present, briefly, two subsections on the areas that have mainly influenced our line of thought: reflective teaching and narrative research.

For more than ten years now, Applied Linguists have brought to attention a great concern about teacher education, especially focusing on English as a second language (ESL) and EFL teaching professionals. The discussions brought in have taken into account a variety of aspects, such as pre-service and in-service education, reflective teaching, the education of critical professionals, the role of narratives in reflection, teachers' conceptual constructions, identities and theories (Richards and Lockhart 1994; Freeman and Richards 1996; Zeichner and Liston 1996; Freeman and Johnson 1998; Richards 1998; Wallace 1998; Almeida Filho 1999; Burns 1999; Johnson and Freeman 2001; Celani 2002; Gimenez 2002; Barbara and Ramos 2003; Liberali 2004; Magalhães 2004; Mello and Dutra 2004; Telles 2004; Vieira-Abrahão 2004).[1]

Following the path set forth by colleagues who have been developing research within the broad areas pointed out above, this chapter is based on two main areas of research: reflective teaching research (Richards 1998; Zeichner 2003) and narrative research (Clandinin and Connelly 2000). Reflective teaching has been a key issue and asset to the area

(Richard and Lockart 1994; Freeman and Richards 1996; Richards 1998) as teacher development is, therefore, viewed as more than just informing teachers of classroom methodologies and techniques. It provides teachers with an active role in their professional profile making up as they explore their experiences in terms of the processes they resort to as they learn how to teach (Freeman and Richards 1996). This brings forth a cycle that is hard to break: reflective teachers are more autonomous and will again and again resort to their experiences and critical analysis of them to reconstruct their practice.

2.1 Reflective teaching research

It was in the 1990s that the paradigm on teaching research became mainstream. This helped shift the area from an outsider's perspective to an insider's perspective. The idea that teachers have their own beliefs and explanations for their classroom behaviour and can interpret their own students' reactions in class (Woods 1996) has contributed to a different point of view to the research agenda in the area. The teacher is not seen as someone who is always simply in need of being updated with the most current methodologies on language teaching, but mainly someone who can make sense of his/her practices and who grows professionally in the process of reflection. Richards (1998, p. 48) suggests that 'teacher development can be seen as a process of ongoing self-discovery and self-renewal, as top-down approaches to teaching are replaced by more bottom-up approaches, or approaches that blend the two.'

Richards claims that different conceptions of teacher education can be put together, gradually, if teachers are still building up confidence in teaching, so that, eventually, they are successful in their profession. He adds that the basis of such an approach should be teacher education as a developmental continuum, which includes the development of technical competence, the interpretation of theories of teaching and the development of personal theories of teaching. This development should not be seen as detached from the environments in which the teacher was educated and works as a professional. Therefore, teacher educators and researchers should consider the social-historical aspects (Zeichner 2003) that influence teachers' beliefs, actions and theories.

2.2 Narrative research

Narratives have been used in several types of research so as to elicit teachers' personal and professional experiences (Clandinin and Connelly 2000; Johnson and Golombek 2002), to create a path in the classroom community (Martin 2000) and to make the elements that influence the second language acquisition process accessible to students themselves (Murphey 1999; Pavlenko 2001).

Narrative inquiry is the process of gathering information for the purpose of research through storytelling. Connelly and Clandinin (1990, p. 2) note that, 'Humans are storytelling organisms who, individually and collectively, lead storied lives. Thus, the study of narrative is the study of the ways humans experience the world.' This guides us to state that anybody's life is constituted by and constitutes complex and intertwined stories, lived, told and heard. Field notes, interviews, journals, letters, autobiographies, and orally told stories are all methods of narrative inquiry. As Connelly and Clandinin (1990, p. 12) also note, 'Research is a collaborative document, a mutually constructed story out of the lives of both researcher and participant.'

Narrative research is influenced by Dewey's thinking (Clandinin and Connelly 2000) about the importance of experience in the understanding of situations. In other words, past experiences mould the way people interpret new life circumstances, and therefore, how educational professionals may see the new experiences they encounter. According to Johnson and Golombek (2002, p. 4),

> inquiry into experience that is educative propels us to not only question the immediate context but to draw connections among experiences – what Dewey calls *continuity of experience* (1933), or how experiences change the conditions under which new experiences are understood so that a person abilities, desires, and attitudes are changed. Inquiry into experience, in this sense, can be educative if it enables us to reflect on our actions and then act with foresight.

The authors cited above use Dewey's set of attitudes in professional development to define the narrative inquiry approach. These attitudes are *'open-mindedness* (seeking alternatives), *responsibility* (recognising consequences), and *wholeheartedness* (continual self-examination)' (Johnson and Golombek 2002, p. 5). This triad is made up of a positive searching for alternative paths to emerging difficulties in the teaching process, the ability to evaluate the consequences of pedagogical actions and the pursuit of a critical view towards one's professional conduct. Consequently, this type of investigation captures both the personal and the professional dimensions (Clandinin and Connelly 2000) and it is a rich source of data for qualitative researchers interested in knowing more about professional development. Narratives should not be seen as a static production, but as a way of understanding the dynamic aspects of our experiences and of encouraging the desire for continuous personal and professional development. Therefore, narrative is a type of research as well as a data collection instrument. In this chapter narratives are used not only as an instrument of data collection but also as a means of self-discovery (*wholeheartedness*), so as to, together with other instruments, further sustain professional understanding and growth through reflective practice.

3 Methodology

In this section we explain who the participants are, the research tools used and the methodology of analysis.

3.1 Participants

The research reported in this chapter involves four participants. The former participants study in a teacher education programme for English and Spanish[2] public school teachers at a large university in the south east region of Brazil. This two-year continuing education programme is organised around methodology and language course modules. The methodology modules are taught by university professors and linguistics graduate students who also advise the undergraduate students who teach the language classes. For these undergraduate students their language teaching works as the practicum as they are pre-service teachers.

The two in-service teacher participants in this research have been teaching for about five years. Neither of them attended private language schools.[3] Amy graduated from a public university and Sophie from a private one. Besides taking part in the programme, they were both involved, for a year, in a collaborative action research project with a research group from the same university where they take part in the continuing education programme.

The two pre-service teachers, Ann and Cherry, are undergraduate students in the same university where the teacher education programme has been developed. Ann studied English in a private language school and Cherry only in junior high and high school. Ann has been in the programme for three semesters and Cherry for two.

3.2 Data collection instruments

In order to better understand teachers' development processes, we carried our data collection based on the contextual approach (Barcelos 2001), which establishes that data should come from various collecting means with the purpose to offer different perspectives on the same individual, at different points in a time line. In order to do so, we employed narratives, journals, non-participant observation of classes, and collaborative reflective sessions about the classes observed.

Both narratives and journals presented in this chapter are among the instruments implemented in the continuing education programme to help teachers better reflect about their learning and teaching stories. Therefore, all the teachers who take part in the programme have written narratives and journals. Yet, due to limitation of space, we present in this chapter the analysis of two in-service and two pre-service teachers. The non-participant observation of classes and the collaborative reflective session were carried out for the purpose of this research.

3.3 Data analysis methodology

The qualitative data analysis was done based on the discursive articulation done by the participants as they narrated their stories in the various moments of our data collection (e.g., narratives and collaborative reflective sessions). The categories to be presented in the next section emerged from the data. It was only after we were able to set the categories that we also noticed that the way the teachers told their stories would fit the set of attitudes proposed by Dewey (1933) when discussing educational experiences.

4 Data analysis

In this section we present the categories that emerged from our analysis of teachers' spoken and written data as we focused on how they connected theory and practice in their re-telling of their experiences and reconceptualisation of categories in their practice. The emerging categories are:

a) language learning experiences;
b) theory and methodology in teachers' discourse;
c) theory conceptualization into practice;
d) theory effectiveness.

We will now present the data and discuss them to better understand the stories our participants have profiled and the aspects of their lives they have chosen to talk about while they retell their experiences. Due to space limitations, we have decided to illustrate the categories above by providing some examples[4] from the teachers' discourse and, therefore, do not bring excerpts from all the participants for all the categories. We have chosen to present the examples that better show the thoughts or attitudes of the pre- and in-service teachers.

4.1 Language learning experiences

In this section we analyse the teachers' stories that revealed their experiences as language learners. The narratives provided the participants with opportunities to reflect about their previous learning experiences. Although the pre-service language teachers took somewhat different learning paths, the in-service teachers had very similar learning experiences. They all, however, shared similar feelings about their language learning. At first, we will consider the experience of the two pre-service teachers. It was mentioned in Section 3 that Cherry's primary experience in learning English took place at junior high and high school. As she remembers it, that was a terrible time during which she made up her mind never to teach like her own teachers had:

> I had really weak teachers who seemed not, even a bit interested in their students' learning. Their greatest challenge was to take 50 minutes of their class to do a 10-minute grammar activity with their students. ... The lesson I learned at that time was: I'll never be a professional like these teachers. (Learning narrative)

Ann, contrary to Cherry, learned English at a language school. Her English learning experiences at junior high and high school were seen as a complement to what she had already learned at the language school and due to that, she saw them as neither crucial nor motivating to her learning: *'it was an opportunity to improve my vocabulary and put my linguistic knowledge into practice. Yet, many times I did not feel motivated as there was nothing new'* (Learning narrative).

Second, the two in-service teachers, Amy and Sophie seem to have had similar language learning experiences. They both learned English at junior high and high school where the focus was on linguistic structures: *'My language classes were limited to the teaching of various grammar topics. ... Language practice was limited to the teacher daily greetings "good morning" when I studied in the morning and "good afternoon" when I studied in the afternoon'* (Amy's learning narrative).

The excerpts of the narratives above show that, in their own account, the four participants had had very disappointing experiences of learning English at junior high and high school. Cherry explicitly mentioned how this had shaped her teaching, and this leads us to hypothesise that the other teachers' experiences may have influenced the kind of teachers they decided to be. Cherry, as well as the other teachers, seem to have started a process of self-discovery, which we hope turns into what Dewey (1933) conceptualised as *wholeheartedness* (continual self-examination). What the narratives have done is to encourage the pre-service and in service teachers to rescue stories that may help them understand their present teaching. Although many teachers may have internalised the teaching methodologies they were exposed to in their experience as students, others might just follow an opposite direction, fostered by disappointment and many times, resentment. The path of reaction to one's entrenched experiences might result in constructive ways of growing and freeing oneself from unsatisfactory experiences, guided by a pro-active, reflective attitude towards the past, as observed in Cherry's excerpt discussed above.

4.2 Theory and methodology in teachers' discourse

The pre-service and the in-service teachers make both explicit and implicit references to theories and methodologies in their discourse. Teaching, learning and language theories help them understand classroom issues or make pedagogical decisions. We have found through teachers' narratives that many times the analytical categories that researchers define in their studies are not clearly separated in teachers' experience. They are lived as a holistic construct, which only gets pieced together as demanded by their remembering and retelling.

4.2.1 Teaching theories

In a narrative about her personal and professional development, Cherry spontaneously mentions the teaching theories that she was exposed to in college: *'For example, when I took the course "Methodology Principles" with Professor Mercer,*[5] *I learned how to work with all the skills (speaking-listening-reading and writing) and now at XX*[6] *I better noticed the relevance of appropriate methodology for students' learning'* (Personal and professional narrative).

It was her experience in the teacher education programme that helped her make sense of the methodologies and teaching theories she had studied previously.

In her class journals, Ann reflects on what she had planned for class, what was actually accomplished, the students' reactions and the comments received in the feedback sessions.[7] She does not explicitly mention the theories she has based her decisions on, but the fact that she is worried about having a clear, real purpose for reading is closely related to teaching theories which emphasise the importance of creating a classroom environment similar to what goes on in the outside world: *'What I think I should really work hard to improve is "reading objectives", something like establishing a real purpose for reading and focusing the activity on that purpose'* (Excerpt from Ann's Journal).

The discourse of the in-service teachers also reveals how teaching theories influence their pedagogical decisions. One of Amy's concerns is to integrate the four skills: *'I'm going to work with writing. How am I going to include the other skills? I want to put this in my planning (...) the purpose is writing but how am I going to include listening?'* (Collaborative session).

In a way the contact the teacher-participants, especially Cherry, Ann and Amy, had with theories has given them alternatives for their practice which could be seen as if they were in a state of *open-mindedness* (Dewey 1933). In other words, their discourse shows that at that moment in their professional lives they were seeking for alternatives and the theories they were exposed to seemed to provide references for them.

4.2.2 Learning theories

Some of the teachers' comments about their classes and their plans for the future clearly focused on learning issues such as the importance of autonomy and process writing in learning.

Sophie, for instance, highlights autonomy development, so that learners become independent and are able to improve on their own: *'The point of vocabulary, acquisition of vocabulary, autonomy is important for them, even if they are in the sixth grade. What is important is that they search, also their own knowledge in the language'* (Collaborative session).

Amy's discourse reveals a more accurate concern with learning and shows how autonomy can be encouraged through process writing. This can be analysed as an interference of the learning theories discussed in the teacher education programme. She realizes how the process in learning can be crucial in students' continual autonomy and, therefore, wants to work with process writing: *'I was thinking about working with that issue that we worked at XX,[8] that they edit their own mistakes, reanalyzing their errors'* (Collaborative session).

As it can be observed in the excerpts above, Sophie and Amy seem to be concerned with students' autonomy, as they believe that their students would improve their learning if they searched for solutions for their language difficulties on their own, becoming therefore more aware of language structure and use. The way the teacher-participants talk about their practice shows that they feel responsible for their practice and the consequence of their choices. The excerpts above show that the teacher-participants' discourse reveals their sense of responsibility (Dewey 1933) since they recognise the consequences of their pedagogical choices.

4.3 Theory conceptualisation into practice

In this section we present excerpts that show how the teacher-participants are able to explain how theory meets their classroom practices. Amy, Cherry and Sophie are the ones who better externalise this.

Amy, one of the in-service teachers, upon discussing how to conduct a writing project with her students, brings up her dilemma of dealing with linguistic structures *a priori* (before the students show the necessity to use them for communication) or *a posteriori* (after the items appear in the process of accomplishing the task):

> And I'll review with them, but there'll be a moment in which they will talk about, for example, their neighbourhood, how you can make a comparison with something else. I know we'll have to work with comparative adjectives, for example. And they'll feel like talking about things that happened in the past, I'll work with simple past, or another verb they need (...) My problem is to address these topics before they come up or wait and see what happens. (Collaborative session)

Throughout the same collaborative session, Amy concludes that linguistic elements should be addressed according to their purpose in the communicative activity. Therefore, her discourse reveals that her conceptualisation of a language theory is based on the communicative function of linguistic structures. She, then, states that her practice should follow this conceptualisation: *'I believe that the best thing is to, as they come up, the necessity, if they have questions, if they don't know what to do'* (Collaborative session).

Cherry, one of the pre-service teachers, seems to have similar theory conceptualisations to Amy's. Yet, she explicitly can trace arguments to recent courses taken as well as her practice. Cherry's critical analysis of what she studied in a course about the communicative approach and what knowing a language involves shows her view that the elements that compose language cannot be seen in separate boxes. For her, it is clear that the linguistic competence is part of the communicative competence and it should not be neglected:

> Prof. Murphy showed us all the positive aspects of using the communicative approach, however, it was not discussed how to deal with grammatical aspects. Therefore, my participation in the language classes [program] was essential for me to see both sides of the coin: we need to work both with fluency and accuracy. (Personal and professional development narrative)

Her awareness of what was taught came with her experience in the teacher education programme and her effort to connect the theory studied and her practice in class.

Despite the theoretical and practical discussions conducted in the teacher education programme, which aims at providing teachers with a more communicative, usage-based oriented approach, teachers might conceptualise language as bare linguistic structures. Sophie, in a narrative about her experiences related to learning and teaching grammar defined grammar as: ... *it is the instrument that guides language, knowing the rules, the norms to be followed.*

This conceptualisation clearly influences her pedagogical decisions:

> Ah, I started with a text and asked them to identify, (inc) if the text was in the present, or if it were in the past (...) from then on I started working with the students the isolated structures, the subject, how the English structure is set (...). (Collaborative session)

The excerpts of this section show that the theory reconceptualisation does not only depend on being a pre-service or in-service teacher. Other issues might influence this process, for instance, the teachers' reflective capacity. Amy is an in-service teacher while Cherry is a pre-service one, yet they have been able to let the theories they have been in contact with influence their pedagogical choices. Sophie, the other in-service teacher, reveals in her discourse a traditional view of language, which is reflected in her teaching.

4.4 Theory effectiveness

In this section we discuss how the teacher-participants show the effectiveness of new and old theories in their teaching as it is expressed in their discourse. After a year with the teacher education programme, Amy and Sophie (in-service teachers) got involved in collaborative action research as mentioned in the methodology session. Despite the fact that they both had similar junior high and high school learning experiences, they attended different colleges and their teaching practice was distinct. Sophie conducted teacher centred classes, translating her instructions and emphasising linguistic structures. The first class observed by a research group member was characterised by Sophie as a class about the linguistic structure of English: *'how the English structure is set (...) it's not so different from the Portuguese grammatical terms, such as the subject, verb and phrasal complement'* (Collaborative session).

After a few months of collaborative action research, Sophie tells the group how successful a reading activity had been, yet she was worried about the structural aspects of the activity. She did not focus her attention on learners' use of reading strategies neither on the meaningfulness of the task for the development of their language proficiency as a whole:

> I planned to start with the text about Pampulha.[9] I did ... we did it, but we did it orally and not in writing ... because they did the reading individually and answered according to the questions and they were able to answer ... I thought about the complete sentence. (Collaborative session)

Amy's first observed class focused on tasks, a feature which is quite different from Sophie's class. Her students were supposed to identify countries in a map and describe them. There was a great deal of elicitation, semantic discussion and group work. Her first stimulated recall session revealed her concern with the focus on linguistic structure but she was able to express that her main teaching focus was not on the structures themselves:

> I'm used to emphasizing the theme, as I wanted to talk about different people, different places. I want to do this a lot, but focusing on writing which is a difficult issue, very difficult at school and I still have questions when I deal with a grammatical point. I try to invent, but sometimes I miss listing the subject, the concepts ... putting what is the verb, the pronoun (... .) But my main objective is to deal with writing. (Collaborative session)

After her participation in the collaborative action research, Amy maintained her theoretical concepts about language learning and teaching and felt more confident about the effectiveness of these theories in her practice: *it became so meaningful to me ... It became real and I could see it clearly.*

After the positive results with a writing project she had implemented (letter exchange among students from two different schools), Amy had new plans to make the school community become more involved in the English projects her students have been doing: *I want to post their drawings of the town at school (...).* Her view of language gives her students a possibility of realistically interacting with the world.

The pre-service teachers have experienced the connections between theory and practice and explicitly write about them. Cherry, for instance, sees that making informed decisions based on theories has influenced her practice positively:

> I had the opportunity to apply theories about lesson planning, teaching multi-level classes, teaching writing, reading, speaking and listening and realized that many theories are good and perfectly applicable (I say this because many of my college friends say that theories don't work in practice). And besides that, I developed a habit of consulting a theory about something I'm going to teach, which I consider extremely significant in my professional development. (Personal and professional narrative)

The excerpts above show that Sophie's, Amy's, and Cherry's discourse does not reveal a dichotomy between theory and practice. Sophie's traditional theories match her classroom choices and Amy and Cherry's more contemporary theories are also used in their classes. Yet, Amy and Cherry are more conscious of the theories behind their pedagogical decisions and, therefore, are able to point out their effectiveness.

5 Conclusion

The analysis shows that the four teachers who have been participants in this narrative research, through their stories, have brought about the constructs named *open-mindedness* (seeking alternatives), *responsibility* (recognising consequences), and *wholeheartedness* (continual self-examination) as proposed by Dewey. They each, in their own ways, are looking for alternatives to the teaching examples they had along their student lives, either by replacing them or fostering the positive aspects they have found and putting them into practice as they have somehow recognised their desirable consequences. Through constructive reflection about past experiences most teachers are able to distance their practice from the kind of English teaching they had at junior high and high school. The two pre-service teachers are able to explicitly make connections between theory and practice as their contact with Applied Linguistics is recent and constant. What they studied in one course is re-analysed in other courses and, together with their teaching, it seems that the parts of the puzzle come together. The discourse of both in-service teachers is connected to their practice. However, while Sophie has difficulties to innovate away from her traditional learning experiences, Amy is able to do that as she has a contemporary view of language and language teaching theories. Therefore, there is not a dichotomy between practice and theory since there is coherence between more conservative discursive views and corresponding more conservative practice in the case of Sophie and the opposite relationship is true for the other three teachers. The analysis of their learning experiences and their practice made all of them aware of theory and practice conceptualisations and the distinct possibilities that their practice may take.

We could state that the use of narrative inquiry as a source of knowledge into teachers' beliefs and conceptualisations about theories they have been exposed to, or have built themselves, and their practice concurs with Clandinin and Connelly's (2000) proposal of narrative as a form of representation rather than a mode of analysis. Human lives, they suggest, are woven of stories. Individuals construct their identities through their own and others' stories. They experience daily encounters and interactions as stories. Every present moment has a storied past and a storied future possibility. Social phenomena become a converging point for individual, collective, and cultural stories. And this is what a teacher experiences daily.

In the programme in which the narratives presented here were collected we continue to use narratives as an instrument of reflection since it can enlighten our understanding of teachers' attitudes and knowledge. The opportunity for self-development that the writing, telling and reflection about the narratives can bring to teachers, along with other reflective activities, has afforded them more autonomy in their professional lives.

Notes

* A version of this paper was presented at AILA 2005 (Madison) with the support of CNPq (*Conselho Nacional de Desenvolvimento Científico e Tecnológico* – Brazil).
1. The purpose of this list of references is to show the strong tradition that has been developing all over the world, including Brazil. Since our work has been done in this country, we provide this list as readers might want to access this

bibliography which has contributed to the theoretical background that supports this chapter.
2. In this chapter we deal with data collected with the English teachers only.
3. Attending private language schools as a way to learn foreign languages is a common practice in Brazil as most people do not believe it to be possible to do so as a regular school student.
4. The excerpts presented in this chapter have been translated from Portuguese which is the participants' mother tongue.
5. The authors of this chapter have chosen pseudonyms to replace the real names of professors mentioned by the research participants.
6. The name of the teacher education programme.
7. After each class the pre-service teachers meet with their advisor (a graduate student) so as to reflect on what was accomplished and to plan the activities for the upcoming classes.
8. The name of the teacher education programme.
9. Pampulha is a landmark in the capital city of Minas Gerais where the schools are located.

5
Brazilian EFL Teachers' Experiences in Public and Private Schools: Different Contexts with Similar Challenges

Laura Miccoli

1 Introduction

Brazilian students and teachers of English as a Foreign Language (EFL) in public or private schools characterise their learning or teaching as *school English* – to students *school English* means limited English skills; to teachers it means that they have not been able to overcome the limitations of teaching EFL in Brazil. *School English* is associated with public schools students for they do not have the means to complement their studies in private language institutes.[1] Qualifying EFL teaching and learning as *school English* is distressing because a federal law requires English to be taught for at least eight years[2] in Brazil.

The National Curricular Parameters (NCPs) (Brazil 1998, 2002) provide the national guidelines for teaching EFL as part of the school curriculum, stating it should promote the development of language skills to be used by Brazilian students' in their personal, academic and professional lives. In spite of that, the NCPs prioritise the teaching of reading and writing skills to the detriment of oral skills, as a way to get around the limitations facing Brazilian education (Brazil 2002). Unfortunately, generalising about this reality is far more common (Moraes 2002) than finding data from empirical research to support the view that EFL teaching is, in fact, limited.

Similarly to research on second language acquisition (Ellis 1994, 2005), whose essentially cognitive perspective has been confronted by systemic approaches (Block 2003; Chaiklin and Lave 1996), understanding

EFL teaching in Brazil requires a contextual view of its challenges – a goal pursued for over ten years through the documentation of students' experiences (Miccoli 1997, 2000, 2001, 2003, 2004) and more recently by complementing them with teachers' experiences (Porto 2003; Neffa 2004; Cunha 2005; Miccoli 2006). This agenda offers possibilities for transcending, transforming and even, one dares to hope, creating conceptions to displace myths and unquestioned 'truths' about EFL in Brazil.

In the course of this chapter 3 objectives are pursued: first, describing the rationale and methodology for investigating classroom experiences; second, presenting Brazilian teachers' experiences in public and private schools as similar and, finally, offering an empirically documented view of the environment in Brazil for EFL as a possibility to rise above the conception of *school English* that still dominates the collective unconscious[3] of Brazilian students and teachers.[4]

2 Background to the study: classroom experiences in a nutshell

Research on classroom experiences has emerged from a gap identified in classroom-centred research (Allwright 1983) that focuses on learners' characteristics and differences, learning styles, competition and outcomes but not on the social-psychological issues faced in EFL classrooms nor on the relationship of these events to learners' past histories. The gap comes from a cognitive, individual view of learning (Ellis 1994, 2005) that clashes with a view of learning as a socio-historically situated phenomenon (Lantolf and Appel 1994; Block 2003), which has developed from seeing the classroom as a culture (Breen 1986; van Lier 1988; Holliday 1994). Early studies on collaboratively structured classrooms have provided insiders' views of the learning process (Budd and Wright 1992; Mohan and Smith 1992; Swain and Miccoli 1994) and led to the identification of *experience* as a productive unit of analysis of students' accounts of classroom events (Miccoli 1997).

When someone's experience is highlighted in research, it acquires a distinctive meaning due to its being narrated in the first person. Thus, narrated experience would seem to be a way to get around Labov's (1972) observer's paradox, stated as that which is observed changes for being observed. Hence an intriguing question emerges – is it possible that the person who lives and narrates an experience transforms it from becoming an observer of her own experience? The tautological nature of the question is intended to situate experience as a fundamental concept for research that aims to document and understand social practices. As such, the construct *experience* is stated as a process of relationships and emotional dynamics that temporally involves experiencer, experienced and context of experience derived from the philosophical theories of Hegel (1991) and Dewey (1938) and those from the cognitive scientists Maturana (2001) and Nuñez (1995).

Hegel and Dewey view experience as organic and intertwined in the relationship of living beings to their environment, including thought, perception, feeling, suffering and action in a process, where both – living beings and environment – transform themselves. Maturana and Nuñez conceive of experience as the cornerstone of knowledge that results from organically based interactions of coexisting organisms that, as observers, distinguish events in their environment. Thus, experience develops as living phenomena properly associated to our biological heritage and communal existence, that is, as a process, which dialectically modifies and is modified. In addition, *experience* is considered the personal manifestation of a continuous developmental process, in which individuals are historically constituted by the experiences of others. In contrast to traditional research, where truth is sought predominantly to establish cause and effect relationships, experience as a process sets research goals at searching for acceptable meanings shared by a community of people at a specific moment.

Ethnography is one of the research methodologies to investigate students' and teachers' classroom experiences (Benson and Nunan 2002). An ethnographic approach to data collection and analysis identifies, describes and relates actions and contributions of participants in intersubjective terms so as to understand their significance. Data collection includes watching, asking, observing and interviewing (van Lier 1988). Thus, a group's cultural behaviour emerges from participants' interpretation of events in context, uncovering the meaning of what they have experienced and making explicit their *emic* theories, that is, views from within that highlight significant features of cultures by internal criteria (Geertz 1973).

Embracing that methodology, my investigations of students' classroom experiences (Miccoli 1997, 2000, 2001, 2003, 2004, 2006) have revealed three categories of *direct experiences*, whose origin can be traced back to in-class teacher-initiated tasks, and four categories of *indirect experiences* as out-of-the-classroom events that explain or influence direct experiences. Direct classroom experiences involve the *cognitive*, *social* and *affective* domains. Indirect classroom experiences have been labelled *contextual*, *personal*, *conceptual* and *future*.

This framework has been adapted to categorise teachers' experiences. In-class experiences are also classified as *direct*. Likewise, reference to out-of-the-class events that explain direct experiences are labelled *indirect*. Direct experiences refer to the domains of *pedagogical, social* and *affective* experiences, whereas indirect experiences refer to the *contextual* domain, that is, to reports about the role of EFL in society, the institution or the classroom and *conceptual* experiences, collapsing references to theories that explain, affect or guide teachers' pedagogical decisions (Miccoli 2006).

Classroom experiences have proven to be insightful in capturing the intricate relationships among professional, social, affective domains of experience as well as the wider contextual, and conceptual dimensions of events that crisscross the EFL classroom. This can be appreciated in Brazilian EFL teachers' experiences in public and private schools in Brazil.

3 The present study: EFL teachers' experiences in public and private schools

3.1 Aim of the study

This study is a follow-up of a previous study on teachers' experiences by Miccoli (2006). The focus of data analysis aimed to find in Brazilian teachers' experiences evidence to support or refute the current belief that in public schools EFL teachers work in far worse conditions from those experienced by their peers in private schools. A secondary goal was to find evidence for the usual association between public school EFL teaching and what is known as *school English,* as a proof of failure of EFL teaching in Brazilian schools. Thus, the research questions that guided us were: (1) Are public school teachers' experiences different from those of private school teachers? and (2) Is there evidence in teachers' reported experiences that *school English* is a product of EFL teaching in public schools alone?

3.2 Data collection and processing

Understanding classroom EFL teaching from teachers' points of view began with the opportunity of conducting two teacher development programmes. The first one lasted for three years with over 20 teachers from 11 private schools working in five Brazilian states from two of five national regions. They granted me the permission to analyse their classroom experiences documented in text productions (Miccoli 2006). The second programme lasted for only one year and involved 14 public school teachers working in urban and rural areas in the state of Minas Gerais. An assignment for an in-class discussion asked them to contribute to a research project by describing the teaching context in which they worked as well as their teaching in such situations. Thus, the experiences that constitute the database used in this study come from narrative reports presented by these teachers in the course of their continued-education programmes.

The same procedures used in the analyses of students' experiences (Miccoli 1997) were followed in transforming these teachers' written narratives into data: (1) identification of experiences; (2) grouping them according to main categories; (3) categorisation refinement by collapsing experiences into their appropriate subcategories; (4) intra and interrater reliability procedures to 'protect our research and theory construction from our enthusiasms' (Lather 1986b, p. 267).

3.3 Findings: EFL teachers' experiences in public and private schools

Our results of the data analysis are presented with excerpts from the data to illustrate differences or similarities in the teachers' experiences in public and private institutions. Given space limitations, only one excerpt from the data in each context is presented. In order to distinguish them, they have been labelled according to context – Private School (Pt. S.) and Public School (Pb. S.).

3.3.1 Direct classroom experiences

The first category of direct experiences is *pedagogical experiences*, whose most frequent subcategory refers to *teaching approaches*. Reports indicate diversity, as the extracts illustrate:

> I told them to open their notebooks and wrote three sentences that I would say in Portuguese...then, I wrote them correctly on the blackboard, asking three students individually how they had responded... after that, I told them to open their books to page 56...I read the activity dialogue, and told them to underline the words they didn't know...told them to complete the dialogue as required and then corrected their mistakes on the board. (Pt. S. Uberaba, MG)

> I began to teach...without textbooks from the school...I looked for help...they [directors] told me to 'do a little something, tell students to color drawings...I tried to create material that would fit the students' age and their reality. I created projects with music, texts...it worked, but there are still many difficulties. (Pb. S. Bom Despacho, MG)

Teaching in the private sector is demonstrably more traditional. The use of Portuguese is usual in class. Teaching is teacher-centred and English use is restricted to formulaic speech in interactions with students. The same happens in public schools, but for some teachers the need to develop teaching materials may lead them to rely on projects with a less teacher-centred approach, as it is the case for this teacher from Bom Despacho (the second excerpt).

These excerpts present similar patterns of pedagogical experiences – the use of Portuguese instead of English for communicating and the teacher-centred approach. However, the production of one's own teaching materials is more common in public schools. Yet, as the public school teacher states, creativity does not resolve all problems.

In the subcategory *teaching materials*, private school teachers report a need for other teaching resources while most public school teachers teach without the most basic supplies:

We need to have access to teaching materials that present practical suggestions for in-class activities. (Pt. S. Rio de Janeiro, RJ)

The school lacks resources; does not offer any materials for EFL teaching; we do not have access to books nor tapes; Xerox copies are virtually unavailable, as the number of copies is limited to two pages per student per term. The library doesn't even have enough dictionaries. The other day I tried an activity using dictionaries and there were only four in the school. (Pb. S. São Roque de Minas, MG)

The data indicate that private school teachers are usually disappointed with textbooks. As for public school teachers, lack of textbooks and other teaching supplies is the norm. These differences do not eliminate the similarity – regardless of the textbook or of the no-textbook situation, public and private school EFL teachers complain about the lack of adequate teaching materials.

In the pedagogical subcategory *four-skills teaching*, teachers from both contexts find it difficult to integrate skills. Some teachers decide not to deal with listening and speaking in class:

As for what cannot be worked out...working with the four skills is a problem that originates in the limitation of the actual number of classes per week, the number of students per class as well as physical infrastructure of the classroom. (Pt. S. Belo Horizonte, MG)

Teaching English in this situation is very difficult, almost impossible, because we have an excessive number of students per classroom (average 45) and individual attention is almost impossible. (Pb. S. Bambuí, MG)

The data reveal the difficulty of integrating the four skills in class. Usually EFL teachers have just one class-hour per week when working with primary students. Two class-hours a week is the average teaching load for EFL in junior high and high school. Added to the large numbers of students they have to cope with, about 45 per class, these teachers lack the approaches and skills needed to integrate listening and speaking activities into their teaching.

The subcategory of pedagogical experiences – *use of new technologies* predominantly contains reports from private school teachers. In this context, finding ways to make better use of the available resources is the problem. In public schools, most reports attest to the common lack of chalk or paper, but when other equipment is available, teachers cannot count on them:

> I regard as important the use of resources such as computers and videos... with all the technology available nowadays, it is inexcusable that the English class be so monotonous and tiresome, but using them well can be a challenge. (Pt. S. Uberaba, MG)

> The school even has a TV and a VCR, but when it is not broken, it is being used, since it is the only one available for the whole school. (Pb. S. Campo Belo, MG)

The excerpts reveal that technological equipment can be found in both teaching contexts. It is true that they are more frequently found in private schools; nonetheless they are not always used. Conversely, when public school teachers have access to technological resources, they cannot use them. Thus, in this subcategory, private schools teachers find better teaching conditions.

The last pedagogical experiences' subcategory includes reports on *evaluation* that comprise experiences with homework correction and grading:

> In a school system that forces us to follow evaluation guidelines, it is difficult to find a way to value individual differences to motivate those who are more advanced, without discouraging those who have limitations or difficulties. (Pt. S. Rio de Janeiro, RJ)

> The student could get an F during the school year and would still be promoted since there is not way to flunk a student in this school.

Students have much difficulty, because they have 'unlearned' how to study with this new approach to assessment. I evaluate them daily, motivating them to feel important and gradually I succeed. If I didn't evaluate them daily and left assessment for last, asking them to study as I used to do some years ago, many would have need special attention to improve their grades. (Pb. S. Formiga, MG)

The excerpts show that evaluation is a problem in both contexts. In private schools, teachers usually are not allowed to develop a plan for evaluating. In public schools, teachers have to deal with incomprehensible policies. In both contexts, teachers lack the skills to conduct an efficient evaluation process.

In the category of *social experiences,* the first subcategory includes reports on the *teacher's role*, revealing how teachers see themselves:

We need somehow 'magic' to meet the different necessities of the students, keeping a good teaching level. As consequence, it becomes difficult to realize any ideal work, which tries to develop the four abilities. (Pt. S. Uberaba, MG)

In order to work in the public school with 5th to 8th grades, the teacher has to be an artist, he has to have a variety of materials, game activities, music to motivate the group... I want to learn more everyday, I don't know everything, but I want to do the best I can and to become a different teacher. (Pb. S. Formiga, MG)

Instead of differences, the extracts have shown similarities between public and private school teachers' definition of themselves whom they characterise as magicians or artists that cope with problems and limitations. These seem far from a professional image.

Another subcategory of social experiences includes descriptions of *EFL students*:

Students who do not have previous knowledge of EFL end up not enjoying the class, not getting involved with it. Then they face it as just one more subject they have to study in order to obtain the minimum grade to be promoted to the next level. (Pt. S. Palmas, TO)

Students are very agitated, hyperactive, and ill mannered. (Pb. S. Formiga, MG)

The data in this subcategory indicates that teachers predominantly see negative qualities in their students. The adjectives more commonly attributed to Brazilian students are: lazy, restless and uncooperative. It may be concluded that EFL teachers in private and public schools share an unconstructive outlook on students.[5]

In the social subcategory *teachers' interaction with students* reports can be characterised as similar since reports from public and private schools show both conflict and collaboration between teachers and students:

> The adoption of an interactive practice with activities in small groups and in a involving way... I'm involved in the development of three projects that I believe will bring extra energy to my classes: 1) cartoon captioning; 2) a mobile library; 3) exchanging mail in English among groups. (Pt. S. Rio de Janeiro, RJ)

> Students who pay attention in class are only interested in grammar (a topic in tests), forgetting about the other skills because those who want to develop a better oral performance look for English courses that make my work seem outdated. Other students couldn't care less. (Pb. S. Formiga, MG)

The similarity in teachers' descriptions of interaction with students comes from having to do so much to engage them. Understanding experiences in this realm demands the consideration of issues that that transcend congeniality. Teachers who invest in knowing their students and in meeting their interests seem to have fewer problems.

The final subcategory of teachers' social experiences is *lack of discipline* – an event that affects them randomly:

> Discipline is a serious problem. We try to act as best as we can, but most times we cannot count on family support, which seems to have lost control over their children and transfer this responsibility to us, expecting us to do what they themselves, as parents, haven't been able to. (Pt. S. Uberaba, MG)

> Lack of discipline is a great problem... I had adults and teenagers as students... some of them were concerned about learning, but the majority were not and only wanted to listen to songs in English. (Pb. S. Itaúna, MG)

Dealing with lack of discipline affects both public and private school teachers – a problem originating outside the classroom. Teachers are left on their own to deal with a problem not limited to the EFL class. Yet, teachers relate most discipline problems to a lack of motivation. Thus, finding meaning in EFL classes may have a positive effect on discipline.

In the category of *affective experiences*, the first subcategory includes reports that refer to teachers' *motivation, interest* and *effort*:

> I love what I do and I want to improve each day, so that I can offer the children a class, which will be as pleasant for them, as it is for me. (Pt. S. Belo Horizonte, MG)

> I do my job positively. In order to do that, I need to have a strict sense of self-discipline for preparing classes and teaching them. I have to keep my enthusiasm constantly so that I can positively influence students. I also have to keep up to date paying for short-term courses (which is difficult) to increase my professional knowledge to deserve my job. (Pb. S. Bom Despacho, MG)

Reports show private and public teachers committed to education. They like their jobs and search for professional advancement in spite of their low salaries. These results should be considered with caution since the teachers who volunteered their reports and descriptions were in teacher development programmes, thus the data might not actually portray the broader population of teachers in these contexts.

The second affective experiences subcategory involves *frustration* with the educational system in Brazil and with students' lack of motivation:

> I do want my students to speak and understand English but I confess that in our working environment – 38 students in class, with just a few really interested in learning to speak, with behavioural problems, with only two 50-minute's classes a week and with all the content that has to be taught in that time, without forgetting that from this content written tests must be constructed – I cannot see any real possibility of teaching my students to speak and understand as if they were language-institute students. (Pt. S. Varginha, MG)

> English is still considered unnecessary in our students' education. Therefore, it is almost impossible to teach English and succeed at it. I have only managed to teach a little grammar and vocabulary. (Pb. S. Formiga, MG)

The data reveal that teachers' frustration comes from idealising the classroom. Teaching smaller classes would be better. Yet, what frustrates them is the norm – not the exception. The ideal classroom for the private school teachers is that of private language courses – a belief shared by Brazilians, as Barcelos discusses in this volume. Public school teachers' frustration includes the virtual worthlessness of EFL in the curriculum, the result of an educational policy that remains in force despite legal possibilities for change.[6] Teachers seem to be fighters against all odds in these reports as frustration is recurrent in both contexts.

3.3.2 Indirect classroom experiences

The first category contains reports on *contextual experiences*, whose first subcategory includes reference to *extra-institutional* experiences:

> The EFL teacher should emphasise the importance of speaking the language. The Brazilian teacher is an educator and not a representative of the foreign culture. (Pt. S. Colatina, ES)

> The situation in which I work can be described as poor because there is no interest by the state government in selecting good, updated textbooks; we work with 10-year-old books. (Pb. S. Bambuí, SP)

Private language courses haunt private school teachers. From a different perspective, data from public school teachers reveal disgust with public policies that fail to meet their own goals. Thus, EFL teachers feel the presence of extra-institutional factors in class.

The second contextual subcategory includes reports on *institutional* experiences with references to teachers' schools and the status of EFL teaching in their schools:

> We'd like to discuss what to do to value English in the educational process as a whole since it is equally important for our students' intellectual, moral and cultural education. (Pb. S. Belo Horizonte, MG)

> I face various barriers to finish my syllabus, because I cannot count on the support of the school since it disregards EFL and does not recognize sour work...the school...assumes that it is impossible to teach a new language to students who face difficulties in learning their own native language. (Pb. S. Itapecerica, MG)

Teachers' institutional experiences are similar. EFL is considered less important than maths and also seen as impossible to teach. Thus, institutions usually neglect it by reducing class time given to EFL or using the English class period for announcements and assemblies.

Another subcategory within contextual experience is that of *large groups*:

> We believe that the biggest challenge for teaching EFL in regular[7] schools is the number of students in classroom. (Pt. S. Rio de Janeiro, RJ)

One of the problems I face is the large number of students per class. Pb. S. Bambuí, MG

EFL teachers in regular schools teach large groups of 30 to 45. This is the norm in Brazilian schools, but EFL teachers consider it excessive, probably due to the fact that private language courses' groups rarely exceed 15 students per class.

Another subcategory within teachers' contextual experiences is that of *multi-level classes*:

> One of the problems we face is students who can be grouped into different levels of knowledge in EFL all in the same classroom ... this causes us to have little feedback from the work we do in class. (Pt. S. Patos de Minas, MG)

> Thanks to the 'school inclusion' program and to the system of cycles [system in which a student can be promoted to the next level even if he has failed in adequate achievement] in the same class there are students with learning difficulties, even with mental disabilities, semi-illiterate students who already are in the 7th or 8th grade, students who go to school only now and then and those few ones who take their studies seriously. (Pb. S. Campo Belo, MG)

Difficulty in dealing with multi-level classes is a problem in both contexts. Teachers in private schools find trouble dealing with different levels of proficiency. Public school teachers deal with differences that come from public policies that bring into the classroom students with diverse needs without offering the adequate support for teachers to attend to these needs.

The final subcategory within contextual experiences refers to reports on class *time*, which negatively affects EFL teaching. Lack of time is the teachers' most common complaint:

> Only if we had extra time we could consider preparing students to use English for communication purposes. (Pt. S. Montes Claros, MG)

> Class time is very short: two weekly 50-minute's classes to cover so much content is not enough. (Pb. S. Campo Belo, MG)

Complaints about insufficient EFL class time are found in all teachers' reports – evidence that the usual 100 minutes weekly hampers the educational goals teachers aim for.

The final category of indirect experiences includes reports containing teachers' *conceptual experiences* that explain classroom practices. The most common is – *It's impossible to teach English with a communicative approach in public and private schools*:

> Even knowing that teaching and learning should happen through interaction in communicative approach classes, I think speaking is still a distant goal. (Pt. S. Colatina, ES)

> My approach is not communicative because I don't have textbooks or time to teach. I only teach some vocabulary and grammar and forget about the four skills. (Pb. S. Itaúna, MG)

Teachers' difficulties to implement communicative EFL teaching have multiple justifications – many students, many levels of proficiency, little time, much to teach. It is a theory that predominates in teachers' reports.

Another theory to explain practice is – *It's impossible to use English in class*:

> We rarely use English during the class routine activities... Our justifications of this practice are... number of students in classroom, students' lack of interest in the class, inconsistency of background knowledge among them, lack of a proper environment and the amount of information in Portuguese that enters the classroom all the time. (Pt. S. Rio de Janeiro, RJ)

> Teaching English in this situation is not easy. The teacher has to make an extra effort to invent alternatives so that teaching can happen. In this situation communication in English in class is not likely to happen. (Pb. S. São Roque de Minas, MG)

The data indicate that teachers list justifications for not using English in class. This is recurrent in public and private school teachers' reports.

The final theory that explains practice is: *Beginners are motivated*. Public and private schools teachers see first time English students as more interested, participative and motivated than old timers in English:

> I'm working with 3 to 6 year-old children on average. In this stage, they love the EL classes and learn with enthusiasm. (Pt. S. Uberaba, MG)

> Students who have been my students in 3rd and 4th grades already have some background in English. They are able to construct sentences

and thanks to that I am able to use English during the whole class. (Pb. S. São Roque de Minas, MG)

Public and private context EFL teachers who teach beginners agree that they show more enthusiasm for learning.

3.4 Discussion

A review of these results answers the first research question. Direct experiences are similar for private and public school teachers as far as: (1) pedagogical approach – teacher-centred predominates (2) teaching the four skills – mostly ignored, (3) in evaluation – difficulties are most commonly reported, (4) view of their teacher's role – the teacher as a clown or a juggler, (5) view of students – as uninterested and unmotivated, (6) dealing with lack of discipline – teachers feel helpless (7) their frustration with teaching conditions – never perfect, (8) interaction between teachers and students – conflicted or satisfactory depending on the situation, and (9) teachers' commitment to their professional practice – both groups committed, provided one remembers that the teachers in this study were in teacher development programmes. Differences have been evidenced in: (1) the teaching materials – in private schools teachers can count on the use of textbooks; in public schools teachers rarely use textbooks, (2) the use of technologies – private school teachers want to improve their use of them; public school teachers rarely have access to these either because they are too few or broken.

Concerning indirect experiences, similarities are shared in all contextual and conceptual categories. The context is similar with regard to (1) the far-from-ideal extra-institutional context – private and public teachers are haunted by private language courses and the lack of governmental investments destroy teachers' initiatives, (2) the second-class status of EFL as a school subject – a problem coming from the disbelief in EFL teaching in regular schools, (3) the class size – always large, (4) multilevel groups – something natural yet unaccepted due to the idealisation of classes similar to those of private language courses, and (5) reduced class time – a residue from the 1971 LDB that still prevails. Conceptually, through the theories that explain practice, public and private school teachers agree that: (1) it is impossible to teach English using the communicative approach – due to large class sizes and multi-level groups in class, (2) it is difficult to use English in class to interact with students – justified by the same reasons, and that (3) first time English learners are more motivated than their older counterparts – in spite of the implication that students may lose their motivation from the teaching they receive. Thus, the results indicate that there are more similarities than differences when comparing EFL teaching in public and private schools.

The answer to research question two indicates that EFL teachers' experiences in public and private schools illuminate what the challenges are that teachers have to face so as to revert the state of affairs that explain *school English* as a sad reality. Discussing *school English* as a problem restricted to public school contexts has to be reviewed in the light of the results yielded here. Teachers' reports from private schools attest that they face problems similar to those commonly associated with the public sector. In fact, in spite of the obvious differences between these institutions, when the issue is EFL teaching, they share many more similarities than differences.

Thus, the results contradict the commonly held belief that associates more difficulties in teaching and less interest from teachers in public schools. Surprisingly, for the two groups of teachers in this study, more descriptions from public school teachers of what they do in class comes closer to a communicative approach than their private schools peers, despite working in worse conditions. The data has also evidenced that teachers in both contexts want to improve their practices, which may be an indication that given the opportunity, teachers want to trade frustration for a sense of accomplishment in teaching.

4 Conclusion

The point of comparing EFL teaching experiences in public and private contexts lies in recognising that Brazilian teachers find it difficult to work with the communicative approach. Different limitations explain it – those external to the classroom cannot be overcome since teachers have no control over them. However, problems that originate in class are manageable, which means that *teachers* should find ways to work them out. As Hunt (1987) urges, change begins personally. This implies accepting the challenge to overcome *school English*. For as long as the teachers in public and private schools continue to reproduce partial approaches to teaching English embodied in the use of Portuguese in class and in teaching reading and writing alone, *school English* – that uncomfortable admission – will remain a reality not in-tune with the evolution in EFL teaching and learning research. Specifically, teachers should be encouraged to employ English in class, trusting that students will eventually make use of it. That change alone would have a profound impact on students' motivation. This opens the way for a more communicative approach to EFL teaching, where multi-level classes are not an impediment, but in fact, preferable to provide opportunities for negotiation of meaning. Taking risks in new seating arrangements, exchanging teachers' individual attention for more peer editing and group work, less teacher talk and more teacher feedback – actions that are within any teacher's reach should be attempted in order to achieve the inside-out transformation of Brazilian EFL classrooms when change from the outside is not a reliable option.

Notes

1. The accepted failure of school EFL teaching in Brazil is one of the reasons for a spread in the number of private language courses that provide EFL instruction in far better teaching conditions than those found in Brazilian public or private schools.
2. Some schools introduce English before grade five – the time dictated by law to begin English instruction.
3. In this volume, the contributions of Ana Maria Barcelos and Vera Menezes de Oliveira e Paiva discuss this issue through the use of narratives.
4. Minas Gerais is the fourth largest state in Brazil.
5. Something Barcelos (2006b) confirms.
6. The 1971 LDB, a legal instrument providing the directives for education in Brazil, not only reduced the number of hours dedicated to English in the school curriculum, but also made it discretionary. The most recent 1996 LDB has made foreign languages obligatory, but does not mandate the amount of class time to be dedicated. Most schools continue dedicating to English half of the class time allotted to other subjects.
7. In Brazil teachers refer to regular schools to distinguish them from private language courses.

Part III
Self-Narratives

6
Turning the Kaleidoscope – EFL Research as Auto/Biography

Leena Karlsson

This chapter has arisen from my PhD thesis that I am working on. It is an account of the research process, but it is also an autobiographical experiential narrative of a teacher-researcher.

1 Initial reflections

When I began my doctoral research I was intrigued by the fact that I had come across two different and separate sets of stories in the research literature and in my own professional experience: there were stories about and by teachers on the one hand, and about and by foreign-language learners on the other. They were all about the same place, the language classroom, but the learner stories and the teacher stories remained separate. Even when learning encounters and interaction were described, the focus was on either one participant or the other, seldom on both or on the interaction between them. In particular, the jokes, memories, stories and texts about teachers often assigned them a very controversial and even inhuman role: they were described as tyrants or witches, but also as angels or demigods. These particular metaphorical expressions for describing English teachers also come up in the Finnish learners' autobiographies studied by Turunen (2003) and Turunen and Kalaja (2004). These textual doubles troubled me.

As we moved from teacher-centred pedagogy towards more learner- and learning-centred approaches, we language teachers had, I believed, learnt to better understand our learners and the conditions that make learning possible, even rewarding and enjoyable. In order to understand ourselves and the approaches we had chosen to use, many of us had seen the need to engage in research based on our day-to-day teaching experience. Learners' voices were definitely not missing from teacher-research, neither were the teachers' own voices but there was an absence of research effort in which both voices would come through infiltrated with the other, collected from the same encounters, and voicing the same experience (for a notable Finnish exception see Jaatinen 2003). My inquiry started from the insecurity I felt when considering the separate stories I encountered, and in particular stories in which a teacher figure seemed to loom over all other influences and motivational factors. My own, at times very fragile, teacher identity also gave me an inner urge to work out the tension that I experienced between my way of being a teacher and the image created in the learner stories.

2 The research story begins

2.1 A complex quest

My research process has been motivated by a need to understand how the nature and meaning of English as a Foreign Language (EFL) interaction is experienced by learners and counsellors. My quest has been for a mode and language of researching that is not distancing, that is, that makes it possible to ease the tension between analytic distance and lived experience. My aim has been to discover a way of linking experience and intellect, emotion and theory, thought and action, communication and analysis, reading and writing, and most importantly, learner and teacher/counsellor. I have sought a method of inquiry that would be pedagogically sustainable, and suitable for researching autonomy and counselling; a method that would make room for lived experience, meaning-making and narrating, which in my view characterise encounters between learners and counsellors. There must be a way of researching that would honour the past and be respectful towards the participants, that is, be ethically sound. I wanted to develop a way of researching learner-counsellor dialogues, and autobiographical narratives as part of the dialogues, that is relevant and reflective, as well as self-reflexive. Self-reflexivity became the very starting point of my research, and I hope to show how it has guided my ongoing effort. I will be looking at research as a complex internal quest in which reflexivity has helped me to recognise my own preconceptions and to monitor their influence.

2.2 Narrative and experience

I have chosen to interpret educational experience through a narrative lens because, like Clandinin and Connelly (2000), I argue that narrative inquiry arises from experience and that it is the closest one can come to it. I understand lived experience as the meaning that we read into our life situations. Experience in my view is ambiguous, it is complex and multilayered; it can be interpreted but only in ways that will remain non-conclusive. I also take my own understanding to be experience. The meanings we read into past experiences may change because the present, the moment of telling, guides our interpretation. Thus when constructing an experiential narrative we open our past to reflection and reappraisal. Moreover, the same process of bringing in current perspectives to illuminate and even change the past may take place when we listen to the experiential narratives of others (Conle 2006). When one story causes us to make metaphorical links with another, that is, through resonance (Conle 1993), we respond to the memories and stories of others with memories of our own, and together these stories will open up possibilities for our future. This is how narrative will help teachers/counsellors and learners to meet. Resonance is also the process that carries the inquiry along by producing yet further stories.

I understand narrative as both the phenomenon and the method (Clandinin and Connelly 2000). Life is filled with narratives or stories, and so are educational encounters. Language-learning experiences, like other life events, are organised in stories, and autobiography guides this lifelong development. I have been interested in how language learners and counsellors story and re-story their experiences. Their telling is filled with narrative fragments recalling events that happen in time and space, and which are prone to change, context-bound and meaning-bearing. Narrative helps in linking the fragments: it shows their interdependence but not necessarily the cause-and-effect dependency. I have made broad use of emplotment as an interpretative process of linking narrative episodes, of searching for and understanding them while listening to and reading the stories in my data and when re-storying myself (Ricoeur 1984).

In my analysis and interpretation I take the telling and the narratives to be dialogical in that the stories are shaped in the co-telling. My interpretation is based on a dialogic reading of my data, and should be seen as a suggestion that will leave room for the reader's meaning-making. The reader has the possibility to test the verisimilitude and credibility of my interpretation through vicarious experience: could I have been part of this, could this have happened in my classroom/counselling session? My narrative is intended to help the reader to enter the world I am describing, and to meet an experience other than her own.

2.3 Auto/biography

The concept of auto/biography as presented by the sociologist Liz Stanley (1992, 1993) has enormous analytic potential for teacher-researchers attempting to understand the classroom experiences and memories of their learners, their colleagues and themselves, and more importantly, wanting to write about those experiences. We have all been learners in various language classrooms for quite a number of years in our lives – as children, teenagers and adolescents. We have been teacher trainees and teachers in yet other language classrooms as adults. These experiences are bound to have influenced us deeply and, uncomfortable as it may feel, they are probably a strong driving force in our interpretation of our students' educational experiences, both past and present. As Stanley (1992, p. 158) puts it: 'biography and autobiography are inseparable dimensions of the same experience'.

Talking and writing about life, or learning experiences, means that the researcher is active in constructing knowledge; that research is auto/biography in the sense that the researcher is using his or her own life to understand and interpret the lives of the research participants. The auto/biographical I is the very agent who is actively producing knowledge, knowledge that is contextual, situated and specific (Stanley 1993). The teacher-researcher thus needs to search the research and writing process carefully for accumulating layers of understanding and temporally located acts of biography (Stanley 1993; Jaatinen 2003).

2.4 The kaleidoscope metaphor

When looking for ways of representing the experiences and voices in the data, I chose to use a metaphor to assist with the telling. Metaphors make it possible to bring in what we know, but they also challenge us to see the already familiar in a new way, in a novel constellation, and from a different point of view. The kaleidoscope metaphor also comes from Liz Stanley (1992). The kaleidoscope encompasses my way of researching, and of conceptualising the phenomenon of language learning and teaching, and teacher knowledge. Although this metaphor is probably painstakingly familiar to those working with life-story research in sociology, I find it a novel enough way of picturing language learning and teaching/counselling. Stanley (1992, p. 178) writes: 'You look and you see one fascinatingly complex pattern, the light changes, you accidentally move, or deliberately shake the kaleidoscope, and you see – composed of the same elements – a somewhat different pattern'.

For me, finding a research methodology and metaphor meant finding one for teaching and counselling, because I look upon teaching as a way of doing research (Jaatinen 2003). Both teacher-researchers and counsellors, in my view, need a kaleidoscopic picture of their learners and of themselves, not a microscopic one, in order to appreciate the complexity and variability of learning encounters. They need to see the kaleidoscopic effect of every new encounter, every new dialogue of autobiographies, every new telling, every re-storying, and every new interpretation.

3 The study: thesis as auto/biography

3.1 Aims and motivation

When looking into the kaleidoscope of EFL stories my basic motivation has been to describe how the past learning and teaching/counselling experiences of the participants (students and their counsellor) organise themselves into texts and into talk, both counselling talk and research-interview talk. I have also wanted to describe how I as a researcher, but also as a counsellor, read these texts and the talk. There is no single story that would encompass the individual experiences of the participants. The ones I have chosen to tell in the thesis should be viewed against the background of my pedagogical and personal autobiography, as should those that have remained untold. I collected the data on various occasions and in various settings during a one-term ALMS module (Autonomous Learning Modules, an English course at the University of Helsinki Language Centre based on learner autonomy). There are two types of data: (1) student documents (open-ended personally inspired reflection texts written by the students in their histories, student logs and diaries), and (2) additional research documents (video-taped group and individual counselling sessions, and biographical narrative interviews).

3.2 Working with the data

I have based my work on the insight that we always look at past events from where we are at the point of telling. Moreover, I have aimed at avoiding a technical interpretation of the past as a series of events that we can control and explain away. Varto (2005) writes about how an experience, in fact, has no beginning in the sense that each moment we experience can give rise to unexpected and strange constellations of experiences, meanings that are new and unpredictable. When experience is looked upon in hindsight, this beginningless beginning is no longer clear, but we only need to think of our everyday experiences to realise how the only link between the fragments is the I, the one who experiences. For me, autobiographical experiential narrative has provided a way of approaching and appreciating experiences, their remaking and retelling.

I have conceptualised narrative inquiry as a three-dimensional space: temporality forms the first dimension, the personal and the social the second, and place the third (Clandinin and Connelly 2000). A narrative study thus focuses on both the personal and the social: it moves both inwards to include feelings and outwards to include the environment and other people. It has temporal dimensions: it moves backwards and forwards, it has a past, a present and a future reference, and experiences grow out of other experiences. Moreover, the context is a specific place or sequence of places. I have attempted to build this three-dimensionality into the research process as part of my double narrative process in which one and the same process includes the narratives generated by all participants in interaction and the voice of the researcher, myself as the narrator (Kyratzis and Green 1997).

In turning the kaleidoscope I have posed questions to my data at various points in time and place, and have addressed different aspects of learner/counsellor experience. I have considered the data from various angles, positioning different bits of it in the kaleidoscope, then testing and retesting the new emerging patterns and the old ones against each other. This dialogic relation will appear in the way I write about these turns of the kaleidoscope in one story from my thesis, Johanna's story, which follows. My writing in this chapter, like in the thesis, is fragmentary, but I have attempted to show the links between the fragments and how these links have come about. I will be storying and acknowledging my shifting interpretative position in each story fragment. The story I have chosen to tell in this chapter has to do with the need to understand the teacher's role in my students' narratives, and the need to understand the role of autobiographical elements and emotions in language learning. It concerns how we use them, hide them, but act on them no matter what we say or write, and how it is often difficult if not impossible to interpret them. The reporting, the researcher's writing process, is yet another example of autobiography meeting autobiography.

3.3 Johanna

3.3.1 The storyline

The storyline goes through the following stages, which are represented by the kaleidoscope fragments in the auto/biographical re-storying in Section 3.3.2:

1. The researcher reads Johanna's pre-course questionnaire and stops short at one of her memories from school.

2. Later she reads Johanna's reflection text and meets another version of the memory.
3. In the group interview Johanna has tears in her eyes when she briefly mentions her experiences from school.
4. The researcher watches the video of the group sessions. Johanna has a minor role in this episode, but she is the one with the most dramatic message.
5. In Johanna's research interview the researcher takes up the school experience, new details come up and the relevance of past experience to later learning is discussed.
6. The researcher interviews the group counsellor and understands the connection between Johanna's memory and her own teacher vulnerability.
7. In a conference presentation, the researcher tells Johanna's story in order to highlight teacher memories and her auto/biographical approach to interpretation.

Presenting the chronological storyline first is a way of inserting my researcher-self into the story, but it is also meant to give the reader a sense of how the memory moved chronologically through the thesis inquiry, and to show the different contexts in which it reappeared. By using the historical present all the way through the story I am emphasising the fact that these events continue to preoccupy me, both as a researcher and as a counsellor (Ochs and Capp 1996).

3.3.2 Johanna through the eyepiece of the ALMS kaleidoscope

Johanna's vivid teacher memory resonates strongly with my own autobiography as a learner, which is how I situate and position myself at the beginning of this story. It is a story with qualities that put it in danger of becoming what Conle (1999, p. 18) calls 'a one-liner', or 'a hardened story'. By this she means a story that can be readily made to suit new purposes of a new teller. A researcher's telling voice can acquire the quality of an all-knowing narrator who uses a story for her own purposes by detaching it from its experiential moorings and from its true context. According to Conle, this can easily happen if this voice is distant from the characters in the story. Johanna's story should not become my instrument, nor should I use it to generalise. I hope to show in my emplotment how, in fact, it changed in form at every telling, but kept its lasting non-changing non-linguistic/experiential qualities as well. In the following turnings of the kaleidoscope I will not only chronicle events, as in the listing of the memory's movements above, I will also narrate, and in that way be both a narrator and a character in my story (Conle 1999). This means that I am as much subject to temporal and contextual changes in the story, as are my research participants, which in turn will help me to maintain a sense of their agency. Significantly, my interpreter's position is shifting in relation to Johanna.

I will now turn the kaleidoscope slowly to bring one auto/biographical fragment into view at a time.

The first fragment
The students are asked to answer email questions concerning their foreign-language learning background before the course begins. Johanna writes about a significant learning experience in German, which has affected her as a learner of English as well:

> Negative. The German teacher in upper-secondary school was a tyrant who made everyone cry in turn. I haven't opened German textbooks since – and I won't open one! We started checking our homework together before going to class so that no wrong answers would come out. No more German, please! (email, translated from Finnish)

Johanna's words resonate with an experience I had as a pupil, and so my story is immediately evoked as a response to Johanna's. I remember having to stand between rows of desks, being cross-examined for what seemed like hours while the other pupils were gazing at me. It was a maths lesson, I was crying and I was only 11 or 12. Conle (1993, 2000) sees resonance as a major structuring principle in narrative research. The metaphorical understanding that she claims connects parts of stories works in my case: there is an adult in Johanna's story, as there is in mine, who uses her power to question up to the point of breaking the child's will and making her cry in shame. The resonance is the powerlessness and victimisation of the one being questioned. Conle suggests that these story-to-story connections work by linking clusters of images in one to clusters of images in others. The connection is not constructed, but automatic in that a metaphor is not consciously created or asked for.

Johanna's memory is from her school days about ten years earlier. While obviously based on a very intense experience, it has all the qualities of becoming dismissed by many as another sob story. However, it echoes scenes in many of the stories about Finnish schools and teachers recently analysed by Salo (2005). Feelings of inferiority, of shame, of lacking knowledge or skills, are all part of the popular imagery of teaching and learning. Obviously, the plot in stories about school and teachers in Finland is often built around how stigmatising takes place, and how a learner is labelled as somebody who does not know, does not have the skills, does not qualify. The popular image of how teachers and teaching stigmatise is readily recycled and thus in danger of hardening into generalised and even stereotypical narratives. It could also give rise to frozen stories that become prisons for those telling them. As a teacher, I see a pressing need to take the story in my hands and to study my professional identity from the perspective of reinventing and recreating. I do not wish to succumb to the stereotype of a tyrant teacher in a hardened story, but I do wish to leave my learner victim's cage now that I know the power of the story over me.

The second fragment

It is evident that in each telling of her personal story, Johanna is evoking new details of the lived experience. Ochs and Capp (1996) point out that every telling of a narrative provides not only the narrator but also the listener or reader with an opportunity for fragmented self-understanding. Each telling only evokes certain memories or concerns in both partners. We only apprehend our partial selves, and only fragments of experience are accessed on each occasion: it is never complete self-understanding on the part of the narrator or the listener/reader. Johanna is continually building novel understandings of what she is as a language learner as she tells and retells her story. Her presentations of her partial language-learner selves are integrated into a collective voice (*made everyone cry, we started checking*) in the email extract quoted above. In this second fragment the pattern becomes even more extended: more language teachers enter the picture, but in the same role as the first, as tyrants:

> As a learner I was lazy I admit. I did my homework but nothing more. Its partly cause of the teachers. They were horrible in every languages. If someone didn't know the answer they made her cry in front of everybody. It really killed something inside most of us. That's also why I didn't want to learnt any language for a while. (Johanna's reflection text, written in English, not edited).

This account of the experience is in a text written for the first individual counselling session. The story here is firstly about what Johanna does and secondly about how she feels. Undoubtedly, the consequences of what she feels are more significant: she loses her interest in all foreign languages for a few years. Bruner (1986) suggests that narrators construct a dual landscape, one of action and one of consciousness. In the former they focus on action and in the latter on beliefs and feelings. The landscape of consciousness categorises and rationalises the actions and beliefs for the reader: something died in Johanna's learner self and so she lost interest in learning.

The lasting non-changing emotional quality of Johanna's story is the experience of shame. Salo (2005) suggests that two themes in particular recur in the telling of negative school memories: (1) bad experiences and (2) monotony and routines. These are stories that need telling in that they characteristically revolve around unresolved events. What is equally important, they are stories that need to be listened to. They gain novel meanings in the active listening and in the sharing of the experience. The turn in the road might come for a troubled narrator who keeps reliving one and the same experience over and over again if he or she has somebody who will listen. As a counsellor at this point, I should be able to accept this listener responsibility, my part in the student's meaning-making process. Thus, the counsellor's true dialogic relationship to the learner becomes crucial in the narrator's process towards coherence.

The third fragment
I now look at Johanna with tears in her eyes in the group interview when she mentions having had 'bad experiences' at school. For me, her reaction is an indication of how the autobiographical event is stored in our memory as sensations, as bodily reactions (Jaatinen 2003). Johanna's experience has guided her in making decisions about what to learn (*not German, ever*) and how to learn (*I hoped ALMS would be a different course*). As a counselor, I need to listen to and to try to understand Johanna's emplotment of her story, her active construction of the past in the light of the present. I need to listen for the narrator's truth, the truth as it appears to her.

The fourth fragment
Then I turn the kaleidoscope to show an episode in the first group session of the course. I am following the researcher's chronology here because although this session was the very first thing on the course, it only came into my knowledge when I was watching the video and editing it. The transcription of the extract is a pale image of the episode on

the video. I have added comments on gestures, tone of voice and facial expressions before sliding the fragment into my kaleidoscope.

Timo:	and if you are too worried about grammar you won't open your mouth and talk.
Counsellor:	that's right that's right and again many students have this fear say at school I daren't open my mouth because the minute I made a mistake the teacher was there (wagging her finger) how many of you have had that experience. (most put up their hands and laughter follows)
Johanna:	we were all crying at least once, it was terrible (shakes her head)
Counsellor:	and that's sad. (continues to talk about student experiences of ALMS courses)
Mia:	we were talking a lot about being at school and studying English at school that although our faces get older the little girl inside (laughs, gestures) there is remembering how it was to sit and wait your turn to read that one sentence and counting and thinking if that one sentence is too difficult.
Counsellor:	and so by the time when you were so busy counting and worrying about your turn you totally lose whatever everybody else is saying.
Mia:	you don't hear anything you just think it wasn't so important, only my turn matters
Counsellor:	exactly I remember doing that on my Finnish course when I first came.
Timo:	(jokingy) nightmares coming back.
Counsellor:	absolutely.
Mia:	and I understand that you are all the time saying that you are not looking at our mistakes it's very good to say it so maybe we ah. (hides her face in her hands when she can't find the word)
Counsellor:	believe it.
Mia:	yes thank you.
Counsellor:	please believe it. (ALMS group session)

The counsellor accepts Johanna's story here and legitimises her experience by weaving it into stories about student experiences from ALMS modules. The counsellor is the primary recipient of the story, and Johanna and the other students are gazing at her at this point. What

Johanna and the counsellor are co-telling resonates with Mia so that she tells her own story. Interestingly enough, Salo's two types of negative school memories are intertwined here: Mia brings in the routines aspect. *Counting and worrying about one's turn to read out the one sentence in the text or gap exercise* is remembered by Mia and her group members, and the counsellor readily relates to it and replies with a story of her own.

The fifth fragment
The next time the memory appears in Johanna's research interview:

> She was an old-fashioned teacher who demanded that we learn a certain rigmarole by heart and then moved on to do some exercises. She did not accept mistakes or incorrect answers. It was not enough that we had done them, they had to be correct. And she did not ask who would like to answer, who knew the answer, but she made us speak in turns, row by row, in order and then someone made a mistake and they were then cross-examined for as long as it took them to give the correct answer or until they burst into tears. And if someone tried to whisper the correct answer it meant that two people were in a nice mess. It was absolutely unreasonable. (translated from Finnish, research interview)

It is noticeable here that Johanna has not been individually targeted as yet in the various tellings of the story. In the interview, she adds another scene in which she was the sole target of the teacher's rage: *'I got ill in the third grade and missed most of the lessons. She got mad and shouted at me because she didn't know I had been ill she thought I had skipped the lessons and I was really embarrassed I just turned and walked away'.*

Johanna later accepts the teacher's apology but still continues, *'I remember her forefinger it was oh no it left us all such bad memories'.*

In the interview I move back and forth between being a researcher and a counsellor, especially when we discuss Johanna's programme in ALMS. As a researcher I am glad to recognise an alternative story about language learning developing, but the counsellor in me finds it important to offer Johanna practical support for her perceived problem with listening.

The sixth fragment
The interview with the group counsellor helps me come to an interim conclusion as a researcher:

> *Leena:* these memories are kind of strong they have always bothered me I've always sort of seen myself as a memory in somebody's head

Group counsellor: as a teacher you talk about now
Leena: yes as a teacher I talk about this as a teacher now and somehow this line between myself as a teacher and myself as a learner is so blurred and I think that you know all the things that happened to me all the things that happened to my friends and then what I hear from my students and what I know happened having been in the teachers' rooms has made me very aware that I might well be a memory in somebody's head

With the help of Johanna's memory I am in the process of doing what Denzin (2005, p. 10) suggests narrative researchers should do: 'In bringing the past into the autobiographical present, I insert myself into the past and create the conditions for rewriting and hence re-experiencing it'.

In the same article, Denzin uses the words 'the sting of memory', an expression that vividly describes my inquiry so far, and which I suspect many recollections of classrooms and language learning and teaching encounters are all about: a memory stings and we need to do something about it. When I think of the beginning of my research process I can see a researcher fighting back an unconscious eagerness to focus on victim stories. Looking back, I understand that the victim story needed to come out to make it possible for me to move on with my inquiry.

The seventh fragment
The circle closes when I talk about Johanna at a conference:

This time, the intertwining of emotions with the rational is my concern all the way through the research process, not stopping short at the data collection and preliminary stages of the analysis and writing. Johanna's memory had me go back to my maths class as an eleven-year-old: I was cross-examined and finally crying.

But I continue my talk. In what follows I am describing the writing process and its relation to the whole research process:

I have become even more aware of the interpersonal dynamics of an interview encounter, and naturally a counselling session. The talk shapes and defines the self and other of both participants and can leave the researcher/counsellor, as well as the interviewees/learners, feeling vulnerable. My focus consequently is also on the letting be, on what is best left untouched, the emotions and the unspeakable, on what is beyond words. And despite the difficulty or impossibility, how to try and write about what I see in my kaleidoscope and how the various patterns have been constructed.

The circle that has once closed opens up again when I write this chapter: I am active in moving the eyepiece of the kaleidoscope and have now added yet another fragment to the researcher story.

4 Discussion: implications of writing experiential narratives

My research started from a need to understand the nature and meaning of EFL interaction as experienced by learners and counsellors. In the course of my writing, I have become aware of how significant my internal quest was to the meanings I gave to the research participants' experiences and memories: it was always my hand turning the kaleidoscope to bring into view the changing novel patterns.

It has also become clear how the very writing has taught me and has profoundly changed my thinking. First and foremost, I have learned to understand the complex implications of the choice of a research method: theory informs method, hence the method is not separate from how we conceptualise the phenomenon, how we know and how we work with the knowledge. Narrative and story-telling has helped me put teacher and student perspectives in the same picture. Moreover, the writing process has, by its very nature, been a feeling process and a narrative autobiographical process in which I have been in dialogue with myself and with my research documents and reading matter (Elbaz-Luwisch 2002). The whole researcher experience of language learning and counselling would be inconsistent with the writing mode if at the end of a process full of slippages, inexactness, indeterminacy, ambiguity and changes of plans, the researcher were to end up neatly writing an objective, precise, unambiguous and non-contextual report. I believe that our writing should reflect the way we have researched: in conceptualising knowledge and knowing as partial, local and situated we have given up on the role of an omniscient narrator. A commitment to a personal and subjective narrative follows the recognition of the close link between our own being in the world and the mode of narrative inquiry.

The process of telling a narrative history of experience is extremely complex. Writing is a way of finding out, of learning, of knowing, of discovery and analysis, and of telling, but it is also a process wrought with ethical dilemmas. All the way through the thesis process I have been concerned about consent, about confidentiality, anonymity, representation and participation. At the beginning the students and the counsellor gave their consent to the full use of the videos, and of the written and audioed documents. Yet, as narrative inquiry is contingent and unfolding, my text is in progress all the time. This chapter is yet another interpretation in which bits of data from the thesis are put into a different context, which means creating another, new experiential narrative. Consent is therefore an ongoing and open-ended process.

Lived experience is evoked in stories, in the telling and in the listening. My research hinges on listening to the stories, on seeing the participants as knowledgeable and active, not as mute objects. The meaning-making process will continue with you, the readers, because the 'results' of a narrative inquiry are for the readers themselves to find in the text. Some results will be found in this short text, others only in the chapters, stories, episodes and fragments of the thesis, which will be yet another story.

7
'To Speak English Is Tedious': Student Resistance in Japanese University Classrooms

Keiko Sakui and Neil Cowie

1 Introduction

Teachers sometimes find that students do not behave in the way we expect them to behave. Student resistance is a well-researched topic in general education, but there are relatively few studies about this issue in English as a Foreign Language (EFL), especially in Japanese tertiary institutions. Two exceptions are studies carried out by Escandon (2004) and McVeigh (2002). McVeigh (2002) defines resistance in the following manner: 'By "resistance" I do not mean a conscious, organised and systematic insurrection against the socio-political order. Rather, I employ this term to designate actions and attitudes that do *not directly challenge* but *scorn* the system' (p. 185). Using McVeigh's definition, Escandon (2004) categorises student resistance into seven different patterns. They are (1) bodily dispositions such as male and female students sitting separately, (2) absence from classes, (3) not responding, (4) neglect or forgetfulness, (5) indifference such as sleeping, (6) inaccuracy such as failing exams, and finally (7) rudeness such as chatting or personal grooming (pp. 6–8).

Following the above definition and seven categories, the present study will explore student resistance as experienced by the two authors, Keiko and Neil, in EFL classrooms at two separate Japanese universities. We will first tell of our respective experiences of student resistance, and then analyse these personal narratives (Clandinin and Connelly 1995) from the perspective of social theories in teacher emotion and critical pedagogy. In order to do this, we will move from the traditional 'author-evacuated' text (Sparkes 1996) of a research report to one where we are speaking as individual authors and also as a joint voice. In this way, as Holliday (2002) points out, we are able to take responsibility for our own ideas by explicitly pointing at ourselves and others.

There are several factors that influenced us to use personal narrative for this research. Following Bell (2002, p. 209), we feel that narrative allows us to understand the impact of our experiences, allows our deeply hidden assumptions to emerge, and helps us to see how our understanding of people and events changes. In addition to these broad reasons for using narrative, we had two specific reasons for examining student resistance in this way. Firstly, at separate institutions and on different occasions, we happened to experience particularly difficult student resistance. Although both of us felt that managing classes and dealing with this resistance was an important part of our professional life we thought that this 'dark side' of our profession had not been discussed much at the conferences and teacher workshops that we had attended. Therefore, in order to share our personal experiences of this often difficult topic, we needed to study our own teaching situations, and to tell and then interpret our own stories of resistance.

Secondly, handling student resistance can be a very emotional experience. In order to illustrate how the experience of struggling with student resistance affects teachers' feelings, a narrative is an appropriate way to describe the complexity of being a teacher in a specific societal and cultural context. By using a storied format for part of this research report we will enhance its readability and give coherence to a complex combination of teacher experiences, thoughts, reflections and emotions. In this way 'narrative serves as a source of information ... as well as a method of interpretation and reinterpretation of experience' (Craig 2007, p. 162).

2 Data collection and analysis

As data for this research, we both kept notes of our experiences and reflections throughout the academic year 2005. In addition to this, Keiko examined the student evaluation results administered by her university. Neil collected students' journal writings about the class and read the transcripts of post-course interviews that Keiko conducted with five of Neil's students. Based on these different data sources we separately wrote about our experiences in a narrative form. For the analysis, we then read each other's stories in order to check their coherence and clarity, and to independently analyse what issues and themes emerged. We then jointly discussed what we could learn from these separate stories about how to better understand student resistance from our two perspectives. From this interplay between our classroom experiences, our various data sources, our two narratives, and our joint reflections, three salient themes emerged: the particular types of resistance that we faced; the emotional impact of that resistance on us; and finally, the realisation that resistance is bound up very tightly with issues of critical pedagogy, especially those of autonomy and investment.

But before sharing our ideas on these themes we would first like to share our stories of student resistance. We do so in the hope that readers will recognise something of their own students and own teaching contexts, and that this shared recognition may be of value in its own right in addition to any theoretical insights we might have.

2.1 Keiko's story

In 2005, I first started working as a full-time teacher at a women's university. I was pleasantly surprised at the friendliness of the students. The students were not the most academically gifted, but I could tell that a lot of them had grown up in good homes where they knew how to have faith in life, where they trusted people, and were optimistic about their life in general. But there was an exception to this atmosphere. I was assigned to teach reading to 25 non-English majors studying fashion and interior design at the 2-year junior college attached to the 4-year university. When I first went into the classroom in April, I was stunned to see what I saw. The students were wildly dressed with lots of make-up, extrovert hairdos and fashions, and they were all sitting at the back of the classroom. Some of them were chatting among themselves very loudly, some others had their faces down on the desk, and some of them were putting on even more make-up. Only a few seemed ready to have a lesson.

I did not know what to do, especially as I was overwhelmed by the loud noises that the students were making. It was very obvious that these girls did not want to be there and most of them did not have the faintest motivation to learn English. I also felt intimidated because I could sense some of them did not like me – not 'me' personally, but they did show some antagonism to a teacher figure.

For the next several weeks, I hated the idea of going to this class on Wednesdays and Fridays. I had to overcome two emotions: fear and misery. I felt fear because I knew that they outnumbered me and I was not sure whether I could control their behaviour. My heart pounded faster as I went to the class. I had to be tough to face the students and I could not run away from them, or my job, or my responsibilities. At other times, I felt sorry for myself. While I was in the class, I sometimes thought, *'What am I doing with my life? Is this the best thing I can do?'* I had to brush these 'evil' thoughts aside, and I had to be interested in what I was doing, even if no one else was! I had to be perky all the time, even if that meant that I was the only one who was like that in the class.

In order to survive I had two mind sets that I went by. The first was that 'I am the boss around here.' I thought I needed to show the students my expectations, both academically and socially, through my teaching. I hate the expression, but I thought that I needed to show that I was the boss, not by overt power that some teachers assume, but by showing the students what their limits and boundaries were, and what my expectations were for the class. The second mind set I went by was that 'I am human too'. I was determined to show the students that I was also a human being; a woman who shares similar interests such as clothes, make-up and hair styles, and who has a life beyond the classroom.

Building on these two mind sets were two main developments in my structuring of the class and in my attitude towards the students. First, I changed my teaching style radically. I decided that I was not going to focus on grammar at all. These girls had had a very difficult time learning grammar points all through their previous school experience and I did not want them to struggle even more. Instead, I encouraged them to understand meaning from the text by relying on their vocabulary knowledge. I also tried to make their progress more tangible by asking them to buy a notebook and assigning each page for writing vocabulary, meanings, exercises, and opinions. As well as helping the students structure their class-work I thought that the notebooks would help them to review the lesson materials for tests. A further point that I emphasised was to encourage and praise the students and their abilities, no matter how small their progress might have seemed. After seeing how the students' resistance was a reflection of their lack of confidence, I realised that my ultimate goal for this class should be to enhance their self-esteem. Teaching English became secondary.

Another change that happened to me was that by seeing these students I started to reflect on my own life. It was eye-opening to realise that there were some students who had not done well at school, and who, as a result, did not feel good about themselves. I had thought that I could get along with different kinds of people wherever I was. But when I reflected on this, I faced the fact that I was perhaps socialising with only one narrow sector of the population, that is, mainly with people like myself. I went to an academic high school, where 99 per cent of the graduates moved onto higher education. Since then, I had worked and had attained higher degrees. I realised that *all* my school-friends had done well in education. And whichever country I had lived in

(Japan, New Zealand and the US), I felt more comfortable socialising with these type of people than with any other. I know I had not selectively chosen friends exactly like me, but time, association, and convenience brought us together. From this perspective, I could not imagine how detrimental school grades can be to some people. I felt ashamed for this lack of knowledge and at the same time I felt how cruel our education system can be to some.

In order to make sense of the fact that education systems often stream people, rather than provide equal opportunities to everyone, I started reading books on sociological aspects of education (e.g., Willis 1977; Heath 1983; Bourdieu 1998). As a result of my reflecting and reading I realised that my students were really smart – maybe not in an academic sense, but more in a street-wise way. The students knew, perhaps intuitively, that doing well in English classes at this stage of their life was not the cleverest thing to do; their energy should be spent elsewhere in order to do well.

I did struggle to teach this class, but in the end, I gained the students' trust and truly began to respect them as students and as young women. As the course progressed, they all sat at the front of the classroom, they all stayed on task, and we all enjoyed occasional chats about personal topics. Throughout the semester I wanted to show that I was not the only information giver in the class, but everyone has valuable insights and information to contribute. Inside the class, I taught English and gave advice on various issues and I often asked for their advice after the class had finished. For example, when I told my students that I was thinking about getting a mobile phone they told me lots of information about it, and one of them brought a brochure the following week.

This became one of my favourite classes in the end. The students did learn some English, and they were pleased with their own progress. I had thought that the student evaluation at the end of the semester would show how much they enjoyed the rapport and atmosphere in classroom, and there were such comments. But the majority of them wrote that they enjoyed it because they could understand the lesson and they had learned some English. They were, ultimately, interested in learning.

2.2 Neil's story

In April 2005, at the start of my second year teaching in a large provincial university in the west of Japan, I was looking forward to my first class of medical students. As in many countries, these students had the reputation of being the best and brightest in the university, and I imagined that they would be intelligent and perceptive and eager to join in with the activities I had planned for them. However, from the very beginning it seemed to me that there was something 'wrong' with the lessons and I was surprised to see how my attitude changed from one of eager anticipation to one of puzzlement and annoyance, and then to anger, and finally resignation.

First lessons are always something of a trial for both students and teacher. I expect some resistance, especially from students who have never met a non-Japanese teacher before, although that is getting rarer in Japan nowadays. Although the students were not as open and positive as I had anticipated, the first lesson with this group seemed no more troubling than those with other classes. But, I was taken aback by one student who wrote the following in his class notebook: *To speak English is 'mendokusai' [tedious]. I don't want to use English any more. I learned nothing.*

From the first lesson on this one student came to epitomise the class for me. There was something enervating about this young man, as though all the energy had been sucked out of him and in turn he was sucking it from those around him. He certainly did not want to speak with any of his classmates and he especially did not want to talk to me. His unwillingness to engage in the lessons was difficult for me to face but actually in terms of other behaviours he was a 'good' student: he always came on time, he always did his homework, and he could communicate in English when I asked him directly. For example, he once told me that he didn't want to be a doctor, but he was only doing it because his father had a clinic and he was expected to carry on the family business. I knew that this was not an uncommon situation for many medical students in Japan so there was a clear reason why he in particular might be a reluctant language learner. But there were other students who appeared bright and intelligent and should have been a joy to teach. But they weren't!

One clear problem that emerged was the reluctance of the students as a group to mix with each other, especially for the male students to talk to the female students. However, there was not just a problem with gender mixing as there also seemed a reluctance for many of the students to talk *at all* with each other, whether their partner was male or female. A student, Yuki commented, *In general it is a quiet class. I heard [another] class is a lot more active ... I wish there were some small number of 'good speakers' in the class. Then we will perhaps start speaking more.*

I do not want to be a disciplinarian in a classroom, and certainly do not want to hover next to students to make them talk. But as each lesson went by I felt more and more angry as I perceived that the students were not 'playing the game' as I wanted them to. This class was so quiet and the students showed such apparent lethargy that I started to wonder if it were not their lack of willingness to cooperate but that there was something fundamentally wrong with my approach. I talked to the students about the homework and decided to change the schedule to introduce more medical-related issues – about diet and healthy lifestyles for instance. For some students, in the short term, there did seem a greater spark of interest. Another student, Mariko confirmed that *Gradually learning about medical English was good because that is what we are interested in.*

But, although it seemed that there may have been greater interest in the classroom content, I still perceived a lack of cooperation, both amongst the students themselves and in communicating with me. I finally began to lose my temper. This is rare for me to do once – but three times I 'lectured' the students on how important it was for them to actively participate; that they couldn't just sit back and let somebody else do it for them. Readers are probably all familiar with the scene of the language teacher finally 'losing it' with their students and shouting at them in a language that they don't understand completely about a topic that is probably irrelevant to them. Well, that was me – and of course it didn't work. There were many more uncomfortable silences, many of the students were as lethargic as ever, and lateness and absence increased.

There was no happy ending to this class. It may not strike many readers as a particularly resistant or unusual case, but for me it was a troubling and puzzling issue. I have a lot of experience with Japanese students and even the most reluctant of classes have a positive atmosphere in the end. But for this class of medical students, composed of students with some of the highest test scores, I feel that I had failed and I didn't know why.

3 Discussion

We could hastily judge that the student behaviour described above demonstrates that our students are 'bad' or that they are not motivated to learn English. However, that was not our sentiment. Rather, these two classes, although very different in many ways, taught the two of us so much about teaching that we would never experience with a 'good' class. In this section we would like to draw upon these experiences and examine three related issues: the types of resistance we faced; the emotional impact resistance has; and, what we have learnt about student resistance from the two critical perspectives of investment and autonomy.

3.1 Types of resistance

These narrative descriptions mirror what Escandon (2004) and McVeigh (2002) described as student resistance, regardless of the different types of institution and student population. The main type of resistant behaviour Keiko faced from her students was rudeness (Escandon's category 7) such as chatting and laughing whilst she was talking, as well as personal grooming by the students such as fixing their hair and looking at a mirror. In addition to rudeness the students also had resistant bodily dispositions (category 1) expressed mainly by sitting at the back of the classroom or by putting their heads on the desks.

Neil, on the other hand, did not experience rudeness particularly, but he perceived his students resisting through their bodily dispositions; they were not willing to mix with other students and appeared apathetic and indifferent. Some were also late or absent. However, on the surface, even the most resistant or reluctant student was well-behaved and did what they were told. The overall perception that Neil had was that the students, as a group, resisted in the lessons but it was difficult for him at the time to describe exactly what was wrong. Only after reading McVeigh's (2002) description of students 'scorning the system' (p. 186) did the students' behaviour make sense to Neil.

3.2 The emotional impact of resistance

For both Keiko and Neil, meeting student resistance was a very emotional experience. Keiko initially found the students' behaviour very difficult to deal with and was in turn, shocked, fearful, and depressed about what she thought she might have to face for the rest of the school year. Neil, too, described his emotional response to his students as ranging from anticipation to puzzlement and annoyance, and then anger and resignation. Keiko finally found ways to cope with her class and stated that in the end it was one of her favourite ones – for her there was a sense of discovery, almost enlightenment, about the lives of the young women in her class. She got to know them well, could explain to herself why they behaved as they did, and found effective strategies with which to teach them and overcome their resistance. For Keiko there was a sense of satisfaction and closure to the class. For Neil, on the other hand, for the duration of the class he did not know how to deal with his students' resistance and his overall emotional state was one of frustration with both his students and with himself.

It is clear then that student resistance engenders many different types of emotions in teachers, but what is less clear is how teachers should respond to these emotions. There is a vacuum in the EFL literature on this area with very few studies examining the impact of emotions on teaching (Arnold 1999; Cowie 2004). In the wider educational field, however, there have been a much larger number of such studies; the work of Hargreaves (2000), and his co-researchers, Lasky (2000) and Schmidt (2000) has been particularly important in identifying theoretical frameworks with which to look at the emotionality of teaching. One such framework is that of 'emotional labor' which was originally developed by Hochschild (1983) and has been further explored by Winograd (2005).

Emotional labour is the kind of work we all have to do in jobs where we have to influence others' emotions. One example from this study is where Keiko said that she had to make herself 'perky' in order to interact with her students. This is a typical example of self-talk that many teachers go through before and during a lesson in order to put themselves in an appropriate emotional state. Winograd claims that teachers can respond to their emotional states in the classroom in a 'functional' or 'dysfunctional' way. The former is where an emotion, such as anger or fear, leads to action to try to improve a classroom situation. Keiko showed this functional response in adapting her teaching approach to overcome her students' resistance and to create a very positive relationship with them. A 'dysfunctional' response, on the other hand, is one in which teachers do not adjust well to the emotional demands of teaching, and if this happens frequently can lead to stress, depression and burn-out. Neil showed this kind of response during the term as he moved from anger to resignation. However, partly as a result of writing this chapter, he eventually came to understand his students more deeply even if he did not change their resistance. Neil's response to his emotions, although not totally successful, was in the end a functional one.

3.3 Issues of critical pedagogy – learner autonomy and investment

The current study reveals that a language classroom is not just a place where a language is taught, but is far more complex where many kinds of factors and issues meet and interact. It is a place where both teachers and students bring their own baggage of various social and cultural assets; gender, ethnicity, race, nationality, and previous educational experiences all mix in the language classroom. The social and cultural factors that both teachers and students bring can gel in nice ways at times, and at other times they can clash.

Viewing student resistance from these factors has relevance to critical pedagogy (Freire 1970; Canagarajah 2005). Norton and Toohey (2004) contend that 'language is not simply a means of expression or communication; rather, it is a practice that constructs, and is constructed by, the ways language learners understand themselves, their social surroundings, their histories, and their possibilities for the future' (p. 1). This study reminds us that each student has a varied identity and sense of investment in language learning (Norton 2000). Or, as Holliday (2005) argues, students are already autonomous beings when they come to our classes. Student resistance can, therefore, be interpreted as a reflection of the clash between a teacher and students' different sense of autonomy and investment. We will now look at our classes from these perspectives.

3.3.1 Learner autonomy

Learner autonomy in language learning has been defined from a number of different, and often contested, perspectives (Benson 2001; Palfreyman and Smith 2005). We will refer to autonomy simply as our perception of our students' willingness to take responsibility for their own learning. We both felt that our students were not independent and that this was a problem; however, we approached this problem differently.

Keiko believed that her students had very little motivation to learn English and that they were unwilling or incapable of taking much control over their own learning. Keiko accepted this lack of independence and adopted several ways to structure her lesson to compensate for it. These included focusing on vocabulary learning and assigning notebooks to make learning outcomes as tangible as possible. Keiko could accept her students' lack of independence quite easily because she reasoned that the students had not experienced a successful academic career and, unfortunately, perceived themselves as failures.

This was not the case for Neil. It seems that for all his students' success in gaining acceptance to medical school – one of the most difficult academic achievements in a very academic achievement oriented society – their apparent lack of independence was a puzzle. On reflection, after reading the post-course interview transcripts, Neil thinks that his students were making the transition from a tightly controlled school environment to a looser, and probably very foreign, way of working in a language classroom. Intellectually, they could see what Neil wanted them to do but emotionally they were dependent on him to push them. They expressed the desire that the teacher should be in control: they wanted Neil to enforce regular seating arrangements, for him to be strict regarding sleeping in class or being late, and, above all they wanted him to make them speak in English.

Neil perceived that all through their lives these students had been trained to jump through academic hoops, and that they had learnt for tests and had become good at them. But once in the university language classroom they were genuinely lost. It is probable that Neil's less structured style, which is based on his own previous educational background and preferred learning style, did not provide clear enough goals and guidelines and so the students resisted. At the same time these are 'good' students who wanted to conform and felt shame or embarrassment about their attitude. The students were aware that Neil wanted them to act independently; but Neil was not aware of his students' preferred ways of learning and, instead of accepting what had worked very well for them previously, got angry.

Resistance, then, can be seen as a clash between different views of what autonomous learning is. Keiko accepted that her students were not fully independent learners and so provided clear structures which allowed them to succeed and their resistance diminished. Neil did not see such structures as necessary and consequently his students continued to resist.

3.3.2 Investment

A second theoretical approach applicable to the present study is that of investment (Norton 2000). In an investigation of immigrant women's motivation to speak, Norton argues that learners invest (or not) in learning English in various ways, depending on their identities, their projected images in the future, and the community that they left behind and they are entering into. It seemed clear to everyone in Keiko's classroom that it was unlikely that her students would need a lot of English for their future. Painfully realising this, Keiko decided to try to empower her students by raising their self-esteem through language learning, rather than focusing on language learning as a primary goal.

At the very beginning of the term, Keiko did not deeply appreciate exactly what kind of educational background her students were coming from. She is also Japanese, and had gone through the same grammar-based, rigorous test-oriented English education. She assumed that her students had had the same kind of successes she herself had experienced. But over time, she began to understand how little confidence they actually had in learning English. Although she did not have any belittling experiences of the Japanese educational system, Keiko came to sympathise with her students who might have gone through it negatively. As a woman she felt saddened to see these young women not having confidence in their learning experiences; and, as a mother, she believes that having high self-esteem can help women do well in whatever they might set their minds to in the future. These factors of gender, race and shared cultural background greatly influenced the decisions that Keiko decided to take in her classroom.

Such empowerment did not happen one-way. Her students – unconsciously – forced Keiko to accept the fact that her own experiences were limited because of various educational, cultural and socio-political factors; and made her more aware, both of the deeper sociological aspects of education and of the limits to an identity that she shared with her students through her gender and race.

Keiko admits that she did not (initially) understand her students' educational experiences, despite sharing much of their social and cultural background. Neil, however, felt that he could understand the type of elite environment that his students had benefited from, which is one reason why he was puzzled by the apparently contradictory and frustrating nature of his students' resistance. It seems that the students were invested in the classroom community but not in the language itself. Ironically, in view of how negatively Neil felt about the class, many of the students expressed how they enjoyed the lessons, and were especially grateful to make lots of friends. Although the students did not appear to mix easily during the classroom activities they were still able to forge new friendships in an environment which was not a strict part of their medical training. They perceived the content of their English lessons to be relatively unimportant and their resistance was a reflection of their lack of investment in the language. However, it is significant that they saw themselves as part of a future 'imagined community' (Norton 2000); not an imagined community in an English speaking country, as Norton refers to, but their future medical community in Japan. So, to the students, making future contacts was important but language learning was not.

4 Conclusion

In this chapter, we, Keiko and Neil, have shared our stories of student resistance and how we made sense of what we experienced. Using personal narrative as a research method we compared two very different classes of Japanese university students. Although different, these two groups of young people taught us so much about what resistance is, and how we need to get to know our students and ourselves. We found that it was especially important to know how to deal with the strong emotions that resistance can engender, and the importance of critical theoretical issues such as learner autonomy and investment.

Winograd (2005) suggests that formal opportunities for teachers to discuss emotions and negative aspects of our profession need to be provided, especially for teachers new to the profession who need as much emotional support as possible. Ideally this should take part in a collaborative and non-threatening atmosphere in which the darker emotions of student resistance can be acknowledged and examined. Unfortunately, this is often not possible in many institutions in which 'teaching (occurs) behind closed doors' (Day 1999, p. 78). This is where reading narratives of student resistance and teacher emotion, and raising awareness of how our students may differ greatly from us in their views of autonomy and investment can be very useful to individual teachers as examples that can be shared and learnt from. The resistance reported in this chapter is not particularly unusual, and so we hope that other teachers who are going through something similar, who may feel isolated and angry or fearful, can learn something vicariously through reading similar experiences.

Finally, a brief comment about personal narrative should be made. Some theorists criticise it as self-centred, narcissistic or self-absorbent (Amos Hatch and Wisniewski 1995). However, we have found that by narrating our experiences, by reflecting on and analysing them, and by trying to relate them to social theories, we have come to understand ourselves, our teaching and our students in a much deeper way. We support claims that narrative is a natural way for teachers to express their, often tacit, knowledge (Clandinin and Connelly 1995), and as self-researchers it has been a natural tool for us to use, too. We should leave readers to make judgement on this issue.

Part IV
Oral Narratives

8
Passion and Persistence: Learning English in Akita

Sara Cotterall

1 Introduction

Accounts of individual language learners' learning experiences began appearing in the literature more than 20 years ago (e.g., Bailey 1983; Schmidt 1983; Schmidt and Frota 1985), many of them deriving from a research paradigm which aimed to explain the impact of individual differences on outcomes in second language acquisition. More recent reports have explored the nature of learners' day to day class activity (Block 1994), learner uptake (Slimani 1989), the relationship between the learner and the target language community (Norton 2000) and the impact of the curriculum on learner motivation and success (Cotterall 2005).

Such accounts are valuable for a number of reasons. Firstly, they offer teachers a mirror image of the reality they co-create in their classrooms. For researchers, they present important variables in second or foreign language acquisition from the perspective of the learner. For learners, they offer the possibility of *making sense of it all* as one of the informants in my 2005 study (Maberly 2004) wrote after reading the chapter describing his struggles with Spanish at university! But most importantly, they privilege the perspective of the central actor in the drama of language learning – the learner!

This chapter also focuses on individual language learners. It tells the stories of three adult Japanese learners who are learning English in a setting which boasts no teachers, no language instruction and no external assessment of learning. These learners are operating in a resource-rich environment with access to a team of language professionals who offer guidance, support and feedback on their learning efforts. My aim in telling these stories is twofold: firstly, to highlight the persistence and capacity of individual learners; and, secondly, to illustrate the rich potential of this novel mode of learning.

I begin the chapter by briefly sketching the background to English language learning in Japan. I then describe the independent language learning facility of which the three learners are members. Next I introduce the learners and their motivations for learning English, before explaining how the data were gathered and analysed. In the central part of the chapter, I tell the learners' stories as they were revealed to me during 18 months of one-on-one meetings. I conclude with comments on the significance of this type of investigation for language research, and the relationship between the findings of this study and previous studies of learners' experiences of language learning.

2 Context

Japan is a particularly interesting setting in which to study independent language learning for two reasons. Firstly, a great deal of time and money is devoted to language learning in this country; and secondly, independent language learning is a very recent and unorthodox arrival on the English teaching/learning scene. Martin (2004, p. 50) claims that 'despite the great amount of time, energy, and money spent on English teaching, it is rare to find a Japanese student who, after six years of English, is able to engage in even a marginal dialogue with a speaker of English.' She proposes a number of explanations for her somewhat severe assessment of the effects of formal language education in Japan. These include cultural and linguistic influences, the belief many Japanese hold that it is impossible for them to communicate effectively in English, attitudes towards mistakes in the classroom, and the use of *katakana* script as an aid to transcribing English.

In Japan, English is a compulsory subject for three years at junior high school and three years at senior high school. Yet six years of compulsory English study seldom produce competent users of English. Gorsuch (1998) suggests some reasons for this: firstly, the prevailing methodology relies on translation and teacher control. In addition, there is significant washback on high school English teaching from grammar and translation-oriented university entrance exams. Furthermore, many high school teachers of English in Japan believe that 'intensive reading, translation, and appreciation of literary works' are core elements of a good foreign language programme (Gorsuch 1998, p. 28).

However graduation from high school is not the end of foreign language learning for many Japanese. According to figures published by the Japanese Ministry of Economy, Trade and Industry (2005) 1,096,952 Japanese individuals learned a foreign language at a private language teaching institution in 2005, the vast majority of whom (91 per cent) were learning English. Furthermore, the English language industry in Japan accounted for ¥192.8 billion in 2005 (Japanese Ministry of Economy, Trade and Industry, 2005) without counting fees spent on standardised English language tests. Significant numbers of Japanese people sit such tests every year. Between April 2005 and March 2006 as many as 2,489,414 Japanese people sat the Eiken test of English language proficiency (Eiken n.d.), 821,510 sat TOEIC in 2005 (TOEIC 2005) and 82,235 sat TOEFL in the 12-month period between July 2004 and June 2005 (ETS 2005).

Methods of studying English in Japan abound. Informal discussions with Japanese university students and adult learners of English indicate that in addition to attending private language schools, many Japanese follow local television and radio programmes to learn English, as well as subscribing to commercially produced courses delivered via the internet, telephone or other forms of technology. Clearly, the national appetite for learning English is keen.

3 Background

The three adult learners whose stories are told in this chapter live in a small provincial city in northern Japan. All three registered in July 2005 as members of the newly opened Centre for Independent Language Learning (CILL), established by Akita International University (AIU) to promote independent language learning in the local community. This facility is located in the city centre and offers weekly language advising sessions (see Cotterall 2006), a seminar programme, a collection of documents on independent language learning including a book (Murray and Cotterall 2006) commissioned by the Japanese Ministry of Education which explains key concepts associated with independent language learning. The Centre is equipped with 12 personal computers, satellite television, an excellent library of authentic books and a wide range of pedagogic and authentic English language learning resources (such as DVDs, computer programs and magazines with MD recordings). The Centre is staffed by three support staff and two professional language educators (the Director of the Centre and myself), who work in the Centre as language learning advisers at various times during the week. In December 2006 the Centre had 80 active members, down from a peak of 134 in October 2005, shortly after the opening of the Centre.

The stories reported here were gathered between July 2005 and December 2006 principally by documenting 'learning conversations' I had with the case subjects in my capacity as a learning adviser at the Centre. Each advising session lasted approximately 30 minutes. Additional incidental data were gathered during informal conversations with the learners and, in the case of one of the subjects, from e-mail exchanges.

Two of the three case subjects were part of a group who had agreed to take part in a research project aimed at investigating the experiences of learners registered with the Centre; the third subject (Sato-san) was invited to participate in this project because of the frequency with which he made appointments for advising sessions. All three subjects registered with the Centre during its first month (July 2005) and renewed their membership every four months from that time. At the time of writing this chapter – 22 months after their initial registration – Harada-san and Sato-san are still regular users, but Taguchi-san decided not to renew his membership after returning from abroad. In addition to visiting the Centre whenever they wanted (within the Centre's six day per week schedule), all three subjects attended almost all the seminars delivered by CILL staff. These seminars focused on learning to learn, reading skills, language learning strategies, vocabulary development and writing.

4 Case subjects

4.1 Sato-san

The first learner, Sato-san, is a 36-year-old male who had been learning English in various ways for 20 years prior to registering at the CILL. Sato-san reported having first begun studying English seriously around 1988 when he became interested in ideas in popular psychology emanating from California. At that time he listened to English language broadcasts on the radio, listened to music in English and read books. In 1995, in the second 'important period' of his learning of English, Sato-san began listening regularly to the NHK English conversation programme on the radio and attending local English Speaking Society meetings. At these meetings he had the chance to speak to native speakers of English who were working at local high schools as Assistant Language Teachers.

Sato-san decided to join the CILL in 2005 after hearing that AIU was to open a language learning centre in Akita City. He had grown tired of attending the English Speaking Society meetings since the *English language spoken there was too easy for me*. What appealed to him about the CILL was the possibility of speaking English with native speakers. The most positive aspects of the CILL for Sato-san, according to a discussion we had in December 2006, were the Centre's collection of authentic materials and the skilled staff from whom he could obtain advice on his learning. What he did not like about the Centre was that he was unable to borrow materials, and that the Centre was located far from his home.

Sato-san's conversational speaking and listening abilities were good when he first registered at the Centre, especially considering that he had never been abroad, nor had he studied English formally beyond the high school level. Sato-san visited the CILL regularly throughout the period described, spending on average 1 hour per week there in 2005 and 3 hours per week in 2006. However the demands of his job and intermittent health problems meant that his ability to spend time at the Centre fluctuated considerably during the year. Sato-san's preferred activities were watching the BBC channel on satellite TV, listening to EFL materials prepared for Japanese learners, reading test practice materials and talking to native speakers of English on the CILL staff (the two language advisers and, at the beginning of the study, one of the support staff).

4.2 Harada-san

Harada-san is a 31-year-old female learner of English. She is a university graduate, with majors in English Literature and Psychology. Harada-san attended a small private women's university in Tokyo where all her classes were taught in English, most of them by native speakers of English. In her first few weeks at university, when she discovered that her English was not as good as that of her classmates, she registered at a private language school which she attended for three years. By the time she graduated, she had achieved a TOEFL score of 575, her English was fluent (according to her) and all her English language skills were strong. However, when she returned to Akita, Harada-san no longer had an opportunity to practise her English and her fluency declined.

At the beginning of the study Harada-san was employed as a high school English teacher. However in December 2005 she was asked by the Principal of her high school to begin teaching Japanese as a Second Language in the school. Harada-san was a very regular visitor to the Centre. In the first year of her registration, she spent on average 2.6 hours per week at the Centre; in 2006, this figure increased to 3.4 hours per week. The maximum number of hours she spent at the Centre in one week was 8.5 in April 2006. Harada-san's goals changed several times during the study as her work situation and plan to pursue further study emerged. While she originally joined the CILL in order to regain her conversational fluency, by mid 2006 she was focused on improving her academic English. As a result, during the study Harada-san used a wide range of materials including computer programs, DVDs, vocabulary learning materials, 'talking books' and academic writing materials.

4.3 Taguchi-san

Taguchi-san is a 42-year-old male learner of English. He is the most proficient of the three subjects, having completed his university studies in California approximately 15 years prior to the study. A few years after returning to Japan from the USA, Taguchi-san moved to Indonesia where he worked in the tourism industry, using his English at work and in his private life. Taguchi-san's preferred activity at the Centre was reading. During the 18 months of the study, he read a number of books including *The Da Vinci Code*. Taguchi-san spent on average 1.3 hours per week at the Centre in 2005; this figure increased to 3.5 hours per week in 2006.

Taguchi-san did not identify as a language learner, explaining in November 2006 in an interview: *'for me it's not like learning, not like studying. I just come here to enjoy reading books, listen to the music and watching DVDs and seeing people, chatting or joining discussion groups. I don't think I feel like I'm formally learning something but rather I say I enjoy'*.

During the latter period of the study, Taguchi-san began planning an extended holiday in New Zealand. As a result, he began to spend time at the CILL reading reference books and researching volunteer opportunities. These activities defined Taguchi-san's relationship with English; it was a tool that he used in his daily life, rather than an object of study.

5 Data collection and analysis

Contact between myself and the participants was constant but erratic. Data were gathered primarily during language advising sessions initiated by the subjects: Sato-san, Harada-san and Taguchi-san initiated 12, 15 and four advising sessions respectively between November 2005 and December 2006. Records of the advising sessions consisted of my notes and, in the case of Harada-san, occasional e-mail exchanges. Two additional interviews (one each in March and November 2006) were recorded with Harada-san and Taguchi-san as part of the wider research project; these interviews were later transcribed and analysed. Data gathered from these additional interviews have also been used in writing this chapter.

I began the study with the aim of producing case studies of a number of CILL members as a way of exploring the learning context. My aim in offering advising sessions was to offer assistance in the planning, management and evaluation of learners' individual programmes. The questions underlying my interactions during advising sessions (including those with the three study participants) were:

- What are the learners' goals in learning English?
- What issues do they face in their experience of learning English independently?
- How do they react to these difficulties?
- What action (strategies) do they take in order to overcome the difficulties?

These questions derived from a framework developed in an earlier study (Cotterall and Crabbe 2008) which was used to analyse the discourse of the advising session. Essentially this framework consists of two non-sequential elements:

1. representing the problem
2. exploring a solution

The second element incorporates attention to goals, strategies, resources and constraints. This framework was successfully adopted in analysing a second corpus of interviews, conducted at another university in New Zealand (Cotterall 2006).

My analysis of the CILL data began with reading and re-reading notes made during and immediately after the sessions, and, in the case of Harada-san and Taguchi-san, transcripts of the interviews. Subsequently I began coding the data, identifying references to 'goals', 'problems', 'strategies', 'resources' and other elements in their learning. My interpretations of key utterances and episodes were checked according to conventional methods of triangulation (see, e.g., Stake 1995, pp. 112–14) including asking follow-up questions, seeking input on transcribed comments from my colleague and reviewing comments recorded in the learners' learning portfolios.

Once all the data had been coded, I wrote up the participants' stories and asked them to check my accounts for accuracy. Subsequently, I conducted a further round of analysis, looking for dominant themes in each of the case subjects' contributions, and generating new interpretations of the views and events they reported.

6 Findings

6.1 Sato-san

Sato-san's story illustrates the need for learners' goals and strategies to be aligned. During his first advising session, Sato-san stated that he wanted to improve his English so that he could gain entrance to Akita International University as an undergraduate student, and subsequently become an interpreter. In order to achieve these goals, I talked to Sato-san about the importance of developing academic reading and writing skills and a command of academic vocabulary. A test of Sato-san's vocabulary had revealed that his knowledge of the 2000 most common words in English was excellent, but his knowledge of less frequent words and particularly those in the University Word List was weak.

However during subsequent advising sessions it emerged that Sato-san was spending more than 70 per cent of his time in the Centre on speaking activities. These activities consisted of talking to the three native speakers of English on the CILL staff, taking part in conversation groups, participating in Movie Club discussions and participating in language advising sessions. Sato-san's ingenuity in managing to spend more than 2 hours per week speaking English in a city boasting so few native speakers of English was commendable!

At the same time, Sato-san continued to work with Japanese-language materials aimed at preparing candidates for formal English language tests. In February 2006 he reported with great satisfaction that he had passed the STEP Pre First Exam. During our advising session on 23 March 2006, we discussed Sato-san's interest in sitting standardised tests and, in particular, the relationship between this goal and his goal of entering an English medium university. Sato-san explained that he felt that by achieving a high score on a recognised test of English language proficiency he would be moving closer to his goal. At the end of this advising session, I raised with Sato-san the possibility that a conflict might exist between his stated goal and his preferred learning activities, and signalled that we might talk about this again in a subsequent session.

On 11 May 2006, Sato-san asked how he could expand his vocabulary so as to be able to pass the AIU entrance examination. When I pointed out (once again) that in order to achieve this goal he needed to focus attention on academic vocabulary, he indicated that he was committed to spending time on vocabulary learning. We then worked together to develop a plan detailing which words Sato-san should focus on, how he might go about learning them, and when he might fit these activities into his existing programme. However at our next meeting, Sato-san reported that he had not spent any time on vocabulary learning.

Consultation with the other learning adviser confirmed that Sato-san's approach to other activities at the CILL reflected a similar pattern. While he regularly attended seminars and other additional activities organised at the Centre, he consistently failed to complete associated follow-up work. Furthermore, the other learning adviser considered that Sato-san's motivation in requesting advising sessions appeared related more to his desire to obtain speaking practice than to his interest in discussing his learning.

Subsequent analysis of my notes convinced me that Sato-san's stated goals and his preferred learning activities were in conflict, and that this needed to be acknowledged. Therefore I raised the issue with Sato-san at our next meeting. However, the potential conflict did not seem to bother Sato-san. Several more meetings took place during which he explained that he had been unable to follow the plan, and had further reduced the amount of time he was spending on reading, writing and vocabulary learning. However at no time did I sense that Sato-san was discouraged or frustrated by the modifications he had made to his plan.

The tension was finally resolved in October 2006 when Sato-san announced at an advising session that he had changed his goal. He no longer aimed to enter AIU in the short term or to become an interpreter. Instead he had decided to recalibrate his learning programme so that he would spend much more time on activities he enjoyed, such as listening to the news and reading for pleasure, and less time on expanding his language resources. It is not clear what prompted this change of heart, but Sato-san's decision appeared to release him from a burden. At the time of writing, Sato-san appears greatly pleased with his change in focus and the re-alignment of his goals and learning activities.

6.2 Harada-san

Harada-san's story is one of constantly shifting priorities and motivations. Many of these changes were driven by external events over which she had no control. Initially she was motivated by a desire to regain the fluency that had characterised her English during her university days. Consequently she began working on her listening and speaking skills through participation in Conversation Group activities, watching DVDs and using interactive computer programs aimed at developing conversational fluency.

However in December 2005 Harada-san was invited by a former professor to take part in a four-day workshop on the work of psychologist Carl Rogers at the University of East Anglia the following March. As a result, she modified her goals, deciding to focus on developing her academic listening and speaking abilities so that she would be able to discuss complex ideas during workshops and understand lectures. Unfortunately in February 2006, Harada-san learned that her trip to the UK had been cancelled.

About one week later, Harada-san informed me that the Principal of her school had just informed her that from April 2006 she would be responsible for teaching Japanese to international students at the high school. From that time on, Harada-san often spoke to me during advising sessions about teaching issues, since she was acutely aware of her lack of training in teaching Japanese as a Second Language. The following month, Harada-san reported that she had decided to apply for a postgraduate course in teaching Japanese as a Second Language. As a result, she modified her goals once again, and began to focus specifically on developing her academic literacy skills since she expected to be asked to read articles about language teaching research in English.

Harada-san's constantly changing goals and needs resulted in her raising a wide range of language and learning issues during advising sessions. These included difficulty finding opportunities to practise speaking, advice on strategies for improving her academic reading and listening skills, problems with expanding her vocabulary, frustration at being distracted by her former students and finally, anxiety that her conversational listening and speaking skills were deteriorating. These last two issues are discussed at some length below in an attempt to illustrate the way in which the advising sessions offered Harada-san an opportunity to articulate and solve her problems.

During the 18-month study, five students from the high school where Harada-san was teaching joined the Centre. Within the context of a typical teacher-student relationship in Japan, it is appropriate for students to ask advice of their teachers about a wide range of matters outside the classroom. Therefore, when these students registered as members at the Centre, they began to seek advice about their English learning from Harada-san, rather than from the CILL staff. The situation was compounded by the fact that these learners were weak in English, and therefore were less well catered for by the CILL materials than were more proficient learners. Eventually, during an advising session on 8 June 2006, Harada-san expressed frustration at this situation, saying – *It's a really big problem to my students … . Before I'm really like a teacher but now it's not teachers, it's really like I'm M … H …* When I commented that her role appeared to have changed, and asked why that was difficult for her, Harada-san replied – *Ohh, because they are my former students, not present students, I must change the rules.*

I had frequently observed Harada-san at the Centre talking in Japanese to these young learners. However her outward appearance gave no indication of the frustration she was experiencing. Japanese social norms made it difficult for her to modify this situation. However once I explained the situation to the Japanese-speaking CILL staff, they approached the high school learners with offers of assistance and support. Soon after, the problem was resolved.

Another interesting exchange occurred with Harada-san late in September 2006. Initially she spoke of feeling worried that her listening and speaking skills were deteriorating because she was concentrating on her academic reading and writing skills. On the face of it, Harada-san's anxiety was difficult to understand, since her future studies would demand far greater competence in academic language than in conversational ability. When asked for more information, Harada-san explained that sometimes when she came to the Centre, she turned on a computer, started watching a DVD and then found that her time was up for the day. In the context of her earlier comments, I took this to mean that she was losing motivation for working on her more cognitively demanding academic language needs.

I initially responded by encouraging Harada-san to plan her time in the CILL, to ensure that she would spend adequate time on activities that supported her learning goals. This suggestion was received with only mild enthusiasm. I then asked if she was feeling anxious about her postgraduate course, and suggested that she begin adopting some strategies to measure her progress. We then had a general discussion about methods of measuring progress in academic reading and listening. This and other suggestions appeared to go some way to overcoming her feelings of anxiety.

However, after the advising session, I continued our discussion of the issue via e-mail because I was not confident that our discussion had addressed the difficulty she was experiencing. Harada-san's reply to my e-mail revealed that indeed she was suffering from a lack of motivation. As she put it – *read, listened, and wrote English seriously. I suddenly faced big wall. I didn't enjoy English.*

This was a very significant admission for Harada-san who, from the outset, had been motivated in her learning of English by enjoyment. Another key motivator was her contact with other CILL members, usually initiated during Conversation Group activities. Apparently Harada-san's new goal – to improve her academic English skills – was threatening to overwhelm those positive feelings. Fortunately the advising exchange seemed to have helped her identify this tension, so that the rest of her message was more positive. She continued – *But last week you told me not only learning English, but also measuring my skill. I saw myself objectively. I felt like inhaling new air. I divided my time there. Yesterday I read an essay and watching DVD 'I've got mail'. I changed my way. I do my favourite thing there.*

Harada-san had found her own solution, realising that she need not spend all her time on activities aimed at improving her academic language skills. In fact, by balancing her time in the CILL between activities she found enjoyable and those more closely focused on her future language needs, she had found a way of reviving her earlier motivation.

One other aspect of Harada-san's involvement with the Centre is central to her experience. During the study, Harada-san formed close friendships with a number of other CILL members. She spoke about these relationships in the interview in November 2006. In response to the question 'What do you like best about the Centre?' she explained – *Talking with my friends. They have dreams, really the same like me. In the future they want to move to a foreign country and first, of course only for business or secondly for life ... We can talk about and dream. It's so difficult for us to the other place.* When I asked her to explain this last comment, she continued – *Yes, especially the dreams. They [other people] like to talk about shopping and traveling ... yeah and boyfriends ... but we like to talk about the dreams.*

For Harada-san, the community of learners at the Centre represented *a kind of shelter from my real society* [Interview, 26 November 2006]. At the Centre she found it possible to talk about topics that were difficult to discuss with others in her regular social network. As such, the CILL represented more than a venue for language learning; it became an important part of her social identity.

6.3 Taguchi-san

Taguchi-san's story is different from that of the other two learners in almost every way. Firstly, his high level of proficiency meant that his language needs were quite different. Secondly, his relationship to English was very different. At no time did Taguchi-san give the impression that his membership of the CILL was associated with study. Rather he appeared to be a member of the CILL in much the same way that someone might belong to a gym. His association with the CILL centred on relaxation, interest and leisure. When I asked him what he liked best about the Centre, Taguchi-san replied [26 November 2006] – *Well I can come to the Center and start enjoying English any time I want during office hours and they are open 6 days a week.*

As indicated above, Taguchi-san did not at any time seek an advising session to discuss his language learning. He did not identify as a language learner at all. Instead, he appeared to consider English a means of pursuing various projects. In November 2006, in answer to a question about whether he had discovered anything about how languages can be learned from his experiences at the Centre, Taguchi-san replied – *Probably, for myself English, like I told you before is only a tool of communication not progress. So if I use the tool without hesitation and I quite enjoy that, I think I can improve, you know, the skill.*

Reading was one of Taguchi-san's passions. Therefore, quite naturally, reading was the major activity he engaged in when he came to the Centre. However he also attended all the additional seminars offered at the CILL. He explained his motivation this way:

> If I go back in time when I was a university student, at that time I spoke English every day, and I was kind of OK ... kind of fluent. And after I came back to Japan I hadn't had the chance to talk in English a lot so my speaking skill I kind of lost. Then after coming to the Center my speaking skill came back. (November, 2006)

Taguchi-san also regularly attended the Movie Discussion sessions and the Discussion group activities organised by members of the CILL staff.

During the last six months of 2006, Taguchi-san spent most of his time at the Centre preparing for a trip to New Zealand. All this activity involved the use of English, whether it consisted of reading reference books on New Zealand, surfing the net for useful websites or writing letters or applications. Taguchi-san had set himself a goal of producing two versions of his Curriculum Vitae in English before his departure. Accordingly he spent time (at home) searching various English language websites for model CVs, and then drafting his own. Taguchi-san's draft CVs became the focus of three advising sessions with me – one in July 2006 and two in November 2006. Our discussion during these sessions focused less on language than on cultural expectations of employment and employment interviews in New Zealand. We also discussed strategies for seeking voluntary work in New Zealand during his visit.

One other significant feature of Taguchi-san's experience at the Centre was his participation in the community of learners. Late in 2006 I learned that CILL members who attended the Friday afternoon discussion group frequently adjourned to a café or a restaurant afterwards. Taguchi-san was a key member of the core group taking part in these and other social activities. Accordingly, he assumed the role of MC at the CILL Christmas Party in early December 2006. Taguchi-san's membership of the learning community of the CILL was a significant, if unstated, aspect of his experience of the Centre.

7 Discussion

In this final section, I wish firstly to comment on the potential of narrative research for expanding our understanding of what language learning involves, especially over the long-term. Secondly, I will relate the findings of this study to previous investigations of learners' stories explored by analysing the discourse of advising sessions. Finally, I will comment on the significance of these stories in understanding the potential of independent language learning.

For many decades research into learner differences has focused on explaining why individuals with a similar cognitive capacity achieve variable outcomes in second or foreign language proficiency. Yet, a growing number of researchers are motivated by a different question. They wish to understand how individual learners manage their language learning over time and how their learning fits into and (possibly) changes their lives. The ultimate goal of such research is not to produce generalisations about learners, factors or outcomes – but to understand the experiences of the individuals.

One recent collection, edited by Benson and Nunan (2005), includes examples of such research into five important psychological factors – learner motivation, affect, age, beliefs and strategies and the construction of identity – all presented from the perspective of individual learners. In the conclusion to their chapter in the collection, Shoaib and Dörnyei (2005, p. 36) eloquently explain the benefits of this approach:

> We have found that learning histories can shed new light on the L2 motivational complex by presenting the various motives that are normally considered in isolation in a contextualized and interrelated manner. In addition, the contextual information concerns both the environmental and the temporal context, thereby offering a genuinely

'rich description'. Finally, there is a further layer of biographical/ autobiographical data that is unique: the emphasis and value that the informant inherently assigns to the various episodes by placing them in the whole life sequence and outlining their consequences and corollaries.

In other words, narrative research treats learners as whole and complex persons. It does not hone in on one aspect of their experience to the exclusion of all other elements; rather it seeks to tell their stories in all their complexity, imprecision and idiosyncrasy.

The case studies presented in this chapter also offer insights into issues canvassed in more conventional second language research. Sato-san's story highlights the importance of realistic goal-setting, and the alignment of goals and strategies in a coherent language learning programme. Sato-san's and Harada-san's stories shed light on the dynamic nature of motivation. Taguchi-san's story offers insight into the instrumental role that English can play in the life of a sophisticated foreign language user of the language.

There is one striking difference between my analysis of the advising sessions I conducted with the three participants in this study and those I have conducted in the past. The problem-solution framework developed in Cotterall and Crabbe (in press) was able to describe only **part** of the interaction which occurred in the CILL sessions. I believe this was due to the relationship that developed between me and the participants. Because of the frequency of our meetings, particularly in the case of Harada-san and Sato-san, I came to know a great deal more about their learning and their lives than I could ever have done with the university students whom I advised at Victoria University of Wellington. As a result, the margins between learning and life became blurred in our talks.

Finally, as an advocate of independent language learning and learner autonomy, I believe that these stories present positive evidence of adult learners' ability to learn within a novel structure. Japanese learners are often stereotyped as passive, shy and lacking in initiative (Saito and Eisenstein-Ebsworth 2004). But the data gathered for this chapter provide evidence of successful independent programme planning, effective strategy use and insightful reflection. Within a learning setting such as the one described here, dialogue between learners and advisers is a superbly flexible tool for supporting independent learning.

9
Communities of Practice: Stories of Japanese EFL Learners

Garold Murray

1 Introduction

A principal tenet of sociocultural theory is that learners do not just conform to their world but that they actively seek to transform it (Donato 2000). This notion has wide implications for our understanding of foreign language learning. For example, Canagarajah (2004, p. 117) posits that 'what motivates the learning of a language is the construction of the identities we desire and the communities we want to join in order to engage in communication and social life'. The desire to transform their world and to participate in other communities was a strong motivating force for a group of adult Japanese who participated in a life history project designed to explore their experiences learning to speak English while living in Japan. As a part of the learning process, these learners became members of small communities of foreign language speakers within the larger Japanese community.

In this chapter I employ the theoretical perspective of 'communities of practice' (Lave and Wenger 1991) in order to better understand the learners' experiences. After outlining the theoretical framework and describing the research methodology, I introduce three of the participants and present abridged versions of their stories. I then explore the types of communities they accessed and the range of learning opportunities these communities afforded. The chapter concludes by considering the implications of the participants' experiences for other learners and educators.

2 Background to the study

Whether we are aware of it or not, most of us belong to any number of communities of practice (Wenger et al. 2002). In their most general form, 'communities of practice are groups of people who share a concern, a set of problems, or a passion about a topic, and who deepen their knowledge and expertise in this area by interacting on an ongoing basis' (Wenger et al. 2002, p. 4). There are three basic components which set a community of practice apart from other social groups: 'a domain of knowledge, which defines a set of issues; a community of people who care about this domain; and the shared practice they are developing to be effective in their domain' (Wenger et al. 2002, p. 27). We participate in these groups at work, at school, and even at home.

Lave and Wenger (1991) contend that we learn by becoming members of a community of practice. We work our way from being newcomers accepted into the group, 'legitimate peripheral participants,' to being full participants by gaining access to a wide range of ongoing activity, other members of the community, and information and resources upon which the community depends. We learn through opportunities to engage in practice and over time make the culture of practice our own.

Elaborating on this theory, Wenger (1998) introduces the concept of imagination as a 'mode of belonging' to a community of practice. For Wenger, it is imagination that enables us to conceptualise our place in the world and in history, to see ourselves as members of communities beyond the realm of our everyday experience, and to 'include in our identities other meanings, other possibilities, other perspectives' (Wenger 1998, p. 187). Wenger's notion of imagination as a mode of belonging was inspired by Anderson's (1983) concept of 'imagined communities'. Anderson argues that what we think of as nation is an imagined community. We can have a sense of belonging, yet the national community is too vast and diffuse for us to have the kinds of relationships that we would normally have within a community. Kanno and Norton (2003, p. 241) define imagined communities as 'groups of people, not immediately tangible and accessible, with whom we connect through the power of the imagination'. They contend that 'these imagined communities are no less real than the ones in which learners have daily engagement and might even have a stronger impact on their current actions and investment [in language learning]' (Kanno and Norton 2003, p. 242).

In language learning research, the concepts of communities of practice and imagined communities have been used to enhance researchers' understanding in a number of areas. For example, the notion of communities of practice has been applied in studies investigating Asian female students' participation in graduate school courses in their second language (Morita 2004), adults learning Japanese as a foreign language in a classroom setting (Haneda 1997), and children learning English as a second language in kindergarten (Toohey 1996). Researchers have also explored how relating to imagined communities can affect the trajectory of individuals' language learning (Kanno and Norton 2003), be a source of non-participation in the classroom (Norton 2001), and influence the social construction of learners' identities (Murphey et al. 2005). In this study I use the perspective of communities of practice – both immediate and imagined – to explore the experiences of Japanese adults who became affiliated with a variety of groups in their efforts to learn English in their local milieu.

3 The study

3.1 Aim and participants

The three stories discussed in this chapter are drawn from a life history research project which documents the experiences of Japanese who have learned to speak English in their own country. The initial aim of the research was to explore the belief that in order to become orally proficient in a language a learner needs to be immersed in the target language and culture. Therefore, the main criterion for participation in the study was that the individual had learned to speak English without having studied or lived in an English-speaking country.

3.2 Data collection and analysis

The methodological design of the study drew on the principles and procedures of life history research, a form of narrative inquiry (Riessman 1993; Lieblich et al. 1998; Clandinin and Connelly 2000; Janesick 2000; Kouritzin 2000a; Cole and Knowles 2001). Data collection centred around two life story interviews (Atkinson 1998). However, carrying out life history research is a long process which involves establishing a rapport with the participants (Measor and Sikes 1992; Janesick 2000). Therefore, prior to the first interview I usually met the participants on a couple of occasions to get acquainted, gain their trust, and explain their role in the research process. Mindful that a life history interview should not be overly structured (Atkinson 1998), in the first interview I asked the participants to tell me how they learned English. However, I had prepared a list of questions primarily informed by the literature on autonomy, motivation, and learning strategies which served to probe and round out the participants' stories.

In life history research the separation of data collection from data analysis is an arbitrary distinction because in reality the procedures often overlap. In this study the analysis began as I transcribed the first interview and began jotting down questions for the second interview. Once the transcription was complete, I read through the interview several times isolating individual utterances or segments of responses and attaching codes to these units of text. The codes were inspired by the literature which I referred to earlier and by the learners' experiences – for example, classroom learning, e-mail, church, etc. After the second interview had been carried out and transcribed, I coded the text in the same way. From the outset, I used the constant comparative method (Glaser and Strauss 1967), that is, I compared new units of text or experience to those that were already coded to see if the same code might apply. As I did this, new codes emerged, and existing codes were grouped together to eventually become categories.

Coding the interviews was an important preliminary step in preparing the stories because the codes indicated which segments of the interviews were related to a particular topic or aspect of the participant's language learning experience. To create the stories I configured these segments of interviews into a coherent narrative structure following a chronological order. At this juncture, I began to consult with the participants in order to clarify points or get additional information. The completed stories were sent to the participants for their input and feedback, that is, a member check (Lather 1986a).

When I got the stories back, I began isolating segments and labelling them according to the categories that emerged from the analysis of the interviews. (For a more detailed account of categorical-content analysis, see Lieblich et al. 1998). I grouped segments of text from different stories according to the categories. For example, I grouped all the segments labelled with the code 'church' together, and did the same for the other codes such as 'work,' 'language use', and so on. Cross-referencing, or noting how one segment of text could be placed under more than one category, drew my attention to the possible links between the various categories. For example, cross-referencing enabled me to see how church, work, and language use were related: Church and work provided opportunities in the local community to learn or use the target language. From this, the new category, 'community', emerged. Then, of course, the data had to be re-analysed from the perspective of this new category. Through this circular process, connections and patterns emerged, and eventually took the form of themes. In this case, the emergent theme was the role of community in the participants' language learning.

4 The stories

In order to learn English, the participants in this study become members of a variety of communities of practice both immediate and imagined.

To illustrate this point I re-tell and analyse the stories of three learners – all of whom chose pseudonyms: Mable, a 54 year-old secretary in a university English department; Francis, a 47 year-old university professor; and Yuichi, a 29 year-old front desk clerk for an international hotel. According to the performance-based language proficiency scale Canadian Language Benchmarks (Pawlikowska-Smith 2000), at the time of their interviews, Mable and Yuichi had attained an intermediate level of listening and speaking proficiency, and Francis, an advanced level.

4.1 Mable's story

Like all Japanese, Mable started to study English in junior high school. Throughout her schooling, the English courses consisted of reading and grammar study; there was no speaking or listening. However, outside of class she grew up watching American TV programmes and listening to her elder sister's collection of American music. She saw the movie *West Side Story* ten times and memorised all the songs. All through junior high school she wrote her diary like a letter in English to her favourite American television character played by Clint Eastwood in the series *Rawhide*. Around this time Mable decided she wanted to live and work in the United States.

After she graduated from high school, Mable studied at the YWCA English Language School in Tokyo for one year. Then she got a job as a secretary with the Audio Visual Christian Society in Tokyo, where she worked every day in an office with a unilingual American lady. After two years she got a job with IBM. At IBM she was the only person in the office who could speak English so she had to take telephone calls from foreign companies. In this job she met her future husband and together they joined their company's English club. Mable held this job for two years before she left to get married.

For the next 16 years she was at home raising her two daughters. During this time she listened to the NHK Radio English lessons and took a course – mainly reading and translation – once a month for five years. As a Christian, Mable had access to English conversation classes through her church and contact with English-speaking missionaries, one of whom did a six-month home stay with her. When her children were old enough, she got a job as a secretary in the English department of a university. When I interviewed Mable she had been working in this position for 11 years. When she and her husband retire, they hope to live overseas for a time.

4.1.1 Mable's story: analysis

Mable's story can be viewed as participation in a succession of communities of practice. Her year of English studies at the YWCA English

Language School followed by her work with the missionary society are examples of engagement in communities of practice that afforded Mable opportunities to learn English and western cultural practices. In her job at IBM, although her immediate work environment was Japanese, through her telephone conversations with workers at foreign companies, Mable was part of a multinational-corporate or 'distributed' English-speaking community of practice (Wenger et al. 2002). Also, in this position Mable joined the company's English club, another community of practice which provided her with opportunities to learn English. During the 16 years while she was at home raising her two daughters, Mable continued her language learning by associating with communities of practice that evolved through her church. There she studied in the English conversation programme and had contact with the foreign missionaries – one of whom lived with her family for six months, enabling Maple to improve her English through a community of practice that evolved in her own home.

After she raised her daughters, Mable went back to work as a secretary in the English department of a major university. She says, *If I can speak English now it's only because I'm working here four days a week for over ten years...I've learned English through my work.* In this department there was a strong sense of camaraderie among the English-speaking teachers. They travelled together by bus to the campus from a nearby train station, gathered for morning coffee in the departmental lounge, and had lunch together. During this time they discussed their practice, shared ideas for lessons, and chatted about personal topics. Mable, who was well-liked and highly respected, was an important member of this community of practice. Yet, linguistically she often found herself sitting on the periphery. Mable said, *The more I work here, the more I feel depression. The foreign teachers, especially at lunchtime, use slang or idiomatic expressions. Then I totally don't understand.* To this she added, *I still can't understand English movies without reading the Japanese subtitles.*

Movies and television programmes played an important role in Mable's early language learning. There is strong evidence to suggest that for Mable her favourite movies and television programmes represented imagined communities that she could participate in from a distance through the media. Watching *West Side Story* ten times and writing her diary everyday to the main character of the television show *Rawhide* afforded Mable peripheral participation in these imagined communities, which gave rise to her desire to become a part of actual American communities. She said, *Through those experiences, I decided when I was in junior high, someday I will be in the United States and work there.*

4.2 Yuichi's story

Like Mable, Yuichi's interest in movies played a significant role in his language learning. Although Yuichi did not like English in junior high school, that changed in high school when he discovered his love for American movies and to his surprise his name appeared on the honours list for having a high grade in English. These two events reinforced his motivation to learn English and encouraged him to join his high school's English Speaking Society (English club).

When Yuichi was at university, he went to the movies once a week. He often took a lunch box and stayed all day at the theatre, watching the same movie at least two, maybe three, times. Yuichi also joined the mixed choral society which performed many English songs. Through the society he became friends with some exchange students, two of whom became his roommates for six and eight months consecutively.

Several months after leaving university, Yuichi got a job at an international hotel in Tokyo where he worked for six years. He worked his way from a job in housekeeping to a position on the front desk, primarily to increase his opportunities to use English. At the time of the interview he had been working in the personnel department of an English conversation school company for two years. In this job he could use English most of the time.

From the time Yuichi moved to Tokyo, he more or less stopped studying English. However, he developed a series of strategies for learning English from his favourite American movies and television programmes which he viewed repeatedly. In addition to this, he used English with his foreign friends and his English-speaking companion of two and a half years.

4.2.1 Yuichi's story: analysis

After leaving high school, Yuichi never took a course in English, the only exception being a brief period of work-related English training at the international hotel. Yuichi has taught himself English primarily through his favourite movies and television programmes and through participation in a number of communities of practice including the English Speaking Society in high school, the mixed choral society at university, the international hotel, and the language school company where he worked primarily in English. Yet, perhaps the most striking aspect of Yuichi's English language learning was his peripheral participation in imagined communities.

For Yuichi, his favourite movies and television programmes represented imagined communities which he visited frequently through repeated viewing. Speaking of his love of movies, Yuichi said, *I like to see other worlds, even if the story is real or not. So, I thought, if I am going to understand movies, I need English. I think what attracted me to movies was the culture.* Yuichi not only wanted to see 'other worlds', but he wanted to participate in the actual communities they represented. A long held dream of his has been to live in the United States. Explaining his desire to be a part of these other worlds and to take on a new identity, he said, *I think maybe when people are young they like to be something else, not themselves...I was dreaming and I was thinking about my future, so I just needed some place to go. Through movies I was attracted to the people and the culture.* The movies and television programmes enabled him to imagine a future self and communities to which he hoped to belong. Through his imagination Yuichi became a peripheral participant in the communities presented by the media. Although he could only access these communities through the media, the language features available on VCR and later DVD technology enabled him to develop a series of strategies for improving his English skills.

However, Yuichi did not uniquely rely on imagined communities to improve his English; he also created a small English-speaking 'world' or community in his home. When he was in university, he had two American exchange students share his apartment. Yuichi's comments suggest they were engaged in the practice of making a home-life and through this process of mutual engagement were learning about each other's culture. Speaking of the experience, he said, *What I remember is that I just enjoyed the atmosphere. So, even though we were in Osaka, it made me feel like I was living abroad. I learned a lot of cultural things, differences between their way of doing things and our way of doing things.* Through this experience he was learning to be a participant in the target language culture in the hope of realising his dream of living in America.

Yuichi has had to content himself with learning English through participation in communities of practice both actual and virtual within the larger Japanese community. Sadly, he has not been able to fulfill his aim of living abroad. He said, *If I could, I'd like to study abroad, even now, but I just had no opportunity to go to America or anywhere to study English.* Reflecting on his English language learning over a period of 18 years, Yuichi said, *What helps me the most is conversation in real life. I never had any interest in going to English class because I think that is not life, but in this moment you ask me some questions, or when I cook with my friend, that conversation is real life. It's from real life.* Yuichi has created his opportunities to communicate in 'real life' by seeking out English-speaking communities or by taking action which led to the emergence of his own communities of practice.

4.3 Francis's story

Francis, who grew up in one of Japan's major seaports, was first introduced to English in junior high school. His second-year English teacher often went to the harbour and invited English-speaking sailors and tourists to visit the classroom. Being able to talk to these people in English encouraged Francis to learn more about their country and culture.

To compensate for the lack of contact with English-speakers, Francis joined the English Speaking Society in his school and also memorised passages from his textbooks which he recited on his way to and from school. In addition to this, his junior high school teacher organised a pen pal club which gave interested students an opportunity to correspond with their teacher.

Later at university, he did a degree in English. Although his main interest was rugby, he joined the English Speaking Society whose activities included the recitation of famous speeches and drama activities. When he finished university, he got a job as a high school English teacher. During this time, he studied English at a community centre two or three times a week. When his fellow learners discovered how good his English was, they insisted that he teach the class. He also went to a Mormon Church for a one-hour English class. There, not only did he have contact with English-speakers, but he had the possibility of participating in cultural events. The next year he was transferred to an island where he had no contact with English-speakers.

The following year he went to a bilingual university to do his MA in Old English. There he was immersed in the English language. After that he taught English in a junior college for eight years before returning to the same university to do a PhD in language testing. A year after completing his degree, he got a position at the university where he was teaching at the time of the interviews.

4.3.1 Francis's story: analysis

Francis's English language learning can be traced through participation in a series of communities of practice. The first community Francis refers to is the junior high class where he acquired his interest in English and other cultures. His teacher fostered a sense of community by bringing in guests from the outside. Francis said, *I think that was the most striking thing that I remember about my early contact with English – when I spoke to the sailor and first made myself understood in English ... Encountering those native speakers of English made me study more about the background of their country and culture.* The other thing the teacher did to reinforce the sense of community in the class was to create a 'pen pal club' enabling his students to communicate with him in English. Excited by his emerging ability to communicate in English, Francis joined the pen pal club and the English Speaking Society.

English Speaking Societies, which are common in Japanese schools and universities, offer a good example of the model of communities of practice put forth by Wenger et al. (2002) and typify learning as peripheral participation (Lave and Wenger 1991). These are groups of young people passionate about learning English, who interact on an ongoing basis to share their knowledge and improve their skills. New members, peripheral participants who are guided and informed by their *senpai*s – older, more experienced, respected members – move over time to a place of full participation. Francis recalled that members were to speak English on entering the club room and that the *senpais* helped newcomers by correcting their pronunciation. The club members engaged in a variety of language activities including speech contests and drama productions. The *senpai* system strongly reinforces the sense of belonging to a group or being part of a community. The English Speaking Societies are communities of practice which provide pedagogical 'safe houses' for learners, places where they are free to learn the language in an atmosphere of trust with like-minded people and without the intervention of authority figures (Canagarajah 2004).

Over the years another source of communities of practice that have been instrumental in Francis's English language learning was church groups. An insightful example is the Mormon church where he went to study English after he had finished university. There he also participated in cultural events. Speaking of the experience, he said, *They celebrated typical American holidays or events, so I could experience things like Easter and Christmas. (I wanted to participate in their activities, but not religious activities.) That was one of the things which helped me the most. That helped me to understand the cultural background.* While Francis was interested in participating in the cultural practices, he is quite clear that he wanted to remain a peripheral participant and not become a full member of the Mormon community.

According to Wenger (1998), practice entails a joint enterprise, mutual engagement, and a shared repertoire. Francis's experience suggests that learners can benefit from participation without sharing the sense of joint enterprise which characterises a community. In Francis's case he was open to a degree of mutual engagement, as evidenced by his participation in activities surrounding cultural events, such as Christmas. He learned English through the community's shared repertoire of stories, discourses, and artifacts. Yet, he had no desire to become a full participant, that is to say, a Mormon. Nor was Francis expected to become a Mormon in order to engage in these activities. As Wenger (1998, p. 137) notes, 'a community can offer peripheral forms of participation that are considered legitimate without fulfilling all the conditions of full membership.' This point has important ramifications for language learners because it suggests they can benefit from opportunities to join target language communities of practice in spite of their limited language skills and without experiencing coercion to alter their identities in order to meet the expectations entailed by full membership.

Later, when Francis became a member of the academic community, he gained access to a number of communities of practice. Speaking of one such community which has evolved around his research, he said, *Since 1985, I have gone overseas to conferences in the United States or Europe to give presentations, maybe twice a year. I have regular e-mail contact with people I meet at conferences. E-mail has helped me brush up my writing ability. If people are writing in good English, then it provides a good model for me.* This imagined or distributed community (Wenger et al. 2002) is spread around the globe and relies on internet technology as well as conference meetings to maintain its professional and social ties. Nonetheless, this community has played a significant role in the development and maintenance of Francis's English language skills.

5 Discussion

While the stories presented in this chapter highlight the multifaceted role communities of practice can play in the language learning process, it is not always clear how educators can apply this notion to classroom and other learning contexts (Haneda 2006). Indeed, Wenger's (1998) comments suggest that basing a pedagogy on communities of practice may not be feasible. He contends that communities of practice evolve; therefore, deliberate attempts to create them might well be doomed from the outset. Despite this caveat, this section of the chapter explores how the community of practice model might inform practice and benefit learners in institutional settings.

Wenger does offer hope for applying this model in the language classroom and other learning environments when he suggests that communities of practice can be 'cultivated' (Wenger et al. 2002). In order to cultivate communities of practice, educators must first recognise their existence in the environments where they work. Then they can take action to support them. By engaging learners in activities which foster a sense of community, it may be possible to nurture existing groups and enhance the likelihood that others will evolve. For example, Francis's junior high teacher seems to have done this by inviting in outsiders and offering his students the opportunity to communicate with him by letter. Today's teachers might facilitate the development of a learning community by employing on-line discussion groups or entire e-learning platforms such as *Moodle*. However, teachers do not need to look solely to 'high tech' solutions. Project work based on a mutual concern or interest can also provide opportunities for students to work together and learn from each other. As Lantolf and Pavlenko (2001, p. 157) point out, educators need to find ways 'of organising the classroom community...that allow students...to be actively engaged in co-constructing their own learning with others in the community'.

Language educators working in other environments such as self-access centres might facilitate a sense of community by providing opportunities for learners to meet in small groups to talk about their goals for language learning, what they are doing to meet these goals, and how successful they are. Centres might also offer theme-based discussion groups bringing together learners with similar interests and goals – for example, a book club, a movie club, or a news discussion group. Another possibility is to organise social events based on target language cultural themes. These activities could actually be organised by learners working with the staff, thereby enhancing the sense of engagement and joint enterprise. Activities such as these have the potential to transform the centre itself into a community of practice.

As language educators we also need to explore the possibilities presented by imagined communities. One way we can do this is by giving a greater place to pop culture in our curriculum. Both Mable and Yuichi made use of movies and television programmes in their learning. Pop culture has been a source of motivation for the people in this study to learn English (Murray 2008; also see Menezes in this volume). The concept of imagined communities provides a possible explanation for the power of pop culture as a motivating force. Movies and television programmes vividly portray imagined communities to which learners can aspire to belong, thus enhancing their motivation to learn the language of these communities. Furthermore, these imagined communities have the potential to offer engagement and peripheral participation. Mable and Yuichi repeatedly viewed their favourite movies and television programmes, suggesting that through repeated viewing they were revisiting these imagined communities and learning the language through strategies inspired by this peripheral engagement. Language educators need to recognise the power of narrative and media to excite learners' imaginations and to provide language learning opportunities.

Looking to the future, the notion of imagined communities and the community of practice model coupled with advances in interactive computer and gaming technologies have the potential to inspire a new generation of computer-assisted language learning programmes. We now possess the technology to create virtual target language communities which learners can enter as peripheral participants, assume an identity, engage in a joint enterprise, exercise their agency, and at the same time experience a variety of language learning opportunities (Murray 1999). There is a need for research and development projects which will make this type of language learning software available to people around the world who are learning foreign languages in their first language community.

6 Conclusion

Mable, Yuichi, and Francis have learned English by becoming participants in a variety of communities of practice. They participated in these communities at school, at work, and at home. Oftentimes the communities were English-speaking groups that existed within the greater Japanese society. At other times the communities were imagined, in the sense that they were diffuse, such as Francis's community of scholars, and at times the imagined communities were virtual, as in the movies and television programmes that were so instrumental in Mable and Yuichi's learning. Engagement in the practices of these communities afforded these learners a wide variety of opportunities to improve their language proficiency and to learn about the target culture. Mable, Yuichi, and Francis did not just belong to one or even several communities of practice, but rather they belonged to a series of communities. Their English language learning can be characterized as participation in a succession of communities of practice that spanned their entire language learning history.

10
EFL Narratives and English-Mediated Identities: Two Ships Passing in the Night?

David Block

1 Introduction

In recent years, there has been an increasing interest in identity as a key construct in applied linguistics research focusing on second language learning and second language use. In research monographs and collections, such as Goldstein (1996), Norton (2000), Pavlenko et al. (2001), Pavlenko and Blackledge (2004), Block (2006a) and Omoniyi and White (2006), the interrelationship between the individual's evolving sense of self and emergent second language proficiency is clearly established. As I note elsewhere (Block 2007), when these and other publications focus primarily on naturalistic contexts, there is compelling evidence that 'being there' is not always a guarantee that individuals will have substantial and unfettered access to the language they are putatively immersed in. However, at the same time, there seems to be, in most cases, some scope for intensive – and often extensive – access to local languages. Norton (2000) provides an interesting combination of both of these views of naturalistic contexts in her study of five immigrant women in Toronto over a period of some two years.

For example, Norton examines the case of Eva, a Polish woman who immigrated to Canada at the age of 20. Norton shows how she was able to re-invent herself as an English speaker over a period of several years. Initially, Eva was happy to be in Canada, seeing it as a country of opportunity. However, as she settled into life there, she began to see that her path to full acceptance by Canadians was impeded by her Polish immigrant status. One of the main places where Eva was regularly exposed to English was in the restaurant where she worked. At first, Eva reported that she was marginalised and even exploited by her fellow workers, who ensured that she did the worst jobs, such as cleaning up. Observing that she tended to do the jobs which required no speaking, the restaurant manager assumed that she could not speak English well enough to do higher prestige jobs requiring direct contact with customers, such as taking food orders. Thus, being in what was theoretically – and effectively – an English-speaking environment did not automatically afford Eva opportunities to practise her English. However, matters changed when she began to socialise with her colleagues away from work and they, in turn, began to see her as more than just a silent immigrant worker. Feeling more accepted, Eva began to engage in far more interactions in English, both on and off the job. Eventually, she established herself as a fully functioning co-worker who was deemed by her colleagues and others to be a worthy interlocutor in English.

In this way, second language identity research like Norton's has brought to the fore the intensity of identity work taking place in naturalistic contexts and the multitude of possible target language-mediated identities that emerge therein. The question I aim to explore in this chapter is whether or not the same state of affairs can apply to adult foreign language classrooms, and relevant to this volume, EFL classrooms. In other words, what prospects are there in such contexts for English-mediated identity work to take place? I begin with a consideration of what I mean by identity before moving on to examine in detail the case of Silvia, an adult EFL learner in Barcelona in the 1990s. I conclude that the kind of English-mediated identity work that can take place in an adult EFL classroom tends to be very limited.[1]

2 Poststructuralist identity

Space does not allow a detailed account of what is meant by identity in current applied linguistics research and therefore I will be brief here (see Block 2007 for a lengthier discussion). In recent years, there seems to be a consensus emerging, which in very broad terms, I would call 'poststructuralist'. In this poststructuralist approach, identity is generally pluralised as 'identities', which are seen, not as phenomena fixed for life, but as ongoing lifelong narratives in which individuals constantly attempt to maintain a sense of balance. The latter is what Giddens (1991) calls 'ontological security', which he defines as the possession of 'answers' to fundamental questions which all human life in some way addresses' (Giddens 1991, p. 47). The ongoing search for ontological security takes place at the crossroads of the past, present and future, as in their day-to-day interactions with their environments and those around them, individuals are constantly reconciling their current sense of self with their accumulated past, with a view to dealing with what awaits them in the future. This process involves a dialectic whereby often-contradictory forces must be synthesised in what Papastergiadis (2000, p. 170) terms 'negotiation of difference'. Individuals are thus seen to strive for a coherent life narrative, seeking to resolve conflicts and allay their ambivalent feelings.

In all of this activity, there is the issue of the extent to which identity is a self-conscious, reflexive project of individual agency, created and maintained by individuals. Surely, in the work of some authors, there is too much talk about individuals making choices, in other words, an overemphasis on individual agency. It is probably more sensible to acknowledge that there are social structures within which individuals exist, such as job markets, educational systems and peer groups that constrain the amount and scope of choice available to individuals as regards what they can and cannot do. Framing matters in this way, we come to see individual agency as constitutive of and constituted by social structure. This means that individuals do not develop their sense of self, working exclusively from the inside out or from the outside in; rather, social environments provide conditions and impose constraints whilst individuals act on those same social environments, continuously altering and reshaping them.

Another way to understand how social structure impacts on identity is to examine identity work inside a communities of practice framework (Lave and Wenger 1991). Eckert and McConnell-Ginet (1992, p. 464) define a community of practice as 'an aggregate of people who come together around mutual engagement in an endeavour'. They note that emerging from this mutual engagement in an endeavour are '[w]ays of doing things, ways of thinking, ways of talking, beliefs, values, power relations – in short practices...'. Ultimately, communities of practice are social spaces in which we observe the emergence of the different identities that people assume and are assigned by others.

Finally, applied linguists adopting a generally poststructuralist approach to identity have tended to emphasise one or more social variables, which include ethnicity, race, nationality, gender, social class and language. However, it is worth noting that these different social variables do not stand independent of one another in the larger general identity of a person. As I explain elsewhere (Block 2006a, 2007), when discussing race, ethnicity, nationality, gender, social class and language, it is indeed difficult to examine one type of identity without mentioning others. In this chapter, I focus on the prospects of an adult EFL learner in Barcelona developing an English-mediated identity, whilst noting that social class mediates her stories of how she is aiming to do this. I understand English-mediated identity to be about how individuals come to develop an expertise in English, which they are exposed to either formally or informally. In addition, it is about an emerging affiliation to English, that is, their attitudes towards and affective connection to English. Finally, when discussing an English-mediated identity, there are issues round gaining acceptance as a valid interlocutor by users of English, in this case, as we shall see, represented by the teacher who acts as arbiter on such matters.

As indicated above, social class issues mediate Silvia's ongoing contacts with English. Class may be framed according to more traditional Marxist analysis, in terms of one's relationship to different means of production and extending from this notion, in terms of the kind of job that one has. Here, however, I discuss it in terms of Bourdieu's (1984, 1991) symbolic capital: economic, cultural and social. Following Bourdieu, I understand these three kinds of capital as follows:

1. economic capital refers to the financial wealth and income of an individual, as well as his/her acquired property and assets;
2. cultural capital is about having valued and legitimate cultural resources and assets, which exist as dispositions and behavioural patterns (e.g. accent and attitude), associations with particular artefacts (e.g. books and qualifications) and connections to certain institutions (e.g. university and professional associations);
3. social capital relates directly to these institutional contacts, as it is about connections to and relationships with less, equally or more powerful others.

3 Identity in foreign language contexts: A case study

3.1 Background

In 1993, I carried out research in which my chief aim was to document and analyse what adult language learners found salient about their EFL classes and how they evaluated their teachers and the lessons they were attending (Block 1995). The context was a large language school in Barcelona. Six students were interviewed on a weekly basis during one ten-week term. Interviews were carried out in either Catalan or Spanish, depending on the individual's preference. One of the cases I examined in this study was that of Silvia. In Block (2000), I present Silvia's case in terms of her 'meta-pedagogical awareness' that is, her knowledge about language teaching, in particular what she considered to be good and bad teaching practices.[2] However, here I will frame some of Silvia's accounts of her experiences as the construction of an ongoing narrative about who she is in the context of her lessons. I examine two strands running through Silvia's comments which relate to two identities that she adopted during her interviews.

Silvia was from a wealthy family in Barcelona and at the time of the study, she was living with her husband and three daughters in one of the wealthiest and most exclusive neighbourhoods in the city. Silvia had studied law at university, but soon after finishing her studies, she got married and for most of the ten years preceding this study, her life revolved around raising her three daughters. Still, she occasionally worked, helping her husband, also a lawyer, at his law firm.

Silvia was attending a Cambridge First Certificate exam preparation course that met on Monday and Wednesday mornings from 10 to 12, during an 11-week term. A pre-course interview, in which we discussed Silvia's previous language learning experiences, was carried out a week before the course began. She and I then met on nine additional occasions, usually on Wednesdays just after class. These interviews ranged in length from 30 to 90 minutes and were carried out in Spanish, the language that Silvia chose to speak with me. In the pre-course interview, Silvia presented herself as someone who valued a good atmosphere in a class and she emphasised the importance of the teacher as well as her classmates in making this possible, although the main responsibility was put firmly on the shoulders of the teacher[3]:

> The teacher does a lot. I think he/she does 70% of the work and the rest [of the work], your classmates, because if you have a class with very few people and they are closed and they don't speak, it's very hard for the teacher to make the class work. In other words, the students are also important, they need to participate and the rest [of the work], the teacher needs to know how to coordinate and make the class pleasant and not boring. (Silvia-22/April/1993)

Silvia's respective relationships with her teacher and her classmates were to come to the fore when she and I began to meet to talk about her experiences on the Cambridge First Certificate exam preparation course.

3.2 Silvia and her teacher

The single most significant issue to emerge in Silvia's ongoing accounts of her lessons was her relationship with her teacher. Fairly early in the course, she told me the following:

> One day I ran into her outside of class and I told her that sometimes she gesticulated a lot and put on surprising eyes and that some classmates might feel a little intimidated. And she told me that it was true and thank you for having told her. And I said: It's just that there might be people who are shyer and anyway, I had noticed this **feeling**, or whatever you want to call it. So the next day she was a little more **soft**, not as aggressive. Because she's a little like that, impetuous and gesticulating and her eyes bulge out. (Silvia-28/April/1993)

In this excerpt, Silvia takes on the role of broker between her classmates and her teacher and she takes the liberty of being rather blunt with the latter. This bluntness may be seen in terms of a certain sense of one-ness that Silvia professed to feel with teachers, something that she commented on both in her pre-course interview and at the end of the course (more on this below). Nevertheless, her desire not only to get on with her teacher but also to be close to her (and perhaps even to be her friend), was upset by one very important mediator of their relationship. I refer here to the way that the teacher corrected her written compositions. The comment below was made about halfway through the course and is typical of what Silvia had to say about this topic:

> If I don't know the word, I shut up. But if I'm 100 % sure, [I speak]. ... It's for this reason that it bothers me so much when she corrects my writing...it's just that she doesn't let anything get past her, not even a comma, a period, or quotation marks...Of course I think that the other teachers have turned a blind eye when correcting. I told her: **YOU CROSS OUT EVERYTHING!** She says it's like swimmers who swim with weights and when the weights are taken off, they fly. So that's what she does with me, but it's hard. (Silvia-5/May/1993)

Three weeks later, Silvia returned to this topic, this time with a harsher critique of her teacher and her correction tactics:

> the other day because it made me so angry that she crossed out things in my **compositions** that I told her that she overdid it with me. And

she says: **yes, I recognize I am very hard with you and...but you should** [do] this and that. ... Yes, the other day it really bothered me, really...she had crossed out things and then in class, she ridicules the errors a little at times and I don't like it...I really don't like it. ... I have a lot of self-esteem, all right, and so I don't like people to correct me, perhaps. Because I already correct myself enough because I am perhaps very demanding, so...Of course, I admit that she's within her rights, she has to do it, doesn't she? But I don't accept it so easily. It's like every time you come and they knock you in the head with a stick, you know? After making an effort...I write with a lot of hope and desire and I always want to improve, right? (Silvia-26/May/1993)

In this excerpt, Silvia manifests a degree of ambivalence as regards her relationship with her teacher as corrector of her written English. The teacher seems to have admitted that she was being tough with Silvia, although Silvia says that she still cannot accept being corrected. This seems to be because on the one hand, she has a 'lot of self-esteem', and on the other hand, because she thinks that the teacher ridicules student errors. However, perhaps in recognition of the teacher's institutional role, Silvia accepts that she is 'within her rights'. She finishes by likening the teacher's treatment of written errors to hitting her over the head with a stick.

In an interview taking place a week later, Silvia returned to the correction of her written work, suggesting that the teacher wanted to keep her in her place and even 'punish' her. She related such behaviour to a tendency she had noted among EFL teachers to take advantage of the power that their institutional position afforded them:

The only thing is that sometimes...I think that teachers, because they speak English and you don't, they are above you. And this infuriates me, actually, because I don't know, but you get this feeling a little and I've mentioned it to other people and they've told me I'm right. I mean it's not just my thing, I'm not going to have any kind of inferiority complex. It's just it's a little... And you say: Well who do you think you are? You're just a teacher. It's true. You might know a lot of English but I know a lot of other things. (Silvia-2/June/1993)

Here, Silvia makes reference to what seems to be a question of social class. A well-educated woman from a wealthy family, with a law degree and a home in one of Barcelona's most exclusive residential areas – in short, someone with high levels of economic, cultural and social capital – certainly does not have to take certain things from someone who is 'just a teacher'. Indeed, she seems to resent the fact that the classroom situation puts her in a less powerful position as regards the cultural capital that English represents. However, by the time of our last interview, which took place just after the last day of class, matters had changed considerably and Silvia explained her reconciliation with her teacher as follows:

> in the end, I also told her what I wanted to tell her and I am at peace with the world because I told her. (DB: What did you tell her?) No, one day I told her that she should write something on my **compositions** and not scratch out everything and only write a check... and I said: **You should have written something here to cheer me up. And the last composition I got a sentence – Good work – or something like this which I appreciate a lot**... and today we were also talking to her. She was asking me what I was going to do next year. (Silvia-16/June/1993)

Silvia went on to make a revealing statement about her relationship with teachers, which seemed less than congruent with her remarks about teachers being 'just teachers':

> I like talking to teachers. I don't know why, but I like it a lot... And besides, we went to the bar and had a glass of cava... But of course since we had never gone to the bar with her, you never get to know her very well. So we were asking her where she was from and how she had ended up here and everything. I don't know, you situate people more when you know a little about their past because if not... (Silvia-16/June/1993)

In these comments about her teacher, Silvia once again manifests an ambivalent attitude. On the one hand, she appreciated the structure and clarity that the teacher provided; on the other hand, she resented the control that the teacher exercised over her via what Silvia framed as draconian correction techniques. In conversations taking place outside of our formal interviews, Silvia's ambivalent feelings towards her teacher seemed to be connected with certain longing for what we might call a missed opportunity in her own life. I often had the impression that she wished she had been able to emulate the expatriate teachers with whom she came in contact in her EFL courses. While the latter left their countries of origin and went to live in another country, usually whilst in their early or mid 20s, Silvia followed routine and tradition, getting married and settling down to raise a family at this age. Her ambivalence may also be understood as a symptom of her struggle to negotiate differences (Papastergiadis 2000) as she produced her ongoing narrative, and her need for ontological security (Giddens 1991) as she strove to make her narrative more coherent both to herself and her interlocutor.

In common with participants in other studies involving ongoing accounts of foreign language lessons (e.g., Bailey 1983; Block 1996; Lantolf and Genung 2003), Silvia was critical of teaching practice and how the teacher made her feel. However, unlike the protagonists in these three studies, Silvia was able to resolve this conflict by talking to her teacher, a move which seemed both to change her teacher's behaviour and satisfy Silvia's desire to be close to her. Silvia's need to be respected was inextricably linked and intertwined with a second struggle going on with her teacher, that is, her quest for an English language textual identity in English. Here I understand an English language textual identity to be about becoming a 'text creator' and gaining a voice in the target language (Kramsch and Lam 1999). In her comments, Silvia constructs her journey from feeling victimised by her teacher, who is said to have ridiculed student errors and made her feel as though she was being physically abused, to believing that her writing was appreciated. Thus, just as she was able to have a person-to-person (rather than student-to-teacher) conversation with the teacher at the end the course, she was also able to gain the teacher's recognition as a competent writer and therefore a validated written text creator in English.

3.3 Silvia and the problem student

The teacher-student dyad captures but one dimension of EFL classroom experiences; another dimension is about the relationships a student develops with fellow students during a course. Silvia's class was a small one, consisting of ten students of various ages with the most important group being a cohort of women like Silvia, who were in their mid thirties. In an early interview, Silvia mentioned in passing that she did not care for one of these women, named Rosa:[4]

> But this one is a little bit of a pain in the neck... no, sometimes she puts you down or she thinks differently and she says that you're crazy to think how you think... and I think it's already the third course I have done with her and I'm a little sick of her and I prefer to

avoid her. If she thinks differently, I think another way and that's it. (Silvia-28/April/1993)

Silvia related how one day she even tried to sit in a different part of the classroom in order to avoid Rosa. However, such a strategy did not work:

> the other day I tried to sit next to someone new and then this person came and she sat next to me. But when we got into groups of two, I sat next to [the new student] and luckily it worked out...I mean I sat next to the student I wanted to and it wasn't noticeable...if I'm lucky, I'll be sure to avoid her because...for me she's kind of a drag. (Silvia-5/May/1993)

When asked exactly why she disliked Rosa so much, Silvia talked about times when Rosa had been rude to her and fellow students. She also told me that she had heard that Rosa had also had problems with her fellow students on other courses that she had attended in the same school:

> So, this girl, they had told me that in her first course here she had a lot of problems with the class, that she ended up falling out with half the class. And at first I thought, she's not that bad, that it must have been the other people's fault and not hers, but now I think it's her fault. I mean I have no doubt that if she fell out with everyone one it's down to her...(Silvia-5/May/1993)

As she did with her teacher, Silvia provided me with an explanation as to why she found it so difficult to get on with Rosa:

> I think she is a self-made person and when people face adverse circumstances they become more demanding and more...If you have things easy in life, more or less, you are more condescending. But if you have them a little [difficult]...then you're very demanding, I think. And I think that's kind of the situation with this girl...and well, she has fixed ideas and I don't know...sometimes things are not black and white. (Silvia-5/May/1993)

Here Silvia plays both psychiatrist and sociologist as she comments on Rosa's state of mind and social background. For Silvia, it seems that if an individual has to fight to improve her lot in life, she becomes more aggressive in the process. By contrast, people who have not had to fight, such as Silvia herself, are more 'condescending', by which Silvia seems to mean amenable and open. As she did when referring to teachers who are 'just teachers', Silvia once again displays a clear class-consciousness here. Thus, if in her comments about teachers she showed a degree of contempt, with Rosa she seemed to object to her status as a relative parvenu. As Bourdieu (1984) notes, parvenus may well manifest the capacity of recognition (*reconnaissance*) of what constitutes distinction and good taste, adopting the outward trappings of legitimate high culture. However, they do not generally have the knowledge (*connaissance*), that is, the acquired and embodied capacity to produce these outward trappings in appropriate and natural ways. In the following excerpt, Silvia seems to follow this logic as she paints Rosa as a graceless and pretentious poser who boasts about prestige elements in her life, such as having Swiss nationality and a son who speaks German:

> she is all the time excusing herself because she says words in German and sometimes I think she does it a little on purpose but...and I think that this girl also does it sometimes because she likes to show off that she was in Switzerland, that she's got Swiss nationality and I don't know...that the Swiss are so perfect, I don't know...and that her son speaks German...Everyone has their things but I don't go around telling everyone...normally if they don't ask me I don't go around boasting. (Silvia-26/May/1993)

However, despite these harsh words, by the end of the course Silvia talked of a reconciliation with Rosa, just as she had done with reference to her teacher. In an interview taking place after her last day of class, she explained how she had made up with her classmate and even suggested that she had perhaps been unfair in her earlier assessment of Rosa.

4 Conclusion

In my view, Silvia's stories about her teacher and Rosa show how in an adult EFL classroom the kind of identity work being done is very different from what goes on in the naturalistic contexts cited at the beginning of this chapter. In the two parallel narratives discussed here, Silvia positions herself as a wealthy and educated person, someone in possession of a good deal of symbolic capital in her day-to-day life in Barcelona and who has a heightened sense of class-consciousness. She deals with the people around her through the prism of this class-consciousness, which leads her to disparage those who are deemed to behave inappropriately by getting above their station. However, ultimately she seems to value harmony over all else and the happy endings to both stories seem to come as something of a relief to her.

At the same time, Silvia works towards the development of an English textual identity via her writing activities, as we see in her accounts of her exchanges with her teacher during the course about these activities. Indeed, her accounts of how she struggled with her teacher over her voice in English seem far more convincing as evidence of an emergent textual identity than accounts I have found in other studies where the focus is on written work.[5] However, this struggle for a textual identity was inextricably linked to her larger, more general concern about how she was treated by her teacher. In Bailey (1983), Block (1996) and Lantolf and Genung (2003), the authors show how students had ongoing conflicts with their teachers about classroom management issues such as setting exams, dealing with homework and error correction. However, whereas in these cases the teacher-student(s) relationships seemed to remain poor throughout the language courses, in Silvia's case, there was a happy ending with Silvia saying that she liked her teacher.

Examining Silvia's case, my conclusion is rather pessimistic as regards adult EFL classrooms, namely that the prospects for an English-mediated identity work to take place are minimal. This is not to say that there is no identity work going on; it is only to say that it is not linked directly to English and has more to do with communities of practice emergent inside the classroom which are about the activities engaged in and the interrelationships of participants. Crucially, the latter are not likely to be mediated by English, as it would not appear to be customary for most people in Spain, Japan, Brazil and many other countries to carry out a significant part of their day-to-day international work in English. To be sure, adult students in EFL classrooms in these countries do speak to each other in English if and when they are asked to do so by their teachers. However, such activity is but a small part of their lives and surely does not constitute what I have elsewhere called 'critical experiences', which I deem as necessary for identity work to take place and define as follows:

> By critical experiences, I mean periods of time during which prolonged contact with an L2 and a new and different cultural setting causes irreversible destabilization of the individual's sense of self. There is, in a sense, an element of before and after in critical experiences as the individual's sociohistorical, cultural and linguistic

environment, once well defined and delimited, becomes relatively ill defined and open-ended. (Block 2002, p. 4)

Of course, one could argue that I have focused on just part of Silvia's ongoing narrative, the part that most suits my argument here. While this is obviously true in that I have not been able to discuss some ten hours of interview material in a chapter of this length, I am confident that what I have reproduced here is typical of Silvia's narrative spread over eleven weeks of contact, in particular her almost exclusive focus on what was going on inside the four walls of the classroom. One might also ask if Silvia's experiences are typical of the very broad and varied world of adult EFL teaching and learning. In response, I acknowledge that the actual issues arising in different adult EFL classrooms around the world will obviously be different from those which Silvia brought to the fore (i.e., students will not always have a conflict with a teacher or a classmate). However, I would add that the tendency for adult EFL students to focus on the immediate environment would be the same. In short, when constructing self-referential narratives of their EFL classroom experiences, students will tend to focus on what arises within and from the activities of the emergent community of practice composed of students and their teachers. And these activities will tend to position the students as 'student', vis-à-vis the teacher and 'classmate', vis-à-vis fellow students. As a result, it will always be difficult for adult EFL students to have critical experiences, as I argue above.

However, despite this rather pessimistic assessment of adult EFL classrooms as potential spaces for English-mediated identity work to take place, I have found variations on the traditional EFL class that offer some hope. One such variation involves the introduction of self-conscious reflective work by students about their imagined identities in English, past, present and future. Here space does not allow me to discuss in detail this pedagogical practice which I think has some potential for the emergence of English-mediated identity work. Instead, I refer the reader to Murphey's use of language learning histories, that is, university students' written accounts of their English language learning experiences as a basis for classroom speaking activities (Murphey, this volume; Murphey et al. 2005).[6] With reference to language learning histories, Murphey et al. (2005, p. 99) note that:

[t]hrough writing and talking about who they have been in their different learning situations and who they are (or want to be) now in the present one, students themselves become the topic of the

class...Providing space for clarifying and constructing identities when done in the target language also encourages identifying with the language as a means of self-construction.

In my view, English-mediated identity work will only take place if and when adult EFL classroom activities provide such space.

Notes

1. Here I use the term EFL to refer to contexts in which individuals are learning English, which is not a typical language of communication in their surrounding environment. Although framing Silvia as a learner of English as an international language or English as a *lingua franca* might be preferable to some scholars (e.g., Jenkins 2006), in this chapter, it would not add value to my discussion of narratives and English-mediated identities and therefore, I stick to more traditional terminology.
2. In Block (2000), I do not use the pseudonym 'Silvia' instead referring to this learner as 'GJ'. Also, note that in Block (2007), Silvia's story is presented in a form similar to that found here. In Block (2006b), however, her story is viewed more from a psychoanalytical perspective.
3. All interviews were carried out in Spanish, but here I will only present the English translations of the excerpts I have chosen to reproduce. All excerpts are presented with standardised spelling and punctuation. Suspension points mean either a pause or that a part of the reproduced excerpt has been removed to aid readability. Comments about paralanguage or other relevant additional information appear in parentheses as follows: (laughing). Words I have inserted to add coherence are in brackets as follows: [in the]. Capital letters are used to indicate that the person has raised his/her voice suddenly. Portions that are in bold were produced in English in the original interview.
4. A pseudonym.
5. For example, in Belz (2002), a German teacher at an American university asked students to write essays using their own invented languages, which drew on English, German and any other linguistic resources they had acquired previously, either formally or informally (e.g., Spanish, Russian, etc.). Belz sees the texts produced by students as 'signs of their textual identities constructed in and through language' (Belz 2002, p. 32). However, apart from stimulating language play and developing further multicompetence, the essay writing did not, in my view, significantly move learners in the direction of textual identities in German. I say this because there is no evidence that the new multi-languages developed by the learners actually mediated new identities or served as any indication that the students were engaged in the process of negotiating membership in what might reasonably be called a community of practice.
6. See also Leppänen and Kalaja (2002) for an account of the use of autobiographies with younger EFL learners.

11
Frequent Flyer: A Narrative of Overseas Study in English

Alice Chik and Phil Benson

1 Introduction

According to a recent news report, approximately 2.7 million overseas students were enrolled at higher education institutions in the 30 member countries of the Organization for Economic Co-operation and Development (OECD) in 2004 (BBC News 2006). With the United Kingdom accounting for 16.1 per cent of this figure, the report observed that 'a premium was placed on studying in the English language' in spite of rising fees. According to UKCOSA statistics for the same year, overseas students accounted for 13 per cent (318,000) of the total enrolment, with Hong Kong students (10,000) ranking fifth in number behind students from China, India, the United States and Malaysia (UKCOSA 2007). Based on comparable statistics from agencies in other countries, we estimate that there are currently more than 50,000 Hong Kong students enrolled in English-medium universities in the United Kingdom, North America and Australasia.

For Second Language Acquisition (SLA) researchers in these parts of the world, overseas students are a convenient pool of 'subjects' for research focusing on the difficulties of studying in a foreign language. There are also a small number of studies documenting cultural difficulties, including the 'language shock' experienced when students encounter unfamiliar accents and dialects (Marr 2005), psychological stress arising from the lines drawn between host students and international students (Ayano 2006), and problems of acculturation (Burnett and Gardner 2006) and discrimination (Jackson 2006). From a research perspective, therefore, the overseas student is a problematic figure, one who must struggle to overcome various linguistic and cultural difficulties. But this is not necessarily the perspective of the students themselves, for whom the difficulties of overseas study are often tied up with the ways in which they are positioned as EFL speakers who are liable to experience such difficulties. The problem that we face, therefore, is one of understanding the experience of study overseas from the student's perspective and within the context of the student's life. Every student who travels overseas for higher education has a story to tell, and in this chapter we approach this problem by telling the story of one Hong Kong student's experience of studying Law and Politics at a United Kingdom university from 2003 to 2006.

2   Identity and study abroad

The notion of identity is central to this study because it emerged as the dominant theme within the narrative that we report. Identity is a complex and contested concept that refers broadly to a 'person's understanding of who they are' (Taylor 1994, p. 25). This understanding is, in part, conditioned by social and cultural circumstances – including gender, nationality, ethnicity, language repertoire and social class – and the ways others see us. These factors of identity are largely beyond our control. But we also take the view that identities are, in part, conditioned by individual agency and negotiated through ongoing narratives involving self-reflection and self-thematisation (Straub et al. 2005). This may be especially so for those whose life experiences involve movements across linguistic and cultural borders. For such people, as Bauman (2004, pp. 11–12) puts it, the thought of 'having an identity' arises as they become 'aware that "belonging" and "identity" are not cut in rock', but take 'the form of a task to be performed, and to be performed over and over again'.

There is now a growing body of research using ethnographic and narrative approaches to explore relationships between SLA and identity development in border-crossing experiences (e.g., Kouritzin 2000; McKay and Wong 1996; Norton 2000; Teutsch-Dwyer 2001). But, as Kanno (2000b) points out, this research often focuses on the ways in which identity factors impede the SLA process for migrants to English-dominant countries. Viewing second language learners as 'bilinguals', Kanno (2000, p. 3) argues that 'to the extent that they are speakers of two languages, and therefore by definition members (central or marginal) of multiple language communities, the L1 world and the L2 world exist for them side by side, each just as relevant to them as the other'. While Kanno's research is concerned with English-speaking children of Japanese expatriates returning to Japan, there have also been a number of studies, adopting this perspective, of individuals who have learned English as a foreign or second language in Asia and spent extended periods studying or working overseas (Block 2002, 2006b; Li 2002; Lim 2002; Sakui 2002; Benson et al. 2003). These studies tend to show how, for such individuals, the experience of living overseas is not so much an experience of linguistic and cultural transplantation, as one of moving 'back and forth' between languages and cultures and of developing identities that are 'neither the sum of the new and the old, not half of what they were and half of what they are' (Block 2006, p. 28).

By describing Hong Kong students overseas as 'frequent flyers', we want to foreground this 'back and forth' character of their experience. Most Hong Kong students who decide to pursue higher education overseas are already bilingual, having graduated from elite English-medium schools in Hong Kong with high levels of English language proficiency. They typically study overseas with the intention of returning to Hong Kong as 'marketable' graduates with competitive advantage over graduates from local English-medium universities. These students are frequent flyers in the literal sense that they may fly home as often as three times a year, using mileage points to reduce the cost of commuting. They are also frequent flyers in a more metaphorical sense, shifting between languages and cultures both across and within both their home and overseas settings. Hong Kong students tend to be well prepared, linguistically and culturally, for overseas study. Nevertheless, the experience often turns out to be a disappointing one. By narrating the overseas study experience of one Hong Kong student, Ally, we hope to illuminate how the difficulties they encounter and their ways of dealing with them are interwoven with their experiences of 'frequent flying' and the construction of distinctive identities as Hong Kong people who have studied overseas.

3 Methodology

Lieblich, Tuval-Mashiach and Zilber (1998, p. 7) identify two major areas of interest within the field of psychology: predicting and controlling human behaviour and exploring and understanding the inner world of individuals. 'One of the clearest channels for learning about the inner world', they argue, 'is through verbal accounts and stories presented by individual narrators about their lives and their experienced reality'. Adopting a narrative approach, we explore one aspect of Ally's 'inner world': her experiences of studying overseas, the meanings that she attached to them, and their contribution to her ongoing sense of self-identity.

Polkinghorne (1995, p. 5) makes a distinction between 'analysis of narratives' and 'narrative analysis', based in turn on Bruner's (1986) notions of 'paradigmatic' and 'narrative cognition'. Paradigmatic analysis of narratives, he observes, 'gathers stories for its data and uses paradigmatic analytic procedures to produce taxonomies and categories out of the common elements across the database'. This is, we think, the most frequent approach to narrative inquiry in second language research. The approach taken in this chapter, however, is more akin to Polkinghorne's 'narrative analysis', which 'gathers events and happenings as its data and uses narrative analytic procedures to produce explanatory stories'. As he goes on to observe:

> The outcome of a narrative analysis is a story – for example, a historical account, a case study, a life story, or a storied episode of a person's life. In this type of analysis, the researcher's task is to configure the data elements into a story that unites and gives meaning to the data as contributors to a goal or purpose. The analytic task requires the researcher to develop or discover a plot that displays the linkage among the data elements as parts of an unfolding temporal development culminating in the denouement. (Polkinghorne 1995, p. 5)

Adopting a similar approach in this study, we use data from interviews conducted over a period of four years to develop a narrative of Ally's experience of overseas study, which begins before she left Hong Kong and concludes after she returned. The three interviews were conducted in Hong Kong by the first author of this chapter in September 2003, September 2005 and January 2007. The three interviews, each lasting around 90 to 120 minutes, were unstructured and conducted in an informal style in a mixture of Cantonese and English (data extracts in this chapter were translated into English by the first author).

After transcription, the first two interviews were coded thematically, with Ally's language background and her expectations and evaluations of overseas study emerging as important themes, and the clash between her expectations prior to departure and evaluations after two years overseas emerging as a key to the narrative structure of her experience. Using short narratives of critical incidents within the data as core elements, Ally's experiences were written up in story form. Ally then read this story and commented on it during the third interview. This interview was also coded, with the themes of re-evaluation and awareness of identity change emerging strongly. A summary of this interview was used as a concluding section to the narrative. Although the second author of this chapter contributed to the analysis of the data, he has not met Ally and the story that follows is narrated by the first author, who interviewed her and knows her well.

4 Ally's story

4.1 Leaving Hong Kong

I first met Ally in September 2002, as a matriculation student at the English-medium girls' school that I had just joined. She struck me as a highly proficient student, who was not afraid of speaking out in class. As I got to know her better, I found that she had a cheerful, positive and practical outlook on life. Ally's mother was the head English teacher at the school and her father a secondary school principal, and both were pursuing doctoral degrees. Though Ally's father was formerly a science teacher and, in Ally's words, *not fluent in English*, as a school principal and graduate student he had presented reports and papers in English both locally and internationally and Ally was very proud that his English had improved over the years. Ally's younger sister was studying at an English-medium international school and English had become her dominant language at school and at home. As a result, the family began to use English more and more: watching English TV programmes and often speaking English at home. Ally's parents insisted that when the family spoke English, there would be no mixing of English and Cantonese.

Throughout her school years, Ally attended top ranking schools. She remembered that the first turning point in her English learning came in Primary 3, when she joined the English Speech Festival (a popular Hong Kong-wide event entered by around 35,000 students annually). She joined because she felt it would be a good opportunity for her to shine and receive individual attention. At primary school, she received one-to-one training from an English teacher from India, who taught her a great deal about pronunciation and articulation. Ally also developed an interest in reading at primary school. Hospitalised for a brief period, and with time on her hands, she began to read the English storybooks that her mother brought her. This was the first time Ally remembered reading in English on her own and to this day she prefers English novels to Chinese novels.

Ally had great confidence in her spoken and reading skills, but found grammar difficult from primary school onwards. Though she would not say she was pushed to focus on English, she did say that her mother's help before public examinations had helped boost her confidence. At secondary school, Ally's mother took over her Speech Festival training. Ally felt under constant pressure to perform well, because her mother was the head English teacher in the school. She also felt that she had to learn English well, not just for herself, but because she could not let her mother *lose face*.

Ally also had several aunts and uncles living overseas – in the United States, United Kingdom, Singapore and Australia – and she was used to travelling overseas to visit her cousins from an early age. Having been taught by a variety of teachers, Ally told me that she did not find it difficult to understand different English accents. But when she travelled to the US during Primary 6, her father left her to her own devices when ordering lunch, which led to a *horrific* experience in which she had to use English to instruct the counter staff at a Subway sandwich shop to assemble her sandwich from *several dozen ingredients*. Even though this happened when she was 11, she still hates ordering sandwiches. Ally also observed on these visits that while her cousins tended to speak English among themselves, they would speak Cantonese to her. *I felt that speaking English means belonging to a community*, she observed, *It is not about accent differences... the problem is not being able to speak English at all!*.

In Secondary 3, Ally went on a three-week study trip to Canada and the United States, during which she said she lost her fear of speaking English. In Secondary 6, she attended a two-week youth conference in New York and Washington, DC, debating with delegates from all over the world, an experience that radically changed her views on the use of English. English was the official language of the conference, and everyone spoke English differently. She made friends with a young man from Kentucky and managed to understand about 70 per cent of his speech. The Canadian study tour made her more aware of the different accents, but her experience in the United States gave her insight into the use of English as a global language. It also awakened a desire to become a *native speaker of English*, which became one of her reasons for wanting to study overseas.

Ally's home and school experiences of English are not the norm for young people in Hong Kong. But it is by no means unusual for children in middle-class families to read, watch TV, and speak English at home, and to travel overseas on family visits and study trips, especially among families who send their children overseas for higher education. When I interviewed her shortly before her departure for the United Kingdom, Ally recognised she had more opportunities to use English than the average Hong Kong student. She also felt privileged in this respect:

> I think I was among the best students in Hong Kong, and my spoken English was much better than most students. I speak English with my sister, we watch English TV programmes at home, there are a lot more foreigner teachers in my school and I have been overseas many times. I have had a lot more opportunities than the average local students.

Observing that some of her local English teachers did not use English like native English speakers, she said that their grammar and fluency was alright, but not their usage: *'When two Chinese non-English speakers speak, the way they use English is different. The grammar might be correct, but not the usage. Like, "the library will be closing in 15 minutes time", that's the sentence they use here. British may say "the library will be closing in 15 minutes"'*.

Ally was also very specific on her language learning goal,

> I want to be a native speaker one day. This takes time and a lot of exposure to English in its natural speaking context... and this is not something I can learn in Hong Kong, at least not from secondary school. I want to be as fluent and as native as a native speaker, this is my goal, and I am working towards it.

But although she was excited by the prospect of studying in the United Kingdom, she did have some reservations:

> I am not prepared to let go and just use English as the only communication language. I am worried about my listening. The British speak too quickly. When I live overseas, I had to start thinking in English, not Chinese, I can't afford to translate in my head.

Ally already planned to study in the United Kingdom when I first met her and in the summer of 2003 she was offered and accepted a place at university in Manchester to study Law and Politics. On the eve of her departure, she expressed her strong desire to use this opportunity to improve her English and live *the full life in a British culture, including the fish and chips*:

> There is a big community of Chinese in Manchester, but I don't want to limit myself to that community. But am I going to make friends with an Indian, a Taiwanese, or a Singaporean? There is a Chinatown there, true, but I don't want to meet other Hongkongers. I want to go to UK because I want to be no different from a native English speaker. I want to watch their local TV, live there, understand their jokes and their culture. If I don't know the English culture, I know a lot less about the language. I also want to bring back home a native accent, if that is possible.

4.2 Manchester

Ally left Hong Kong with the anticipation of *starting a new life that I wanted for myself*. During her first term, her mother told me that she was doing well in her study, but she worried because Ally had hinted that she was not happy. Ally intended to return to Hong Kong during the Christmas holiday, but decided to stay on to revise for the upcoming examinations. It was not until the summer of 2004 that she returned and she was so happy to come back home that she cried on the plane when she saw Hong Kong. Ally returned to Hong again at Christmas 2004 and in the summer of 2005 she was especially eager to board the flight to Hong Kong, because she had internships with two law firms waiting for her. We met again in September 2005 for the first time since our interview before she had departed two years earlier. Though she was eager to go back to Manchester to complete her last year of study, she didn't particularly want to leave Hong Kong.

Our second interview took a very different course to the first. My first surprise was that, where she had previously used the terms 英國人 (British people) or 外國人 (foreigners – a term that does not have the same derogative connotations that it has in Britain), she now used the derogative slang 鬼 (*gwei* – literally meaning 'ghosts'). Over lunch, she described two recent assaults on Chinese take-away restaurant owners in London and went on to describe examples of discrimination against herself and other Hong Kong students. On the day she arrived in Manchester, she told me, a bus driver had accused Ally of trying to avoid paying the fare by giving him a ten-pound note. But he did not say anything to *local* passengers who gave him 20-pound notes. On the same day, a British man shouted at her because she was wearing a Beatles t-shirt. She didn't believe that the man would have shouted at her if she was a *gwei*. She also had another unpleasant encounter:

> I was walking down the street and there were these drunken guys swearing at me saying, 'you Chinese blah blah blah' and I swore back. A couple days later, I saw one of them on campus. He was a student there. Honestly, discrimination was not something I anticipated. I feel that I am being treated differently simply because of my ethnicity. It is not just the obvious swearing, there are other more subtle signs, from body language, gestures, the glare and sneer...it was felt rather than verbally expressed. Shop keepers would greet the locals nicely but not we Chinese. We are constantly sneered at and glared at in the supermarket. Maybe as a woman, I am more sensitive to these discriminating encounters.

For Ally, incidents like this showed that racism was the mainstream experience of all Chinese, students or otherwise, in Britain.

Ally lived in the university hall, where she mostly made friends with other Asian students. She felt that the British students and the hall staff were hostile towards overseas students, especially Chinese students. She told me that during an official hall dinner, the five-year-old daughter of one of the hall staff shouted *I never like Chinese* at the Hong Kong students. Ally believed the child had got this attitude from her family. Ally's friends also experienced discrimination in the academic setting, such as their tutors marking essays according to the students' family names, rather than the merit of their work. At university, Ally felt that she was treated first as a Chinese student and second as a Law student. Upon arrival in England, she had suddenly become *a non-European international student and a non-native English speaker*. Her English proficiency, rather than her academic ability, was the first concern of the teaching staff:

> The gweis assume that I am useless. The gweis treated me as invisible, except when they have problems, and then they remember my name. I know that with better English proficiency, it's less likely that they will look down on me or take advantage of me.

While Ally's experiences with discrimination were very real and she was shocked at being viewed as *just another non-local with limited English*, she also recognised the limitations of her English proficiency and was critical of some of her Asian friends for using avoidance as the only strategy to deal with discrimination.

Ally felt, in fact, that her listening and speaking proficiency had improved considerably during her two years in Manchester:

> It took me several months to get used to the Manchester accent ... Now I can understand sports commentary, it is the constant exposure. English learned from conversations, like going to the banks, daily shopping, and small group tutorials. I have picked up different ways to express myself, a stronger British accent and other slang and phrases. I definitely have better intonation and stress, and more vocabulary.

Ally also felt her academic English had improved in terms of specialised terminology, but writing was something she still needed to work on. While she felt comfortable listening to lectures, she saw small group tutorials as battlefields. But while some Hong Kong Chinese students had considerable difficulties with tutorials, Ally fared better:

> The tutors give me more opportunities to speak and treat me as *normal*. It means they don't need to slow down their speech and there is more in-depth discussion. When it comes to group work, the local British students are only willing to partner with foreigners with fluent English. They do not just partner with whoever sitting next to them.

During her second year, Ally also volunteered to be a student advisor at the university legal advice centre:

> I need to interview clients, understand their cases and send them back letters or give advice. It is quite a challenge because I really need to understand my clients' situations and try to find ways to help them. It may be writing a letter on their behalf or advising them on the next course of action. I treat this as my extra curricular activity and it's also a good way to develop my language and academic knowledge. As a Chinese, I have to talk to a British client and try to help them. It was quite something.

She felt that this experience and her fluency in spoken English had set her apart from other Hong Kong students during her summer internships in Hong Kong:

> I felt that I don't need to translate in my head when engaged in daily conversation, my fluency has definitely improved. I have also

stopped using er ... ehm .... to start my sentences. I still don't consider myself a user of English. I am still a learner, especially in academic English. But I have improved my confidence in speaking English, I can respond immediately and spontaneously. Comparing myself to other Hong Kong local interns working in this international law firm, I felt they had delayed reaction to spoken English. It is very obvious.

Ally's two years of overseas study had clearly been a disappointing experience in terms of her initial expectations. But I also observed that she had become a mature and independent young woman, aware of her strengths and weaknesses, capable of dealing with experiences of discrimination and more than capable of holding her own in difficult situations.

4.3 Returning to Hong Kong

During her final year of study, Ally returned home once more for a four-week Christmas holiday. Previously she had stayed with her relatives in London during holidays, but now she was worried that she might be imposing. So, even though she had to prepare for a major examination, she decided to come home. And in the summer of 2006, Ally came back to Hong Kong for good and enrolled as a full-time student on a one-year postgraduate Law programme. When I met Ally again in January 2007, she was looking for a job. Although she had found that some Hong Kong law firms would not even grant her an interview, she felt that her overseas experience and fluency in English would give her a competitive edge with international firms.

During our last interview, I asked Ally to look back on her experience of studying overseas and how it had changed her. Ally said that her sense of who she was had changed a great deal. As a secondary school student in Hong Kong, she had never thought about her ethnic or cultural background. She was just a secondary school student living in Hong Kong:

> In UK, my cultural background suddenly became important. I do not want to be labelled as just a Hongkonger, or Chinese. One thing I do not like about many gweis is that they cannot tell the differences among various Asian cultures. Korean, Japanese, Chinese, Malaysian ... etc, these are all from their so-called 'Asian backgrounds' ... They just group everyone into Orientals. It is like mixing up Londoners with British, or Scots with Brits. It is ignorance.

Her interaction with people from different cultural backgrounds had also led her to believe that *a person has to be sensitive to cultural differences to be mature*. She said that she was young when she first travelled overseas on study trips, and had only begun to *start questioning my cultural and ethnic identity*. But her experiences as a young girl had paved the way for a future affirmative attitude towards her cultural and ethnic background:

> Living in Britain for three years was not a short period of time. When others asked why I wasn't actively making friends with British people, I just laughed. I didn't consider there was a need, as suggested, like improving my English proficiency. If my English was not good enough, I wouldn't be able to participate in tutorials and expressing myself in English. I don't think of mixing with people from cultural backgrounds similar to mine to be a problem. It is natural that people sharing similar cultural backgrounds would make closer friends. I only found a problem with discrimination based on cultural differences. I am proud of myself for voicing my stance when the situation required it. It might not be pleasant, but at least I made myself clear.

Summing up our own observations, Ally had clearly come to understand that her initial expectations of overseas study had been rather naïve. Although she had not become the *native speaker* of English, she wanted to be on the eve of her departure, she had gained a relatively secure sense of herself as a Hong Kong person capable of using English for the purposes that she needed it.

5 Conclusion: frequent flying

Although we intend Ally's story to stand for itself as the outcome of our research, we also want to draw out two key dimensions of the story, which we feel make it a story about language learning and identity. First, we have observed that the published literature, which is largely written from the perspective of the host institutions and communities, tends to treat the overseas student as a person who is liable to experience difficulties of linguistic and cultural adaptation. While we do not want to deny that overseas students often do experience such difficulties, our point is that from the 'host' perspective, linguistic and cultural difficulties become a defining feature of the overseas student's identity. What Ally's story highlights, however, is the extent to which, from the student's perspective, the difficulties may lie more within the attitudes and practices of their hosts. Ally had been overseas on several occasions before, but these had been rather sheltered experiences. Thus, while she anticipated difficulties in adapting to student life in the United Kingdom, she was ill-prepared for experiences of discrimination and racism. Although she started out with self-confidence and a desire to integrate – in fact, to become a 'native speaker' of English – she was surprised by the degree to which her hosts resisted this desire by positioning her as an EFL speaker and treating her as *invisible* unless problems arose. It was this, above all, that made Ally's experience of overseas study a disappointing one. Her perceptions of the ways in which others saw her also destabilised Ally's sense of self-identity, leading her to position herself temporarily on the Chinese side of a Chinese-*gwai* divide that she had previously been unaware of. Here we see evidence of Bauman's (2004, pp. 11–12) notion of identity as a 'task to be performed' in situations where previous identities are challenged by the experience of border-crossing.

Our second point is that Ally's story also highlights how, by focusing on adaptation to the host community, the literature may fundamentally misunderstand how issues of identity impact upon overseas students. Returning, to Kanno's (2000, p. 3) idea of bilinguals inhabiting 'multiple language communities' in which L1 and L2 worlds exist 'side-by-side', we want to suggest that Ally's story of 'overseas study' was very much rooted in Hong Kong and the experience of 'frequent flying' between Hong Kong and the United Kingdom. We also note how this experience ultimately had its greatest impact on her identity as a Hong Kong Chinese person. Being a person who has 'studied overseas' is a recognised social identity in Hong Kong – an identity that involves assumptions about knowledge of English and intercultural competence of the kind that Ally discussed in the third interview. Far from being 'strangers in a strange land', in other words, Hong Kong students overseas do not exactly 'leave' Hong Kong at all. And in order to understand their experiences overseas, it seems important that we understand how the meanings of overseas study are framed within expectations, experiences and possibilities that are specific to Hong Kong.

Having noted that 'paradigmatic' approaches to narrative data is more frequently used in second language research than the 'narrative' approach we have adopted, our final point concerns the rationale for this approach. When narrative data are analysed paradigmatically, the significance of the narrative character of the original data can easily be lost. In this study, however, it seemed important to tease out the narrative threads within the interview data, because we were concerned with the ways in which the experience of overseas study developed over time and across contexts. We are, in other words, concerned with the narrative structure of overseas study, as it is revealed through the narratives of those who experience it. An important assumption that we are making here, however, is that Ally's story, although unique, has much in common with those of other Hong Kong students who travel overseas for higher education and, perhaps, with those of overseas students from elsewhere in the world. In order to test this assumption, we would clearly need to look at more stories of overseas study and examine them from comparative perspectives. But in order for stories to be compared, they must first be told. Our rather limited objective in this study, therefore, has been to bring one such story to light in the hope that others will follow.

Part V
Multimodal Narratives

12
Using Photographs to Access Stories of Learning English
Tarja Nikula and Anne Pitkänen-Huhta

1 Introduction

This chapter focuses on Finnish teenagers' accounts of learning English as revealed *by photographs* representing the role of English in their out-of-school lives, and *in discussions* based on those photographs. The study reported here is a part of a larger project on English in Finnish teenagers' everyday practices (Nikula and Pitkänen-Huhta 2005).[1] In general terms, our project draws on discursive views of language and literacy and makes use of methods inspired by ethnographic approaches. The project is based on the general assumption that language and literacy are inherently social and that people draw on socially, culturally and historically bound practices in constructing their identities as users of language and literacy.

Our main objective in the project is to investigate teenagers' perceptions of the role of English in their lives, but as issues of learning emerge in both the photographs and discussions, they deserve to become a focus of analytic scrutiny. It is hardly surprising that language user and learner identity get intertwined in our participants' stories, as they all live in the EFL context of Finland and study English at school. In this chapter, we focus on narratives – triggered by photographs – of informal language learning outside school contexts and the contacts between school and everyday learning.

We use the term *informal learning* fairly loosely to refer to contacts with the language in everyday settings that arise from the needs and interests of the language users. Informal learning has usually been juxtaposed to formal learning so that any learning not taking place in institutional settings is considered informal (Tusting 2003). Even though the term is often associated with adults as, for example, they acquire languages through participation in workplace activities (e.g., Eraut 2000), young people's language learning is not confined to institutionalised environments, either. Especially if one adopts a social view of language learning, which puts emphasis on participation and socialisation (e.g., Pavlenko and Lantolf 2000; Block 2003; Lantolf and Thorne 2006), it can be argued that language learning is an all-pervasive phenomenon that also connects to people's everyday activities and interests. Because it is so pervasive, it may not easily be recognised as learning by the people involved and therefore access to experiences of informal learning is often best achieved indirectly. Using photographs to trigger personal narratives is a valuable way of gaining insights into learners' subjective experiences with languages, and of revealing aspects of informal learning.

In the following we will first outline the view of narrative adopted in this chapter and briefly describe the methods of analysis. In the sections on the findings we will describe first the narratives revealed by the photographs and then those revealed by the discussions on the photographs. In the final section, some concluding remarks as well as implications for education will be presented.

2 Narratives in identity construction: a discursive approach

Thornborrow and Coates (2005, p. 2) point out that stories have a central role in our lives, which is why narratives have been studied extensively, and their formal properties, such as content, function, and organisation have received considerable attention. Important for our study is the widely acknowledged assumption that narratives are significant in the social construction of identities (e.g., De Fina 2003) as well as in the construction of one's identity as a language user and learner (e.g., Norton 2000). As Meinhof and Galasiński (2000, p. 325) argue, identities are discursively constructed through narratives and analysing these makes it possible to track the processes of identity construction in action.

The narratives we study emerge from the context of photographs and discussions about them. Apart from the teenagers offering their personal accounts of the pictures, the discussions also often involved them answering questions raised by the researchers. Applying the concept of narrative to such data would be difficult if we relied on formal criteria only, for example that narratives have a clear beginning, a middle and an end, or that narratives contain a sequence of narrative clauses, usually in the past tense (Thornborrow and Coates 2005, p. 3). However, rather than focusing on the formal linguistic properties of narratives, we follow Galasiński and Galasińska (2005) in adopting a broad discursive definition of a 'narrative contract' (Barthes 1974 as quoted by Galasiński and Galasińska 2005) between the narrator and the 'narratee' (Galasiński and Galasińska 2005, p. 102). That is, there was a narrative contract between us, the researchers, and the participants so that they were expected to tell stories about the photographs and we were expected to listen to them. Rather than extensive stories of participants' language learning histories (cf. Murphey et al. 2005 and Murphey and Carpenter, this volume), the photographs triggered more specific mini-narratives – often collaboratively constructed by the participants (see Coates 2005, pp. 90–2) – relating both to the situations and contexts represented in the photographs and to the values and attitudes attached to them.

Photographs have been used in language studies to document social realities, such as literacy practices (Hamilton 2000) and linguistic landscapes (Gorter 2006). They have also been used to access discursive constructions of identities (Meinhof and Galasiński 2000; Galasiński and Galasińska 2005; Pietikäinen 2006). Hodge and Jones (2000, p. 317) engaged participants in taking photographs to enhance collaboration in research. As regards research on language learning, visual methods have hitherto been used only rarely (but see Kalaja et al., this volume; Menezes, this volume; Pitkänen-Huhta and Nikula 2006). In the social sciences, photographs have been more widely used, especially in sociology (see Prosser 1998). What characterises sociological studies is the use of researcher-generated photographs as an interview device to trigger memories and stories, which Prosser and Schwartz (1998, p. 123) call 'photo-elicitation'. Our research design is different in that the participants took the photographs themselves (see also Radley and Taylor 2003; Radley et al. 2005). This was done to engage them personally in the process of making sense of the role of English in their lives and to provide them with alternative semiotic means to express their thoughts and feelings.

3 Describing the method

As pointed out above, the aim of the larger project of which the photographs and discussions form a part is to gain an understanding of how Finnish teenagers perceive the presence of English in their everyday lives. In addressing this issue, a teacher we knew put us in touch with seven students, Alisa, Eve, Lisa and Vera,[2] aged 14–15 (in grade 8) and Dave, Erik and Sam, aged 15–16 (in grade 9). The students were known to be friends outside school, but as the boys and girls did not know each other, we had regular meetings with the two groups separately; the regular contact lasted for over a year (February 2005–May 2006).

Taking photographs was one of the ethnographic methods used in the very early stages of the project (Pitkänen-Huhta and Nikula 2006). In our first meeting with the boys and girls, we asked about their willingness to take photographs related to English. The more precise instruction was to take any number of photographs of situations, places and activities in their everyday surroundings where English in their view has some significance. In the following group discussion we talked about issues raised by the photographs. Each boy and girl took a set of about ten photographs. We first conducted an initial thematic analysis of the photographs by grouping them into broad categories on the basis of their content. This analysis was further deepened in the group discussions about the photographs. The hour-long discussions were transcribed to capture both what the participants said about English in their lives and the ways in which they chose to express their views. That is, from a discursive point of view, it is also important to pay attention to linguistic features such as word choices and grammatical constructions in the participants' contributions.

The photographs can reveal two levels of narratives. Firstly, there are the stories told by the photographs in their own right, 'without recourse to words' (Harrison 2002, p. 106). Photographs may reveal both the photographers' individual perceptions and stories and, to the extent that similar themes and objects emerge in photographs taken by many individuals, some general meanings prevalent in the 'macro-stories' in society towards the phenomenon in question. One aspect of our analysis hence consists of analysing the photographs taken by the teenagers in their own right, as indexing (see Blommaert 2005) their personal understandings but potentially also more generally accepted views about learning English, relating to the 'official voices' of education.

The second level of analysis focuses on what the teenagers said about their photographs in the discussions. We thereby wanted to gain a deeper understanding of how they perceive the role of English in their lives. Such meanings lie not only in the pictures but also in the way the participants make sense, reflect on and interpret the pictures while talking about them (see Radley et al. 2005, p. 278). As Harrison (2002, p. 105) notes, 'photographs provide basis for narrative work; there are stories about photographs, and there are stories that lie behind them and between them'.

4 Analysis

In the following section, we will first describe the more general stories revealed by the photographs (Section 4.1) and then move on to the more personal level of learner identities, which were unravelled in the group discussions (Section 4.2).

4.1 Narratives of learning in photographs

Generally, all sets of photographs taken by the participants told a fairly similar story of the presence of English in their lives. In particular, the sets contained photographs relating to their daily encounters with English through the entertainment industry, tourism, and hobbies. In terms of their content, the photographs could be divided into five categories (see Pitkänen-Huhta and Nikula 2006). Firstly, there were photographs relating to the role of English in tourism and travelling. A much larger category was formed by photographs representing the modern entertainment industry, such as TV, music and films. Thirdly, the print media, such as magazines and books, were also present in the photographs, but not as often as pictures related to entertainment industry or to computers, which was the fourth category we identified. The final category included photographs representing hobbies, such as skate- and snowboarding, football, and ice-hockey, and these were common especially in the photographs taken by the boys. Thus, the photographs in these five categories depict encounters with and uses of English rather than learning English.

Nevertheless, learning emerged in the photographs as well. Notably, the visual narrative brought up phenomena related to formal learning in particular. Among the pictures categorised as the print media, there were some photographs of school textbooks and of dictionaries as shown in Figure 12.1.

Thus, the participants readily connected English to school textbooks and dictionaries, that is, to the tools of learning in formal education. That an aspect of their identities is connected to school practices is hardly surprising given their background as students. However, the presence of these photographs can also be interpreted as educational discourses in the larger society intermingling with the teenagers' own discourses of language use, that is, images of textbooks and dictionaries can be seen as indexing the importance granted to the formal learning of English in Finnish society. Their photographs seemed to index socially prevalent facts and values and to 'represent and reinforce the values and beliefs of our social environment', as Meinhof and Galasiński

Figure 12.1 Photographs of school textbooks and a dictionary 'English-Finnish dictionary'

(2000, p. 326) put it. Thus these representations indicate that when young people are constructing meanings for English in their lives and in Finnish society at large, they are nearly unanimous in relating English to education and formal language learning.

4.2 Narratives of learning in discussions about photographs

From the viewpoint of narrative inquiry, using photographs as material for discussions proved useful because when the participants explained the reasons for taking the photographs and elaborated on issues raised by them they also explicitly and implicitly constructed identities as learners of English. In this way we were also able to gain a deeper understanding of issues that would have remained uncovered had we used photographs only.

Three different types of stories of language learning emerge from the discussions. Firstly, the teenagers made explicit comparisons between formal and informal learning and also commented on intentional learning in their everyday lives. However, they also constructed stories of incidental learning and, moreover, their stories touched upon issues related to expertise they gained through their everyday practices of using English. In the following we will discuss each of these in turn with the help of data extracts.

4.2.1 Contrasting formal and informal learning

In their accounts the participants made explicit comparisons between school learning and everyday learning or, more specifically, everyday uses of English. They seemed to associate learning within the educational institution with grammatical correctness and accuracy, whereas informal learning in everyday activities was more about making oneself understood. In extract 1,[3] in her response to the researcher's question about her two pictures of books, Vera explicitly states that the ways books are read in and out of school differ considerably:

(1)
Anne so two kinds of books, you had Harry Potter and English textbooks
Vera [yeah hh]
Anne [are they] somehow different in your opinion
Vera well they **are** 'cos you read them in a completely different way.

The researcher first notes that there are pictures of two different kinds of books: school textbooks and a novel (Harry Potter) and asks Vera whether these books are somehow different, thus inviting her to make a comparison. Despite the fact that this topic was raised by the researcher, it is significant that Vera answers with an emphasis that they *are* different, and continues to further elaborate on the difference by saying that one reads them *in a completely different way*, that is, practices related to the books are considered very different in the formal educational environment and in everyday activities. Also in Extract 2, the boys' talk about a photograph of school textbooks (see Figure 12.1) indicates that they see differences between learning inside and outside school:

(2)
Tarja school English, can that be described somehow or is it similar to what you (use) in skateboarding and basketball
Erik   well no it ain't
Sam   well it's a bit like we practise formal written language here
Erik   yeah and when we talk with our friends we don't much care about grammar or word order or anything
Dave   yeah
Sam   yeah
Erik   we just say it more or less (correctly) 'cos we understand it anyway, I mean here it's more like getting rid of errors and like.

In answering the researcher's question on how they see the relationship between school English and the English used in hobbies, the three boys collaboratively construct a narrative, suggesting that learning in the everyday is about understanding and getting one's message across, whereas learning at school is about accurate and normative use of English. It is also significant how the boys build contrasts between language modalities when they comment on formal learning focusing on the conventions of written language (*we practise formal written language here*) and informal learning happening in and through spoken language (*we talk with our friends*).

Similarly in the girls' discussions, photographs trigger stories with explicit commentary on the differences between formal and informal learning. This is exemplified in extract 3 below, where a photograph of a computer has triggered talk about free time activities:

(3)
Eve well like sometimes you speak English in your free time and get used to talking and then pronuncation gets better, and then of course – well you don't perhaps concretely learn it so much, not things like grammar anyway, you know its more common that we use school stuff outside school
Anne yeah
Alisa but one does – like for example separate words in songs and such, if you don't know a word then you check it in a dictionary
Anne okay
Alisa then those'll stick in your mind.

Eve first explains how using English in the everyday gets one used to speaking and improves one's pronunciation. She also points out that grammar is not something *concretely* learnt in the everyday use of English, implying that this is something happening at school. Alisa, for her part, comments on how she learns vocabulary by listening to music and by checking words in the dictionary. The girls thus explicitly talk about learning in their everyday lives and use concepts from the world of language teaching when talking about pronunciation, grammar and vocabulary. This is in interesting contrast to the boys, who more often describe their use as *ending up speaking English* than framing themselves with concepts arising from educational discourse.

Even when not making explicit comparisons, the voices of education and language teaching could be heard. This was the case in particular when the teenagers told mini-stories relating to intentional language learning in the everyday. These stories often suggested that the participants find certain school-related practices useful also in their out-of-school activities. For example, they give accounts of using dictionaries when they read novels or want to understand lyrics. Both the boys and the girls talk about using dictionaries to check unknown words as illustrated by extract 4, in which Alisa explains the meaning of the picture of a dictionary:

(4)
Alisa   well I took a photo of some books like that, I didn't remember our English text books right then so that's why I took – I mean if you look at song lyrics for instance so you quite often look them up in a dictionary
Anne   right
Alisa   like what the word is.

She says that she uses the dictionary to check unknown words in lyrics. The practice of checking words in a dictionary has most likely been learned at school and is thus connected to discourses of formal learning. At the same time, it is, however, a practice one needs in order to cope with ordinary everyday activities. This implies that the boundaries between different domains and practices – and thus also between formal and informal learning – are not necessarily very clear-cut. Practices learned in formal educational environments can be taken into use in everyday activities when the situation and the needs of the language users so demand.

Another practice most likely adopted at school relates to processes of text comprehension. Extract 5 is a piece of talk around a photograph depicting a Harry Potter novel:

(5)
Tarja   how do you feel it goes, I mean reading in English, do you often need help from a dictionary or
Vera   well as a matter of fact I didn't use a dictionary at all when I read the fifth one like I read it – I mean you do understand when you just read without stopping, you do understand, and there are some words that you don't understand
Anne   [mm]
Vera   [but] you understand it well as a whole and it doesn't – you get all mixed up and don't get on with it if you stop at every word that's a bit
Anne   right
Vera   that you don't know, but I did understand it somehow quite well, part of the things remained a bit unclear but then I did understand the main plot as a whole.

Here Vera describes the activity of reading for pleasure, justifying why she does not use a dictionary by emphasising the importance of understanding the main points and keeping on reading even when there are unknown words in the text. It is notable here that it is the researcher who brings in aspects of formal learning when asking about the use of a dictionary. Thus this story is, in fact, researcher-initiated, but it is Vera who offers an elaboration. When describing how she did not, in fact, resort to a dictionary when reading the novel, Vera seems to echo the voices of formal language education promoted in the curricula, foreign language textbooks, and in classroom practices. She thus seems to occupy a position between a language learner and a language user when drawing on discourses of education while talking about her everyday practices.

4.2.2 Narratives of incidental learning

The photographs also triggered stories relating to unintentional and incidental learning of English in the teenagers' everyday lives. What is significant in these accounts is that learning English is often presented as being effortless and happening almost automatically. This was particularly evident in the way the boys talked about their relation to English when engaged in their hobbies such as skateboarding and snowboarding (see Figure 12.2).

In the following extract, Dave is talking about a picture of skateboarding:

(7)
Tarja why did you end up taking a photo of this
Dave well all the tricks there are in English [and]
Sam [mm]
Dave and also otherwise you just end up using English like, cos they don't have any equivalents in Finnish.

In this mini-story (and in other similar ones), the boys talk about their relation to English in terms of automatic, necessary and purposeful use. They just *end up speaking English*, because the vocabulary they need in practising sports simply does not exist in Finnish and therefore it is more practical to adopt English terminology. This discourse of learning being incidental and arising from practical needs is related only to everyday uses and thus the boys are not perhaps willing to attach these qualities to school learning, as they see it.

Figure 12.2 Photographs of skateboarding and snowboarding

The boys also make more explicit comments on incidental learning in their everyday lives. In extract (8), the boys are talking about learning jokes from TV:

(8)
Tarja how much you sort of pick up English from movies or films and such like
Erik they come like that [a lot]
Dave [quite a lot]
Erik like if there's a really good joke in a film it rarely can even be translated into Finnish, such a good joke in English cannot be translated into Finnish but
Sam [yeah]
Erik [then] it often happens that you end up mulling them over and using them cos they stick in your head.

Again, the boys do not talk about learning in terms of intentionally trying to understand something. Instead, they learn English expressions incidentally, simply because one cannot translate them into Finnish and *they just stick in your head*. In this respect, the boys' accounts were somewhat different from the girls', which were more explicitly connected to intentional learning (and discourses of formal education). Because of the small number of participants, no general conclusions about gender differences can be drawn, but this emerging difference between the boys and the girls is certainly an aspect deserving more careful examination in the future.

4.2.3 Gaining expertise through informal learning

The third type of narrative identified in the discussions is related to gaining expertise through learning English. This kind of expertise seems to be accessed through out-of-school practices only and it is connected to knowledge of the special terminology of hobbies such as skateboarding and snowboarding. This is particularly common in the boys' stories, as in extract (9), a discussion around a picture of skateboarding, in which the boys collaboratively construct a narrative of terminology that justifies the use of English:

(9)
Tarja why did you end up taking a photo of this
Dave   well all the tricks there are in English [and]
Sam   [mm]
Dave   and also otherwise you just end up using English like, cos they don't have any equivalents in Finnish
Anne   right
Dave   take for instance skateboarding rullalautailu but that sounds so stupid
Erik   [mm hmp]
Dave   [cos skate]boarding
(1.3)
Anne   why do you think it is that rullalautailu sounds stupid
Erik   has originally been invented in English=
Sam   =yeah.

When the researcher asks Dave to explain a photograph of skateboarding, Dave says that all the tricks are in English and they *just end up using English* when dealing with skateboarding. The boys also talk about the sport being *originally invented in English* (as if the sport did not exist 'in Finnish'!) and using the right terminology in English is necessary, since comparable words simply do not exist in Finnish. Moreover, they evaluate the languages by claiming that the Finnish terms sound stupid, and say that therefore it is better to stick to the original English words. Through this very natural relation to English as an inherent part of their hobbies, they adopt an expert identity, both in relation to sports as well as to the language used (and learnt) in the practices related to the sports.

The participants also appear to adopt the role of an expert insofar as they feel they are able to criticise bad translations and clumsy subtitles that appear on TV and in DVDs. Both the girls and the boys construct such mini-narratives when elaborating on photographs representing various forms of the entertainment industry. In extract (10), Vera and Eve bring up bad translations in subtitles:

(10)
Vera or then, well otherwise I even don't put on subtitling you know
Anne yeah
Vera cos those subtitles are sometimes so badly, or especially on DVDs they're really badly translated
Eve you're right, the Finnish translations are really weird sometimes.

These expert identities are clearly related to English that they encounter in their everyday activities, especially in various forms of entertainment, but the expertise might also derive from the combination of school and everyday learning. In fact, the participants also extend their expert identities to the school context, when they evaluate their teachers, and the teacher trainees in particular, as in extract (11):

(11)
Sam like when the English teacher in the optional course gave us a word test so that s/he said a word and then we had to write it down in Finnish and in English, and then s/he blurted out 'kossis' [an imitation of the teacher's mispronunciation] and we were like what are we supposed to write when it was like, like caution was the correct answer
Dave and also some teacher trainees they pronounce – say things quite in their own way and
Sam yeah
Erik and when they're a bit nervous then what comes out is something, sounds odd.

Here the boys talk about a test they had in their English lesson, in which the teacher said words in English and the students had to write them down both in English and Finnish. According to the boys, they had difficulty in identifying the words because of the teacher's poor pronunciation and give as an example the word *caution*, which the teacher, according to the boys, pronounced as *kossis*. Similarly they comment on the teacher trainees' idiosyncratic and odd ways of pronouncing words *quite in their own way*.

The teenagers' expert identities in certain areas of language learning seem to be related to issues of empowerment. As learners they feel empowered by the skills that they have learnt either at school or in their everyday activities to such an extent that their position gives them authority to evaluate and criticise the language use of others, who should, in fact, be in a more powerful position as language experts through their institutional roles as teachers or as professional translators.

5 Discussion

Photographs combined with discussions about them proved to be a powerful tool in gaining access to narratives of language learning as a personal and experiential practice. The photographs themselves could be seen as narratives: the sets of photographs were very similar to each other in telling a story of formal learning, thus indexing more prevalent educational discourses in Finnish society. In the discussions, however, these similar visual narratives gave rise to very different kinds of stories, which penetrated into more personal and individual issues of learning.

The narratives triggered by the photographs seem to vary from those dwelling on and indexing the prevalent discourses of formal learning to others creating discourses of informal learning, which emerge from the participants' own activities and practices. On the one hand, the participants made an explicit division between formal and informal learning, connecting the former to written language, grammar and norms and the latter to making oneself understood. On the other hand, in connection with their everyday practices, they also positioned themselves as experts of particular areas of language use, thus suggesting that informal learning can be an empowering experience. Importantly, however, even if they did acknowledge that learning can take place in everyday activities, they seemed to put such learning in a subsidiary role, hence implying that language learning proper only takes place within the school walls. However, the data also showed that the discourses of formal and informal learning intermingle in their narratives, creating mixed identities that fluctuate between school practices and those arising from their own ways of making use of English. Narrative analysis thus provides evidence of teenagers occupying varying positions among discourses of formal and informal learning, suggesting that the conceptualisation of learning is based on personal experience and participation in discursive practices both in and outside the school.

To conclude, even though our participants' narratives portrayed their everyday practices as personally meaningful sites for informal learning, it became evident that they did not value their practices as learning. It would thus seem important for formal language teaching to find ways to acknowledge informal learning, and to prevent value judgements which only deem school learning to be important and serious learning. This may not be an easy task but it is well worth bearing in mind, as young people of today are constantly engaged in a variety of practices which involve English and which thus provide rich learning opportunities, often different from those offered by the school.

Notes

1. A study conducted within the Centre of Excellence for the Study of Variation, Contacts and Change in English (VARIENG), a joint research unit of the universities of Helsinki and Jyväskylä, Finland (www.jyu.fi/varieng).
2. All names have been changed.
3. In the transcripts the names Anne and Tarja refer to the authors. The discussions were originally conducted in Finnish, but to save space, only the English translations are provided in the extracts.

13
Self-Portraits of EFL Learners: Finnish Students Draw and Tell

Paula Kalaja, Riikka Alanen and Hannele Dufva

1 Introduction

Life stories[1] have become increasingly popular in research on second language learning in contexts of English as a second language (ESL) (see e.g., Pavlenko and Lantolf 2000; Norton 2000, 2001; Pavlenko 2004; Benson and Nunan 2005) and more recently in contexts of English as a foreign language (EFL). However, it is acknowledged that these contexts are very diverse historically, economically, socially and culturally. Our study was conducted in one of these contexts, that is, Finland.

So far, research on life stories written by practising EFL teachers in Finland has addressed such issues as the choice of languages to be studied at school and in a university MA programme (Kalaja et al. 1998), and teachers' career paths (Kalaja and Dufva 1997) be these a result of a call from childhood or just a drift. The life stories were an outcome of a national writing contest, with some one hundred submissions. Studies on life stories written by EFL learners have, on the other hand, focused on metaphorical conceptualisations of teachers and learners (Turunen 2003; Turunen and Kalaja 2004), or attributions or discursive explanations provided for success or failure in EFL learning with credit or blame assigned to learner internal or external factors (Heikkinen 1999; Heikkinen and Kalaja 2001; Isomöttönen 2003; Kalaja 2004). In a study by Leppänen and Kalaja (1997, 2002), EFL learners were viewed in terms of heroes, comparable to those found in folktales. As a rule, the data used in these studies have been collected as an assignment in courses that our students have taken with us.

As part of a longitudinal research project, the present study is an attempt within a sociocultural approach to examine the experiences of

EFL learners in a specific context of learning the language, that is, in Finland, where the uses and users of English in various domains have been on the increase in the past few decades. They were asked to account for their experiences in the form of a visual narrative, or more specifically, a self-portrait, and provide their own interpretation of what they had depicted. This allows us, too, to discuss the role of different modalities – verbal and visual – in collecting and analysing data.

We start off by spelling out the theoretical assumptions of the study (Section 2) and placing it in the context of Finland and the learning of foreign languages there (Section 3.1). After this, we report on the study, its aims, data collection and processing and findings (Sections 3.2 and 3.3), and conclude the chapter by discussing its theoretical and methodological implications (Section 4).

2 Background to the study

2.1 Starting point 1: visual accounts

Drawings – or other visual accounts such as photographs (see Nikula and Pitkänen-Huhta, this volume) – have rarely been used as a research tool in the study of language learning or teaching. However, human figure drawings do have a long history, going back to a book of children's drawings published in 1887 by Corrado Ricci, an art critic, who introduced drawings as a means of psychodiagnostics. Since then, drawings have been made use of, for example, in (developmental and clinical) psychology, art therapy and education (see e.g., Harris 2005) where they have been used to examine the skills, abilities or emotions of an individual in various ways. Human figure drawings have also been used as a measure of the developmental stage (e.g., Draw-a-Man Test or Draw-a-Person Test; see e.g., Harris 1963) or intelligence of an individual (as part of Stanford-Binet Test). World-wide studies suggest that that there are considerable cultural constraints in the way human figures are drawn (see e.g., Cox et al. 2001; La Voy et al. 2001; Jolley et al. 2004; Burkitt et al. 2005; Cherney et al. 2006).

With the recent interest in the multimodality of texts (see e.g., Kress and van Leeuwen 1996; Ventola et al. 2004), analysis of various types of visual representations has gained in importance in language studies, too. Based on hallidayan thinking and tools of the systemic-functional grammar, Kress and van Leeuwen (1996) have developed ways of analysing images and drawings. Although we will not be employing their tools in our analysis, we acknowledge the importance of different meaning potentials present in the two modalities – verbal and visual. As Kress et al. (2001, p. 15) put it: 'Each meaning making system – mode – provides different communicative potentials. In other words, each mode is culturally shaped around the constraints and affordances of its medium – its materiality'. This suggests that there may indeed be differences between learners' verbal and visual narratives. Visual representations have also been used to explore how children construct literacy (Kendrick and McKay 2004) or how drawings function as parts of texts they have produced (see e.g., Ivanič 2004 and *Lancaster Corpus of Children's Project Writing* http://bowland-files.lancs.ac.uk./lever/index.htm).

Finally, there are a handful of studies that directly or indirectly involve language learning or teaching. Iddings et al. (2005) analysed the multimodal representation of self by two ESL learners in a multilingual classroom. Andersson (1995) and Aronsson and Andersson (1996) explored drawings of classroom life by children. In her study, Nikula (2000) asked first-year university students of EFL to draw their conceptualisations of grammar: the idea was to trace any developments in these over a school term. In an exploratory study, Swales (1994) looked at metaphors of learning in cartoons drawn by half a dozen ESL/EFL learners.[2]

In our analysis of drawings, we are informed by the sociocultural idea of mediational means and drawing as mediated activity, which at the same time point to the social and cultural constraints present in the task (see e.g., Brooks 2005). When analysing the self-portraits we will be considering two points: firstly, what mediational means *appear* in the drawings and what this may say about the way the learners view themselves as learners (or to put it another way, what this may reveal about their beliefs about foreign language learning), and methodologically, what kind of mediational means *drawings* seem to be in *themselves* (for more specific research questions, see Section 3.2).

2.2 Starting point 2: a sociocultural approach

We rely primarily on a sociocultural approach to study the second language learning process. Central to this approach is the idea that human behaviour, second language learning and development included (Lantolf 2000; Lantolf and Thorne 2006), can be regarded as mediated activity. The ideas of Lev Vygotsky (1978, 1987) and A.N. Leontiev (1978, 1981) form the foundations of this approach, which since the 1970s has been taken in various directions by such notable researchers and thinkers as Michael Cole, Yrjö Engeström, Alex Kozulin, Gordon Wells and James Wertsch.

Most human activity is culturally mediated. The social and cognitive activity in which human beings participate is mediated by a number of semiotic and material tools. Language is of course one of the most powerful tools used in thinking and interacting with other people. But there are other kinds of artifacts, or *mediational means*, available to human beings. Other people, or social mediators as Kozulin (1998) calls them, are the most significant of these. Of course, language as dialogue plays a role, too, since it is through this type of semiotic activity that people most often interact with others. However, there are other kinds of mediational means that can be used in learning, thinking and problem solving: symbols, drawings and metaphors, to name just a few, are also used by people to help them organise their activity and carry out their actions.

In research on second language learning, a growing number of studies have focused on what kind of mediating artifacts second language learners use in the learning process and how they use them. Some of these studies have been concerned with the way other people use speech to scaffold second language learning in the zone of proximal development (e.g., Aljafreeh and Lantolf 1994; Antón 1999; Antón and DiCamilla 1999; Ohta 2000). Others have focused on how the nature and type of the task mediates the learning or research activity or its outcome (e.g., Coughlan and Duff 1994; Roebuck 2000; Platt and Brooks 2002). Most, if not all, of these studies have used recordings of activities in progress (e.g., transcriptions of audio- or video-recordings of activities in the classroom) to identify the various types of mediational means that might be available to the learner.

In this study, we will be making use of drawings to investigate the second language learning process and to identify the mediational means that students consider important in relation to themselves as language learners. On one level, for us as researchers drawing is a tool we use in the research process. On another level, drawing as an activity gives the participants an opportunity to make visible the objects, events or persons they consider important in the learning process. We regard these drawings as a type of *visual narrative* 'told' by the participants in the learning activity. The representations of these objects, events and persons in the drawings made by the students can be interpreted as mediational means they have used or are still using in learning English.

Having spelled out the starting points of our joint venture, it is time to move on to the study, its context, aims, design, and findings.

3 The present study: visual accounts of experiences of learning EFL

3.1 The context of the study: From novice to language expert

In Finland, most children start studying their first second/foreign language in Grade 3, at the age of nine. In 2005, almost nine out of ten children opted for English, studying Swedish – a second official language in Finland – and other additional languages later during their school career. While in the past, knowledge of English used to be a privilege of the well-educated few, nowadays some knowledge of English is practically expected of all Finns.[3] In fact, most Finns can now be characterised as bilingual or multilingual in the sense that basic education involves taking courses in a number of foreign languages. Consequently, the need for EFL teachers is high.

The present study is part of a longitudinal research project *From Novice to Expert*, based in the Department of Languages and the Centre for Applied Languages Studies of the University of Jyväskylä, Finland and launched in 2005. The aim of the project is to trace the development of beliefs about language and language learning and teaching held by two groups of students: *teacher trainees* (those students who have opted for a teacher training programme when entering the university and graduate as qualified teachers of foreign languages) as opposed to *non-trainees* (those students who study to be other types of language professionals) over a period of five years before completing an MA degree programme. More specifically, the idea is to follow the growth in the students' pedagogical and linguistic expertise, their socialisation into academic ways of speaking about these issues, and possible changes in their identity: from an upper-secondary-school student to a university student, and from a learner of English to a language expert (for findings of a pilot study, see Dufva et al. 2007). After graduation the students – working as qualified EFL teachers – will be passing on their beliefs to future generations of foreign language learners in their daily teaching practices over a career of some 40 years. Therefore, as future gatekeepers, their beliefs are worth studying.

In the project, the two groups of students are being followed longitudinally and sets of data will be collected during their first, third and fifth year of study. We will be reporting findings from Stage 1, where, in addition to completing the drawing task, the students have filled in two questionnaires about their school experiences of EFL learning and attitudes towards English, compared with Finnish, their first language.

3.2 Research design

As is evident from Section 2, the present study – conducted within a sociocultural framework – is among the first ones to make use of visual narratives in accounting for experiences of EFL learning in a specific context, that is, Finland. More specifically, learners were asked to draw a self-portrait, depicting themselves not as users but as learners of English, and provide their interpretation on the reverse side of the task sheet. We felt we needed the latter to help us out in the process of interpretation even though we come from the same culture as the participants of this study.

The study seeks to answer two related questions: (1) What kind of *mediational means* can be found in the self-portraits that were drawn by the students (and what these possibly reveal about their beliefs about learning EFL)?, and (2) What kind of mediational means are mentioned by the students in their written interpretations? In addition, we will briefly discuss the issue of using drawings as a means of collecting data: Is there something in the drawings that cannot be made available by other means? Or vice versa, is there something that is easier to express verbally rather than by visual means?

To collect data, each student was provided with an A4 sheet of paper and a set of crayons. The sheet had frames, a title 'Self-portrait' (originally in Finnish) at the top and an explanation 'This is how I look as a learner of English' at the bottom. The students were asked to draw a picture of themselves as learners of English and give their interpretation of the piece of art in a couple of sentences on the reverse side. The task was carried out as part of a compulsory course on Learning to Learn Foreign Languages that the students take during their first year of studies in the BA/MA programme they are attending.

The data were collected partly in the autumn of 2005 (N = 81), and partly in the early spring of 2006 (N = 42). Of the self-portraits, a few had to be excluded from analysis either because they were metaphorical depictions of the learner (e.g., as a glass into which water is poured or as a quilt that had not yet been finished), or because we were not allowed to use the drawing for research purposes. In the end, a total of 110 self-portraits were subjected to analysis. In the analysis, attention was paid to the presence of any other human figures or objects (especially books or other media) in the pictures – in addition to the learner, the main character – or of comments thereon in the written interpretations. Importantly, these were interpreted as symbols for various types of mediational means in activities (see Section 2.2 above).

Two raters coded both sets of data (i.e., the drawings and interpretations) independently, and if there were any differences, these were negotiated until agreement was reached. The data were analysed both qualitatively and quantitatively.

3.3 Findings

The findings will be reported in two stages, first, concerning the drawings, and after that concerning the written interpretations, with comparisons made where feasible.

3.3.1 Drawings: other human beings

In Stage 1 of our analysis, we first noted whether the learner had depicted herself alone or together with others when learning English.[4] Compare Figure 13.1 with Figure 13.2.

In the sub-set of drawings with others present, there was variation in the way they had been depicted: they were placed either in the centre next to the learner or on the periphery, often separated from other objects or activities. They varied in size, too, from tiny figures (in comparison to the learner) to full-size interlocutors (as if of equal status or importance with the learner); and also in appearance, from stick figures to human-like figures, often comparable to the way the learner had depicted herself.

OMA KUVANI

Tältä näytän englannin kielen **oppijana**

Figure 13.1 An EFL learner without others (originally hair coloured brown)

We found only a third of the learners to depict themselves with others (see Table 13.1):

As is evident from Table 13.1, other people do not seem to have a very significant role in EFL learning.

3.3.2 Drawings: books

Next in our analysis we observed whether the student had drawn herself with or without books. Contrast Figure 13.3 with Figure 13.4.

In the sub-set of drawings with books, there was variation in the way they had been depicted: the book (or books) was placed in the centre, the learner holding it in her hand(s), or on the periphery, next to other

OMA KUVANI

Tältä näytän englannin kielen **oppijana**

Figure 13.2 An EFL learner with others (in black-and-white)

Table 13.1 EFL learning: mediational means in the self-portraits

	With		Without	
	N	%	N	%
Other people	34	31	76	69
Books	72	65	38	35
Other media	58	53	52	47

194 *Narratives of Learning and Teaching EFL*

OMA KUVANI

Tältä näytän englannin kielen oppijana

Figure 13.3 An EFL learner without books (originally in blue-and-white)

OMA KUVANI

Tältä näytän englannin kielen oppijana

Figure 13.4 An EFL learner with books (originally in bright colours)

objects or activities. They could appear with or without titles; they could be books needed in studying (e.g., dictionaries, grammars) or read for pleasure (e.g., Harry Potter); they could be open or closed.

It turned out that two thirds of the students had depicted themselves with books (Table 13.1). Interestingly, books would seem to have a more significant role in EFL learning than other people if we judge by the visual narratives alone: they indicate active learning through reading or consulting of books for reference purpose, or both.

3.3.3 Drawings: other media

Finally, we took note of if other media, including television, radio or computers, were present or not in the drawings (compare Figure 13.3 above with Figure 13.4).[5]

Half of the students depicted themselves with other media, and the other half without (see Table 13.1). This means that for some students media (other than books) play some role, whereas for others they do not. However, the inclusion of various media seems to suggest that the students are actively seeking opportunities to learn (or use) the language outside the classroom, too.

3.3.4 Interpretations of the drawings

In Stage 2 of our study, we looked at the interpretations on the reverse side of the task sheets. Sometimes these contained roughly the same amount of information as the drawings: in other words, other people, books and/or media were mentioned as mediational means involved in EFL learning. But sometimes the verbal accounts contained less – or more information about the mediational means.

For example, Figure 13.1 (see above) depicts learning EFL without others, books or other media. Likewise, its interpretation does not comment on any media, printed or other, although it does comment on the learner, providing additional information (translated into English):

(1)
I'm eager and happy but at the same time a little bit naive. So far I've managed well with my knowledge (of English), which has made me (perhaps even too) self-confident. (Therefore the big head). The small body is a reminder that one has to be humble in the face of the heavy workload (ahead).

Figure 13.3 (see above) depicts learning EFL without other people or books but with other media, or more specifically, with television. Its interpretation elaborates on both these aspects at some length:

(2)
I began studying English as a little boy watching Dallas with my big sister. The mountain peak looming through the window is my goal and I might reach it one day. The flourishing plant behind the television set is a symbol for my language expertise in its initial stage as a learner of the English language.[6]

Finally, the quantitative findings concerning the verbal interpretations are summarised in Table 13.2.

Both the drawings and their verbal interpretations suggest that EFL learning tends to be a lonely business and that books do play a major role in EFL learning. There was a significantly higher number of those who chose to draw themselves alone rather than with others, and also of those who drew themselves with at least one book. The analysis of the students' verbal interpretations gave similar results overall, with the exception that the students did not mention books in their interpretations as often as they depicted them in their drawings.

Besides commenting on EFL learning with or without other people, books or other types of media, the interpretations occasionally elaborated on some other aspect of EFL learning. For the most part, these were comments on positive feelings involved in learning (or using) the language, including motivation, and were in some ways comparable to the smiles and happy faces found in the self-portraits,[7] see for example Figures 13.1, 13.2 and 13.4.

4 Conclusion

To summarise, our analysis of the *drawings* indicates that as a rule EFL learners depict themselves alone. We also found that books are the

Table 13.2 EFL learning: mediational means in the verbal interpretations on the reverse side of the self-portraits

	With N	With %	Without N	Without %	No mention N	No mention %
Other people	31	28	71	65	8	7
Books	53	48	57	52		
Other media	50	45	60	55		

primary mediating artifact in the drawings. The analysis of the drawings thus seems to support the view that learners regard themselves as cartesian rationalist agents, that is, as individuals who rely on their own internal intellectual capacities when learning a new language, considering the role of others unimportant and relying on a literacy-based way of learning – receiving knowledge – from books. The book can also be claimed to epitomise the strong tradition of literacy and even the bias towards written language in linguistics (Linell 2005).

Analysing further what the learners actually *do* in the drawings, it seems that they depict themselves as *recipients*: reading, watching and possibly listening. It is not far-fetched to think that the emphasis on receptive skills reflects the idea of learning as a matter of transferring knowledge from an external source into the learner's mind, a receptive vessel. Thus strong, age-old conceptualisations of 'learning' and 'knowledge' as literacy-based, individual and receptive processes are echoed in the portraits of present-day students of our study.

But in addition, as a culturally mediated activity, drawing is also subject to a number of cultural conventions of art and visual representation. Quite a number of the students chose to follow the traditional way of representing the self in such art work: they drew themselves facing the viewer (full-face), often alone.

Is this the whole story then – the story of a lonely learner? One way to answer the question is to turn to the students' written interpretations analysed above, and also to other sets of verbal narratives. Interesting observations can be made. For instance, students often claimed in their verbal accounts that they had learned best by interacting in the target-language environment. Also, in their written interpretations it was possible for them to describe matters that did not easily lend themselves to visualisation, for example, describing their learning process longitudinally. If we compare the drawings with other pools of data we have collected over time (e.g., life stories, for a review, see Section 1), it seems that one very Significant Other is missing in the learners' portraits: the teacher! By contrast, in verbal narratives the teacher is frequently described as a crucial gatekeeper or guardian of EFL learning.

These noticeable differences between verbal and visual representations make it necessary to (re)consider data collection methods. First, although it may be evident, it needs to be said that the different meaning potential present in the visual modality and the particular tools of making a drawing have their consequences: for example, drawings may be more 'static' in their expression, possibly constrained by various factors such as the tradition of self-portraits in art. Besides, the constraints that were present in the research design and task (the wording, the time allowed to complete the task, etc.) also have their effect.

In conclusion, we argue that an individual's beliefs about or conceptualisations of EFL learning are typically situated and multi-voiced (see also e.g., Alanen 2003; Dufva 2003; Dufva and Alanen 2005; Iddings et al. 2005). One research method or modality (verbal narratives vs. visual ones) cannot possibly capture the multiplicity of meanings present in the views held by a learner. In a way, then, there may be no single set of 'authentic' beliefs, or a stance towards EFL learning, but rather a variety of views that emerge in a situated fashion, depending on the task at hand, the modality of presentation, and possibly, some other factors. Besides, beliefs may vary in strength: there may be powerful and even hegemonic views reflecting strong social and cultural ways of thinking, such as the conceptualisations of learning and teaching characteristic of the Western educational tradition on the whole. But there may also be other voices, more subtle, or even suppressed – individual and unique perspectives on what it means to learn foreign languages.

Notes

1. Life stories, also referred to as (self-)narratives or life histories (LHs), are 'based upon first-person accounts of relatively long-term processes of learning and...focused on learners and their experiences rather than the learning activities or situations in which they participate' (Benson 2005, p. 17).
2. Drawings have also been used on courses focusing on learning to learn foreign languages (for a recent textbook, see Kalaja and Dufva 2005).
3. The changing status of English and increase in its users and uses in Finland are addressed in a research project *English Voices in Finland*. It is funded by the Academy of Finland and part of a Centre of Excellence in Research *The Study of Variation, Contact and Change in English* or VARIENG, a joint venture of the University of Helsinki and Jyväskylä, for details visit http://www.jyu.fi/hum/laitokset/kielet/varieng/en/.
4. In Section 3.3, feminine pronouns are used generically.
5. For lack of space illustrations are kept to a minimum, with cross-references in the text.
6. The student does mention another person (that is, his sister) but they do not seem to be interacting (in English). In this interpretation (and in Figure 13.4) other aspects of EFL learning are talked about (or depicted) metaphorically.
7. However, the analysis of these is beyond the scope of this study.

14
Multimedia Language Learning Histories*

Vera Menezes

> We tell our lives as narratives, but we experience them as hypertexts.
>
> Jay Lemke 2001

1 Introduction

Learning English is far from being an easy task in Brazil. Learners face contextual limitations, such as poor linguistic experiences at school and few opportunities to use the language in authentic contexts (see chapters by Barcelos; Miccoli; Dutra and Mello in this volume). In spite of this, it is surprising how some learners achieve a good mastery of English as we will see in some of the narratives in this chapter.

Investigating second or foreign language acquisition processes is a challenging enterprise as we can neither examine what happens in the learners' minds nor observe all their learning experiences. Nevertheless, language learning histories (LLHs) may reveal different aspects of the complexity of second language acquisition (SLA). The personal reflections in LLHs, framed by the 'landscape of learning', encompass educational events, personal experiences, identity issues, beliefs, fears, desires, preferences, personal and institutional relationships. Learners' understandings on how languages are learned, besides revealing particular experiences, can also provide important insights into SLA.

In this study, I intend to look for recurrent patterns in learners' narratives which can help me answer the following questions: (1) What do learners' LLHs tell us about SLA as a complex system? And (2) What kind of knowledge emerges from the interaction among text, hypertext, images and sounds in multimedia LLHs?

In Section 2, I discuss aspects of narrative research, multimedia, complexity and SLA as a complex system. The corpus of LLHs is described in Section 3 and, in Section 4, I analyse selected samples of the multimedia narratives. In the conclusion, I will argue that SLA emerges out of the interaction among different experiences with the language.

2 Background to this study

I have been working with narrative research (Paiva 2005, 2006a, 2006b), theoretically supported by Chaos/complexity theory in order to understand how learners acquire language in a non-English-speaking context. At present, I am particularly interested in multimedia narrative studies (Paiva 2006c) as much more information emerges through the combination of texts, hypertexts, images and sounds.

As pointed out by Larsen-Freeman (2000, p. 169), language learners have been seen from an etic perspective. While working with LLHs and listening to language learners, we aim at changing the etic perspective into an emic approach. By 'etic' I mean the external researcher's interpretation and by 'emic' the learners' interpretation of their learning experience. The focus on learners' experiences helps researchers to make a shift from objectivism/subjectivism to experientialism and then get a better understanding of how languages are learned from the point of view of the learners. In the experientialist perspective, man is seen as part of the environment, in constant interaction with it. Man changes the environment and is changed by it.

Lakoff and Johnson (1980) see objectivism, subjectivism and experientialism as myths.[1] They consider that 'like metaphors, myths are necessary for making sense of what goes on around us. All cultures have myths, and people cannot function without myth any more than they can function without metaphor' (Lakoff and Johnson 1980, pp. 185–6). The authors favour the myth of experientialism which does not oppose external and internal aspects of understanding as objectivism and subjectivism do. In the experientialist perspective, man is seen as part of the environment, in constant interaction with it. Man changes the environment and is changed by it.

The study of LLHs reinforces the experientialist perspective because the narrators talk about their constant interaction with different environments and the changes they undergo.

2.1 Narrative research

LLHs give voice to learners who often talk about their learning experiences in different contexts rather than in the traditional classrooms.

The narrators freely expose their memoirs and their emotions by giving their own explanations on how they learn or have learned a second language. These reports enable us to understand certain aspects of acquisition (e.g., fear, anxiety, family influence, etc.) which are not easily reached by other research tools.

In order to understand learning experiences, several researchers have been making use of LLHs. Pavlenko (2001, p. 213), for example, believes that this kind of narrative is a 'unique source of information about learners' motivations, experiences, struggles, losses, and gains' and McGroarty (1998, p. 598) considers that 'autobiographies and memoirs of highly literate and reflective learners have provided additional poignant observations about the subjective aspects of the language learning experience'.

The growing research interest in first-person accounts has given birth to important publications such as Benson and Nunan (2002, 2005). So far, researchers have been analysing written texts, either already published autobiographies as Pavlenko (2001) or LLHs collected among students (see Murphey 1997a and b, 1998a and Murphey et al. 2005). Some researchers use their own history, for example So and Dominguez (2005), or narratives collected by means of journals, for example Swain and Miccoli (1994) and interviews, for example Shoaib and Dörnyei (2005).

In my own work, I have been resorting to multimedia LLHs because it is my contention that pictures and sounds not only illustrate written texts, but also make up a larger network of meanings. In order to understand the ways in which images communicate meaning, I will use the grammar of visual design developed by Kress and van Leeuwen (1996). These authors understand that pictorial structures 'have a deeply important semantic dimension' (p. 45). I believe that the same can be said about sounds.

Gerard and Goldstein (2005, p. 6) say that '[w]hen you add audio to pictures and text, that's worth a million words'. In a clear reference to one of the characteristics of a complex system – emergence – they point out that 'words and images are much more than the sum of their parts'. In fact, one can say that multimedia portray much more information than each individual medium does, as meaning emerges through the interactions among the different media employed by the text producer.

In Section 2.2, I present some characteristics of chaos and complex systems, including SLA, in order to help us understand the acquisition experiences portrayed in the multimedia LLHs.

2.2 Chaos/complexity

Chaos theory and studies on complexity have been influencing many different research fields, including education. Gilstrap (2005, p. 57) points out that an understanding of chaos metaphors might help us understand complex educational environments and the paradoxes of complex adaptive systems, which, according to Velve et al. (2002, p. 2) are open entities consisting of related elements. SLA can be understood as an example of a complex system. It is open to new information and interactions in a continuous flow which make it evolve into more complex stages. The next section presents an overview of SLA as a complex system.

2.2.1 SLA as a complex system

Larsen-Freeman (1997, p. 141) was the first one to observe that 'there are many striking similarities between the new science of chaos/complexity and second language acquisition'. She understands that SLA shares the same characteristics of other complex systems. They are dynamic, non-linear, unpredictable and adaptive, to mention just some of their features.

In order for a complex system to evolve there are periodic attractors responsible for periodic or repetitive behaviours. Attractors are defined by Lewin (1992, p. 20) as 'states to which the system eventually settles, depending on the properties of the system'. In spite of the stable factors or periodic attractors, the system is open and other elements will play important roles in SLA. As explained by Larsen-Freeman (1997, p. 146), a complex non-linear system exhibits 'a 'strange' attractor because although its cycle repeats itself like the functionless pendulum, no cycle ever follows the exact same path or overlaps any other cycle. 'The orbits can become very densely packed together, and can in fact approach infinite thinness, but are still constrained within the limits of the attractor' (Taylor 1994, p. 203). At the same time that SLA is constantly changing, it also stays within the boundaries of what we call language acquisition. One cannot predict how SLA will develop, although one can tell it is fractal, a smaller copy of the whole, that is, a fraction similar to the whole linguistic system.[2]

When we turn our attention to LLHs, we see that no matter how much teachers plan, teach, evaluate and give feedback, students will react in different ways and unforeseen events will inevitably be part of their learning experiences. Linguistic differences, cultural backgrounds, reasons for learning and many other components of the acquisition system affect and are dynamically affected by other components. Although SLA processes are similar, strange or chaotic attractors will constantly reconfigure its dynamicity, and even within its limits the outcomes will be different, no matter how similar the initial conditions are. Slight perturbations and unforeseen events can cause important positive or negative results. The seemingly orderly world of language learning is in fact chaotic and chaos seems to be fundamental in such a process. SLA depends on the interaction among several elements and as the system is open, it is subject to continuous inflow and outflow of language experiences. Although it is self-organising, it never reaches equilibrium, but only temporary stability.

2.2.2 The edge of chaos

Velve et al. (2002, p. 2) point out that 'phase transitions or the edge of chaos occurs when the system is operating at the border of order and chaos' and that it is at this point that the system is functioning at its highest level of creativity.

Order and chaos coexist in a dynamic tension. According to Ockerman (1997), the system is capable of remarkable things when operating in the narrow zone between order and chaos which is called 'edge of chaos'. He explains that the edge of chaos is a state between order and chaos and that is where 'the greatest information processing takes place, where risks are taken and new behaviour is tried out' (p. 222). He adds that

> There are five factors, or control parameters, that determine whether a system can move into the edge of chaos (or beyond it into disintegration): the rate of information flow, the degree of diversity, the richness of connectivity, the level of contained anxiety, and the degree of power differentials. In human systems, these factors combine into a kind of creative tension where people are linked to others in paradoxical relationships of cooperation/competition, inspiration/anxiety, and compliance/individuality (group initiative to illustrate the process). (Ockerman 1997, p. 222)

In SLA, we can also consider some factors which move the system to the edge of chaos. They are: the amount of second language experience, the degree of input diversity, the richness of interactions, the level of contained anxiety, and the degree of autonomy or control of one's own learning. I take for granted that autonomy also implies the idea of power differentials (Ockerman 1997). Learners are differently empowered individuals and so their capacity to act has a direct effect on their autonomy.

So far, I have presented the theoretical support for this study which aims at understanding SLA by means of experiences portrayed in multimedia narratives. The next section describes the context of this study.

3 The context

Thirty-eight multimedia LLHs were collected at the Federal University of Minas Gerais, in Brazil: 20 in 2005 and 18 in 2006. The writers were prospective English teachers enrolled in two 60-hour online courses which aimed at developing computer literacy and English language skills.

The courses[3] aimed at developing computer skills such as editing images; creating hyperlinks for texts and sounds; and using Microsoft *Word* tools. They used the new acquired skills to write their final papers in the form of multimedia narratives. There were no strict guidelines for the text. They were asked to describe how they had learned English and to include hyperlinks, images and sounds. The students and the teacher formed an online community and interacted through a discussion list hosted by YahooGroups. The students used the list to send their tasks, solve doubts, and discuss any problems related to the course. Feedback was given by the teacher and the classmates and the students had the chance to edit their texts many times before having them published.

Thirty-seven students allowed me to publish their LLHs in the project homepage [http://www.veramenezes.com/narmulti.htm] and these texts formed the corpus for this study. I also included in the corpus my own LLH. One student was also interviewed by email so that I could understand why she had chosen some of her hyperlinks. In Section 4, I present some of the findings.

4 Data analysis

The LLHs were read many times so that I could select excerpts which would help us understand what learners' experiences reveal about SLA as a complex system and what kind of knowledge about SLA emerges from the texts. Some images were discarded because we do not have permission to publish them. I realised that openings and closings followed a general pattern and that the experiences could be divided into two main groups – inside and outside the classroom. The analyses will present an overall description of the way the texts open, present experiences and close.

4.1 Openings

Most of the narrators, inserted their own coloured photographs in the very beginning of the narratives, as in Figures 14.1 and 14.3, and one of them chose a manga[4] style (Figure 14.2).

The images are in the close-up format and the narrators are gazing at the reader. As explained by Kress and van Leeuwen (1996, p. 122), this visual configuration 'creates a visual form of direct address. It acknowledges the viewers explicitly, addressing them with a visual "you" '. Most

Figure 14.1 Close-up    *Figure 14.2* Manga    *Figure 14.3* In a conference

pictures represent the students smiling which is also explained by Kress and van Leeuwen (1996, p. 122) as the viewer being asked 'to enter into a relation of social affinity with them'. In Figure 14.3, the narrator decided to show her academic identity by publishing a photo taken in a conference setting. Her LLH also includes a lot of references to research projects and research groups at the university and image and text present a coherent dialogue around her academic life. It also shows that SLA is an open system and that experiences with the language are not confined to the classroom itself.

The way the narrators start their LLHs also vary. Some of them, especially the ones who did not include their own photographs in the very beginning of the text, introduce themselves by saying their names, talking about their childhood, or describing their early interest in learning English as in (1):

(1)

A long journey

Well, I dare say my interest in English was born on February 12, 1984 (oh yes, that's my birthday!). I say that because I remember very clearly the time when I would ask my *father* how to say such-and-such words in English. I don't know exactly how old I was then, but I'm sure I was very young. I also remember I had *loads of fun* turning my father into a walking-talking dictionary. As he himself has always been a language fancier, he would feel pleased to notice my interest in English and would always answer my plausible questions.

One of the first phrases I learned was 'the end'. Can you guess why??? Just because of *The Woody Woodpecker* cartoon. This phrase would always appear at the end of the cartoon – which, still nowadays, is one of my favorites!

When talking about her father, the narrator inserted a hyperlink to the soundtrack for the movie *Legend of Zorro*. When asked about her choice she explained that when she was a child she and her father used to watch the film together. If one clicks at *The Woody Woodpecker*, one can listen to Woody's trademark laugh. Both sounds are indices of how significant cinema is in her English learning experience. The link attached to *loads of fun* leads the reader to a baby's laugh and emphasises her statement that she has been interested in English since her early childhood. This meaning is also present in the picture of a newborn baby. The choices of the pictures and their position on the page can be interpreted as representing periods of her initial 'long journey': from an illiterate baby to a child being introduced by her father to the realm of literacy. This excerpt demonstrates that learning events are experienced as hypertexts reinforcing Lemke's (2001, p. 80) statement that 'we tell our lives as narratives, but we experience them as hypertexts'. The initial conditions of her SLA – her father's interest in English and her early motivation – had a very positive effect in her late experiences. Her father enrolled her in a private English course and paid for a trip to the United States and she decided to be an English teacher.

We can see in this and in other LLHs that SLA is a complex system as it relates different elements – family, cultural industry, educational artefacts (books, dictionaries), school, teachers, classmates, etc. – in a dynamic non-linear process. In Section 4.2, I present some LLHs excerpts which can help us understand the complexity of SLA.

4.2 Presenting experiences

The experiences found in our corpus can be divided into two groups: inside the classroom – the ones which display periodic attractors, represented by explicit language teaching in school contexts – and outside the classroom – the ones whose dynamicity is constrained by strange attractors created by cultural experiences and unexpected events which put the SLA process into movement. In other words, classroom experiences are predictable and follow a common pattern and outside classroom ones yield disturbances which can change the acquisition route. Several LLHs present both kinds of experiences and we understand that the two are important for the acquisition process. The images associated with the different experiences can be identified as social actions, transactional reactional, mental and verbal processes (Kress and van Leeuwen 1996).

4.2.1 Inside the classroom

In the first group, we can find visual narratives of silent students sitting at their desks and of teachers in front of their students usually teaching traditional boring classes. These can be described as predictable experiences. Boredom is usually represented in the written texts and in the photographs. Some of the images come along with balloons, such as the one in Figure 14.4, with a vector pointing at the bored student. It represents a transactional reaction of a student[5] in the classroom, and, as Kress and van Leeuwen (1996, p. 67) point out, this kind of reaction is not 'represented directly, but mediated through a Reacter, a "Senser" (in the case of a thought balloon), or a "Speaker" (in the case of the dialogue balloon)'.

Figure 14.4 Boredom

Images of teachers usually show predictable actions: teachers teaching grammar items or isolated vocabulary, as shown in Figure 14.5, where the balloons represent the speech process and the stick in the teacher's hand works as a vector. As defined by Kress and van Leeuwen (1996, p. 74), 'the active participant in an action process is the participant from which the vector emanates or which is fused with the vector'. The teacher is the actor, the one who speaks and makes movements. Although one cannot see the students, one can infer that they might be sitting in lines repeating after the teacher the words *ceiling* and *floor*:

Figure 14.5 English teacher[6]

One recurrent complaint in our corpus is that the verb *to be* is over taught as in Figure 14.6. Again we have a reactional process, where the narrator evaluates her SLA. It seems that the students are aware that their SLA systems need something different in order to be put into movement.

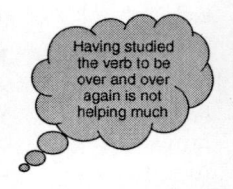

(thought bubble: Having studied the verb to be over and over again is not helping much)

Figure 14.6 The verb *to be*

Through both verbal and visual modes, some students represent themselves as members of a learning community undergoing poor experiences in their regular school classrooms (e.g., in Excerpt 2) as opposed to the rewarding ones lived outside school. Seldom do they report good experiences in elementary and high schools, although English classes at the university and at private language schools are often described as good exceptions.

(2)

> During my two years of English at the High School I tried some private English schools, but they are very boring with old fashioned teaching approaches, as well the High School itself, the type of 'Sit down...' or 'the book is on the table'. The exercise we were supposed to do seemed nonsense and tiring at all. Of course I gave up those.

In (2), the narrator remembers that different schools offered him boring experiences. His statement is reinforced by three images showing repetitive exercises. The first shows an active participant in the action of sitting down, as indicated by the vector. Repetition of tiresome activities is metaphorically represented by the other two drawings of people doing repetitive physical movements (walking and running). The sentences *sit down* and *the book is on the table* represent clichés in the aural oral method which seems to be the one adopted in these schools. They symbolise meaningless repetition which is not enough to move his SLA system.

This LLH and many others show that inside classroom experiences, in general, do not lead learners to the edge of chaos as they seldom offer a good amount of language experiences, input diversity, and rich interactions. When talking about school experiences, students usually show how anxious they were when forced to do boring activities which did not seem to contribute to their SLA. A good exception in the school context is the literature class as it deals with language as a social practice. Some students point out how important literature has been in their SLA processes inside and outside the classroom. Our LLHs also reveal that most learners are in control of their own learning. The next section presents some of these autonomous experiences.

4.2.2 Outside the classroom

The second group of experiences shows that chaotic or strange attractors are the ones which make the most difference in the students' SLA processes. There is enough evidence to say that learners are led to 'the edge of chaos' by strange attractors which do not appear in traditional learning contexts. They run risks, explore the language, and experiment with different language use situations. As Nelson (2004, p. 102) had already realised 'the classroom is not isolated from the world. Rather, students, and the knowledge they embody, cross classroom boundaries in networks that multiply and recycle that knowledge'. SLA networks are formed by students' favourite foreign bands and songs as in (3) and (4) ; literature as in (3); TV shows; the web; video and computer games; RPGs (Role Playing Games); internet chat rooms; travelling, studying or working abroad; interaction with other speakers of English as in (5); and experience abroad as in (6).

Excerpt (3) is followed by photographs of Radiohead, Led Zeppelin and The Doors. The subtitle for this part of the LLH shows how cultural production – literature and music – brings dynamicity to SLA. The words in italics are hyperlinks to lots of sites where the reader can see photographs, listen to songs, read more about several bands and singers and view the trailer of *The Princess and The Warrior*. Several reading and listening possibilities emerge from the unpredictable routes the reader can take and thus have a glimpse of the narrator's experience:

(3)
Literature and Rock'n'Roll: The Best
Literature helped me a lot. I learnt and am learning lots of English thanks to Literature. Including, of course, music!!! I always loved music, and by the time I started my course, I was falling in love with *Led Zeppelin* (see 'In The Light' lyrics), *Creedence Clearwater Revival* (now 'Revisited' – see 'Sinister Purpose' lyrics), *Metallica, The Doors, AC/DC,*

Radiohead, Tool, David Bowie, the craziest of all *Iggy Pop, Leonard* 'The Master' *Cohen* (please listen to 'Waiting For The Miracle' – the images are from the film *The Princess and The Warrior*), and others.

Music increases the rate of language input and it is not surprising to find out that almost every narrator talks about the role of music in their SLA processes. The same narrator in (2) talks about the value of music, referring to a Brazilian TV programme aiming at teaching English with songs in (4). He explains that one could listen to songs and sing following the lyrics on the screen and then attend a lesson with grammar rules and vocabulary explanation. He uses an image to represent a mental process, the metaphor for one's insight, and both image and the statement in capital letters emphasise that the TV programme changed his belief about his capacity to learn English. It was the turning point, the edge of chaos and changed the route of his SLA system.

(4)

> And I'll always remember the day and the music that opened up my eyes to the fact that *I REALLY COULD UNDERSTAND* this language, despite the classes on the schools that were very less effective.
> It was very fun because watching the programme, the English rules and its words made sense, on the contrary, in the classroom it didn't. I still remember the phrases of it, like 'No crisis arises my life goes along as it should...' and at the time I found myself singing it and they are complete sentence that made me think about the language and its rules, because these rules had a superb explanation from the programme presenter who seems to have an entire domain in the matter.

The next excerpt shows an experience which is rarely found in school contexts. The narrator in (5) practices *capoeira*[7] and this was a strange attractor which changed his SLA route. It was a good opportunity for him to speak English with foreigners:

(5)
When I was 16 years old I started practicing *capoeira*, and I also started to have contact with many foreign people. (...) Talking to these people was a great experience for me, because for the first time I was feeling that I could communicate with native speakers, in the target language!!

Excerpt (5) is a good example to show that SLA is open to unexpected experiences and that strange attractors (e.g., *capoeira*) can change its route. We can find similar examples where students' SLA systems were positively driven toward success by interactions with foreigners in sports and work contexts. Traveling seems to be another strange attractor. Several narrators talk about the importance of travelling abroad and included many photographs in their LLHs. One example can be seen in (6):

(6)

I and ballerina near Covent Garden, London	On the end of July 2005 something wonderful happened to me. I went to *London* with mum and there we met my sister that had already been living there for some time. Mum stayed only three months, I stayed eight months. **Amazing experience**. I could finally **experience English Language in its natural environment**...in a place where I would have to either SPEAK or SPEAK. There was no choice. In the beginning I was so ashamed of my English, it was horrible. Then one day, one guy from New Castle said to me, 'You speak very good English,' and I thought he just wanted to make me less uncomfortable, but later on I sometimes heard the same comment from other people and slowly I started getting more and more **confident**.

The events outside the classroom seem to decrease the level of anxiety and to move the SLA system into 'the edge of chaos' because they are responsible for a high rate of linguistic experiences, represented by a wide range of input, interaction diversity and autonomy. In (6), the narrator, ashamed at the beginning, becomes more confident as she keeps getting positive feedback from native speakers. The photograph shows the confident narrator in Covent Garden, London. Using the terms of Kress and van Leeuwen (1996), the narrator's arms form vectors in a transactive action. She has a goal: to hold the ballerina who is in a non-transactive position. She is confidently gazing and smiling at the reader, a visual form of addressing (Kress and van Leeuwen 1996, p. 122), and the image works as a metaphor of her *amazing experience* with the English language where her only choice was *SPEAK or SPEAK*. The embrace seems to symbolise her total integration with the culture and with the language. She also 'embraced' the language and that decision was her edge of chaos, the turning point for her SLA.

Outside classroom experiences offer opportunities for learners to exercise their autonomy, choosing their own acquisition track. Each LLH is unique and the narrators seem to mark this uniqueness in their closing remarks. Let us see, in Section 4.3, how our narrators close their texts.

4.3 Closings

When closing their texts, students usually choose to reflect about SLA. As they have read many versions of other classmates' LLHs, they are aware that there are no similar histories. One of them stated: *I think it's fascinating to realise that the process of second language acquisition can vary so much from one person to another, and that it isn't predictable.* Others close their text by giving advice: one wrote *A piece of advice? Follow your dreams*, a second stated *Only you can write your history!*, and a third one concluded *One thing is very clear for me at this point: when a person really wants to learn another language, she will find a way to make it happen, no matter how hard it might be or how little help she might get.*

Most of them seem to be aware that they are involved in a complex system always in movement by making statements such as *The learning process never ends; I do not think it is over or that it will ever be*; or *To be continued ....☺.* They understand that the system is open, as registered in one of the student's final words: *each day is a new today with new things to learn*, and non-linear as described by another narrator who says *I know that the way I studied English was not a 'normal' one, or a sequential one like some people do in private English courses, but my English knowledge was built up as an 'art-craft' with some different experiences and English accents.*

5 Conclusion

LLHs tell us that the participants' learning experiences oscillate between two phases – classroom activities which are shown as predictable and repetitive and a more creative phase where agency permeates their experiences, but they are interconnected, they influence and are influenced by each other. The former is responsible for metalanguage and the prevalent concept of language is the one of a set of grammatical patterns and lexis. The latter is connected with linguistic social agency as learners use the language to do things: listen to songs, watch movies, read different kinds of texts and interact with English speakers. Language is seen as communication. Competing forces of the convergence and the divergence of the different experiences keep learners' trajectories within the region of the SLA attractor but a higher level of complexity emerges and each state is different from the previous one. Changes and perturbations occur during the acquisition process and they make the system work. The multimedia LLHs show how the SLA process self-organises itself and moves towards success.[8] There is temporary stability, but the system never reaches equilibrium.

The use of visuals, sounds and hypertexts were essential for representing individual identities, anxiety, happiness, discomfort and tensions students experienced during their SLA process. Some multimedia texts use a lot of visual material, others are more economical, but as I have already stated in Paiva (2006c, p. 37),

> words, images and sounds together added up too much more than the sum of their parts. The multimedia texts enhanced the students' creativity and imagination and had profound and significant impact on our learning community, given that participants not only produced and shared a new kind of text, but reflected on their past and present learning processes while helping peers develop and improve language and computer skills.

The LLHs show that SLA is a complex system and that second language does not come out only as a product of formal learning contexts, but it emerges out of the interaction of different social networks (family, cultural production, school) with the individual cognitive and affective factors.

Notes

* I am grateful to Paula Kalaja, Ana Maria Barcelos and Phil Benson for their insightful comments and review.

This work has been supported by two research agencies in Brazil: CNPq (*Conselho Nacional de Desenvolvimento da Pesquisa*) and FAPEMIG (*Fundação de Amparo a Pesquisa*).

1. They explain that they are not using the term 'myth' in any derogatory way.
2. Larsen-Freeman (1997, p. 150) reminds us that language is also fractal because it is not different from other natural phenomena.
3. The syllabuses can be found at http://www.veramenezes.com/call205.htm and http://www.veramenezes.com/literacy.htm respectively.
4. *Manga* is the word for most Japanese 'comic pictures'.
5. The complete image was not reproduced because I do not have permission for it.
6. Drawing by Romulo Lagares, a former student of mine.
7. Capoeira is an African-Brazilian fight-dance and martial art.
8. It is worth mentioning that our data bank also contains narratives which describe SLA systems which did not evolve because they received no new energy either by the school system or by the learner's individual experiences. These are sad stories of unsuccessful acquisition.

Part VI
Conclusion

15
Narrativising Learning and Teaching EFL: Concluding Remarks

Vera Menezes, Ana Maria F. Barcelos and Paula Kalaja

1 Introduction

Using Karlsson's metaphor (in Chapter 6), we can say that the experiences portrayed in this volume make up a kaleidoscope. The volume works as a tube of mirrors and each chapter as coloured beads put into movement by each one's reading, projecting different images of the complexity of learning and teaching EFL. By reading the lived experiences of teachers and learners we can see the reflection of our own anxieties and uncertainties about the realm of EFL.

We have read about several experiences which prove that 'students do not behave the way teachers expect them to' (p. 98) and that 'the language classroom is not just a place where a language is taught, but is far more complex where many kinds of factors and issues meet and interact' (p. 106), as pointed out by Sakui and Cowie in Chapter 7.

In Chapter 4, Dutra and Mello, quoting Connelly and Clandinin (1990, p. 12), note that 'Research is a collaborative document, a mutually constructed story out of the lives of both researcher and participant.' (p. 52, Chapter 4). In this sense, this collection portrays the story of researchers interested in narrative research in their professional lives. In showcasing and analysing the stories here, we are also reconstructing our own learning about ourselves as researchers, teacher educators, teachers and learners.

The hypertexts of this volume show links to the different chapters. Each chapter has a link, a connection, to different or similar concepts in another chapter, thus constituting a multilayered narrative. As such, not only is this concluding chapter a storied event of all the stories told in this book, but this book itself is a narrative composed of many stories which we try to make sense of as we construct this conclusion. Thus, we are being transformed and have been transformed by this storied event.

Important issues were brought into light by several research reports. In this concluding chapter we first comment on the emerging key issues. Second, we briefly highlight some methodological aspects of doing narrative research, and we conclude with future directions and implications for teachers and researchers.

2 Lessons learned from the narratives

Three key issues emerged from all the studies in this collection: identity, communities of practice and agency, and the power of narratives. Each of these will be discussed separately in the following sections.

2.1 Identity

Identity has emerged as one of the main issues that permeates all the different chapters in this collection. As such, it is related to several other aspects touched upon in the different research reports, such as contexts of learning, beliefs, emotions, narratives, agency, communities of practice, imagined communities, experiences, and chaos/complexity. As in a kaleidoscope, the themes overlap and interconnect. Although for organizational purposes the different issues are discussed separately, they are interconnected in a complex way.

Identity in this collection is understood in a poststructuralist perspective: it is described as being in flux and dynamic. This is observed in Chapter 12 by Nikula and Pitkänen-Huhta in which learners' identities shift between that of a language learner and a language user. Their mixed identities, according to the authors 'fluctuate between school practices and those arising from their own ways of making use of English' (p. 184).

In a poststructuralist view, identities are socially constructed through narratives. As pointed out by Block in Chapter 10, identities are 'ongoing life narratives in which individuals constantly attempt to maintain a sense of balance' (p. 142). Narratives are portrayed in the different chapters as ongoing narrative constructions of teachers and learners' selves and identities in certain circumstances and contexts, as noted by Nikula and Pitkänen-Huhta in Chapter 12. The narratives have revealed students' and teachers' experiences as well as their processes of identity construction in action as users of English (Cotterall, Chapter 8), as learners of English in different contexts (Barcelos, Chapter 3), as teachers struggling with a resistant group of students (Sakui and Cowie, Chapter 7), as learners of English in the classroom (Murphey and Carpenter, Chapter 2) and out of the classroom (Murray, Chapter 9) in Japan, as teachers struggling in an EFL context (Miccoli, Chapter 5), and as a learner in an adult EFL classroom in Spain who struggles to construct an *English mediated identity* and an *English textual identity* (Block, Chapter 10).

English mediated identities refer to 'how individuals come to develop an expertise in English which they are exposed to either formally or informally', as pointed out by Block (p. 144, Chapter 10). This type of identity is present in other chapters such as those by Barcelos, Murray, Murphey and Carpenter, Cotterall, and Menezes (or 3, 9, 2, 8, and 14) in which students struggle to construct an English mediated identity by themselves or within a community of practice or imagined communities in informal and formal learning contexts. This type of identity was most salient in Chapter 12 by Nikula and Pitkänen-Huhta in which students develop an *identity of expert* in the language gained through informal learning in their interest in sports or hobbies as well as to the language used in those practices.

Block, quoting Kramsch and Lam (1999), notes in Chapter 10 that English language textual identity, is 'about becoming a "text creator" and gaining a voice in the target language' (p. 149). Silvia, an adult Spanish learner of EFL, was able to construct this identity for herself at the end of the term by having her writing recognised by the teacher. Similarly, participants in the studies by Cotterall, Murray, Murphey and Carpenter, Barcelos, Nikula and Pitkänen-Huhta and Menezes (or Chapters 8, 9, 2, 3, 12 and 14) also tried to gain a voice in the target language, constructing their textual identities.

But how does one construct these two types of identities? Quoting himself (Block 2002, p. 4), Block in Chapter 10 claims that it is necessary to have *critical experiences*, defined by the author as 'periods of time during which prolonged contact with an L2 and a new and different cultural setting causes irreversible destabilisation of the individual's sense of self' (p. 152, Chapter 10). Several chapters showed how students (and sometimes, teachers themselves) went through critical experiences.

In Chapter 11, Chik and Benson, for instance, in narrating the story of Ally, an educated adult learner who has learned English in her own country and moves back and forth between languages and cultures and between developing identities, suggest that her experience abroad was a critical experience. According to the authors, Ally's 'perceptions of the ways in which others saw her also destabilised' her 'sense of self-identity, leading her to position herself temporarily on the Chinese side' (p. 167). In Chapter 7, Sakui and Cowie, on the other hand, dealt with teachers' identities as unfolding and changing in the face of student resistance in class. Although Block´s concept of critical experiences refers to an L2 contact, the episode seems to have been a critical experience for Sakui and Cowie, in terms of negotiating differences with students as they produced their ongoing narrative as teachers. Karlsson's (Chapter 6) and some of Cotterall's (Chapter 8) participants also had critical experiences in their language learning processes.

By listening to Silvia's voice in Chapter 10 by Block and to the reflections of Sakui and Cowie in Chapter 7 about student resistance they had experienced in two different university contexts in Japan, we can make sense of similar experiences in our own classrooms by acknowledging the signs of resistance. Perhaps we can say that Block's study in Spain also portrayed a resisting student. Resistance seems to occur because the behaviour of teachers or classmates does not work in favour of agency. In Chapter 14, Menezes observes that classroom activities are predictable and repetitive and that agency permeates experiences outside school, although both kinds of experiences are interconnected, influencing and being influenced by each other.

In Chapter 10, we can see that Block also believes that it is difficult for the language classroom to provide critical experiences. He recognises that teachers provide 'spaces' for classroom activities such as writing their language learning histories to help the construction of English mediated identities or, according to Murphey and Carpenter (in Chapter 2), to promote agency and pathways thinking. We also relate the concept of critical experiences to the concept of *edge of chaos* mentioned by Menezes in Chapter 14, and defined by Ockerman (1997) as a 'state between order and chaos and that is where "the greatest information processing takes place, where risks are taken and new behaviour is tried out" (p. 222)'. To create an edge of chaos, teachers need to have information flowing, diversity, connectivity, contained anxiety and a degree of power differentials.

In Chapter 8 by Cotterall, learners' identities and experiences were seen as related to their goals and independent language learning. Her study conducted in an informal learning context shows a conflict between a learner's goals and strategies. The results suggest that learners' goals shift and change according to their priorities, contextual constraints and motivation. Changes in external events may lead to changes in motivation, actions, emotions, goals and practices. As these change, so do learners' feelings and emotions (of frustration, anxiety, or positive feelings about themselves). Cotterall's analysis proved that the Japanese learners she investigated were flexible and adapted themselves to an independent learning context, 'exploding some myths' about the way that Japanese learners tend to learn.

To a certain extent, Chapter 4 by Dutra and Mello is also related to identities in construction as they investigate how teachers in a continuing teacher education programme narrate their histories and envision their professional lives and how they understand and recreate their pedagogical actions, and thus, reconceptualise their history and their identities as in-service and pre-service teachers. As they reconceptualise theories in practice as well as their past and present in their narratives, these teachers show agency thinking and pathways thinking as they envision new possibilities for themselves as professionals by reflecting on the place that theory takes in their lives, and how the social-historical aspects influence their beliefs and actions.

To sum up, we can say that identity can also be thought of as a kaleidoscope, as one's identity is constructed by means of several other identities that interact with each other in a complex way.

2.2 Communities of practice and agency

The second aspect which was salient in most narratives of this collection concerns the concept of communities of practice and agency. A community of practice was the focus of Chapter 9 by Murray, and agency of Chapter 2 by Murphey and Carpenter. Yet, these concepts permeate all the other chapters, as we will be pointing out in this section.

In Chapter 9, Murray uses the concepts of communities of practice by Wenger et al. (2002) and imagined communities by Kanno and Norton (2003) to investigate the experiences of Japanese adult learners in learning English. The results show that some of his participants engaged in peripheral participation in the imagined communities of movies and television, similarly to the participants in chapters by Menezes, Kalaja et al. and Nikula and Pitkänen-Huhta (or 14, 13 and 12). His study suggests the need, as Murphey and Carpenter (in Chapter 2) acknowledge, for teachers to create the conditions in the classrooms for learners to engage in communities of practice and become agents of their own learning.

Other chapters, such as Chapters 12 and 13 by Nikula and Pitkänen-Huhta and Kalaja et al. highlight how students can create communities of practices or engage in imagined communities in informal contexts. For the participants in Chapter 13 by Kalaja et al. the imagined communities were composed of books. The authors were concerned with the types of mediational means that appear in the drawings and what these say about the way learners view themselves as learners (i.e., about their beliefs). They employed a sociocultural approach which assumes human behavior to be a mediated activity and culturally mediated by a number of semiotic and material tools, such as language. Their findings suggest books to be the most common mediational tool in students' imagined communities, in which teachers were not present.

Chapter 12 by Nikula and Pitkänen-Huhta focused on students' narratives (as triggered by photographs) of informal language learning. Adopting a social view of language which puts emphasis on participation and socialisation, their results indicate a complex relationship between learning English formally and informally and identities. Students adopted identities of *users of the language* in their daily encounters with English but school practice was also an aspect of their identities, echoing voices of educational discourses in the society at large. Nikula and Pitkänen-Huhta acknowledge in Chapter 12 that 'practices learned in formal educational environments can be taken into use in everyday activities when the situation and the needs of the language users so demand' (p. 179).

Agency permeates most of our narratives. Murphey and Carpenter in Chapter 2 aimed at understanding to what degree students attributed the outcomes of their experiences to external sources or to their own agencies. Although their chapter focused specifically on agency, several other concepts are interrelated to this, such as identity, communities of practice, discourse of agency distribution, social capital, motivation, and beliefs. The authors believe that *'empowering individual agency* may be the most important step for success in language learning as it is for those undergoing psychotherapy' (p. 17). To have agency, one needs to engage in *pathways thinking* or 'the ability to imagine and find possible routes to these goals' (p. 18). In order to do so, teachers have to help students by adopting a *discourse of agency attribution,* that is, 'blaming students for their success' as a source of social capital,[1] since our identities are 'closely tied to the communities in which we imagine ourselves as actors and agents' (p. 18, Chapter 2).

Social capital, agency, identity and communities of practice are related to each other in intricate and complex ways. As Murphey and Carpenter explain in Chapter 2, 'agency interacts with social and cultural capital in a catalytic manner and they can mutually increase each other' (p. 20). In other words, agency is dynamic and 'always co-constructed with those around the L2 users' and 'shaped by particular sociocultural environments', as pointed out by Pavlenko (2002b, p. 293). Thus, according to Murphey and Carpenter, when a student feels part of a community of practice that values her and her knowledge, she starts identifying more with the class and finds it a place she enjoys going to. This creates an 'effective ecology for learning (Hawkins 2005) or an affinity space (Gee 2004)', quoted by the authors, or a place in which 'collaboration, acceptance, and empowerment happen naturally' (p. 20, Chapter 2) or where an edge of chaos can happen.

In Chapter 7, Sakui shows that she herself was able to have pathways thinking – she imagined and found possible routes to her goals as a teacher. By the same token, the participants in Chapter 8 by Cotterall showed pathways thinking when they were able to modify their goals or strategies to find more motivation and have more positive feelings about their own learning. Pathways thinking, however, seemed to be missing from the participants in Chapter 5 by Miccoli, although they showed commitment to teaching. In Barcelos' study (Chapter 3), some participants also showed pathways thinking when they were able to meet their goals in learning English at university, despite the lack of agency thinking in their previous experiences.

The photographs of Chapter 12 by Nikula and Pitkänen-Huhta, the multimedia narratives of Chapter 14 by Menezes and the drawings of Chapter 13 by Kalaja et al. often portray students doing something with English outside the classroom. This indicates the importance of other language experiences besides the classroom, which Nikula and Pitkänen-Huhta (in Chapter 12) name *incidental learning*. They claim that 'it would thus seem important for formal language teaching to find ways to acknowledge informal learning and to prevent value judgments which only deem school learning to be important and serious learning' (p. 185, Chapter 12).

Agency is closely connected to the entertainment industry as a source of English learning. Referring to the power of movies, Murray in Chapter 9 shows the importance of imagined communities and communities of practice. He says that 'language educators need to recognise the power of narrative and media to excite learners' imaginations and to provide language learning opportunities.' He also points out that

> We now possess the technology to create virtual target language communities which learners can enter as peripheral participants, assume an identity, engage in a joint enterprise, exercise their agency, and at the same time experience a variety of language learning opportunities. (p. 140)

In short, the many chapters of this collection provide us with a glimpse of students' worlds in outside-school contexts and contacts between school and everyday learning suggesting the types of communities of practice or imagined communities they are able to engage in. Although the classroom is a complex space and still needs research, the studies here have shown how researchers have started getting out of the box themselves to investigate the communities of practice or imagined communities students engage in and the agency they demonstrate outside the school context.

2.3 The power of narrative

Several authors in this volume have emphasised the power of narratives, exploring the numerous ways in which narratives can shed light onto different issues in language learning and teaching and professional development.

Narrative was shown in the many studies reported in this collection as a tool that allows an understanding of the impact of our experiences, the emergence of deeply hidden assumptions, and an opportunity to understand change in people and events, as Karlsson points out in Chapter 6. Narratives are seen in this volume as pervasive in human experience and in language learning and teaching. According to Karlsson (Chapter 6), language learning experiences are organised in stories and learners and teachers story and re-story their experiences. (p. 85, Chapter 6).

Two chapters in this collection aimed at understanding teachers' and learners' language learning and teaching experiences: those of Miccoli and Barcelos (or Chapters 5 and 3).

In Chapter 5, Miccoli uses the concept of experience as situated within a social/cultural view of the classroom instead of only a psychological/cognitive one. She defines experience as 'a process of relationships and emotional dynamics that temporally involves experience, experienced and context of experience' (p. 66, Chapter 5). She investigated EFL teachers' experiences in public and private schools, in Brazil, through the analysis of their written accounts, and tried to deconstruct the belief that 'school English' is a result of public school English learning. Her results show how teachers' experiences give rise to emotions and feelings such as frustration with the system. Similarly to Barcelos' participants, the teachers in her study are 'haunted' by the private English course, and by *school English*, a concept that permeates the studies situated in Brazilian contexts (by Dutra and Mello, Barcelos, Miccoli and Menezes, or Chapters 4, 3, 5 and 14).

In Chapter 3, Barcelos analysed narratives of language and secretarial science students and tried to identify the kinds of experiences and beliefs they had in two different contexts of learning English in Brazil. The results suggest the influence of different contexts of learning in

Brazil on students' language learner identities and beliefs about these places, about their teachers, about their learning and about themselves as possible agents of their own learning processes. Some of them showed agency and pathways thinking in looking for alternatives to transform what they saw as poor learning in the past and construct different paths for themselves in the present and future. Their experiences with learning English in public schools or private English courses influenced the kinds of emotions they felt as they struggled to develop (or not) their English mediated identities in both contexts. Most of them participated in imagined communities through music and the entertainment industry, similar to the experiences reported in Chapters 12, 13 and 14 by Nikula and Pitkänen-Huhta, Kalaja et al. and Menezes.

In Chapter 8, Cotterall states that narrative research, while treating learners as whole and complex persons, 'seeks to tell stories in all their complexity, imprecisions, and idiosyncrasy' (p. 127). Narratives arise from experience and are the method *par excellence* to investigate experience. Experiences are seen as 'complex, multilayered and ambiguous'; 'its interpretation [is] always non-conclusive', as pointed out by Karlsson in Chapter 6 (p. 85). To Dutra and Mello in Chapter 4, narratives are not static but dynamic. They are a way of understanding experiences and of continually developing oneself. Thus, in Chapter 4, 'narratives are used not only as an instrument of data collection but also as a means of self-discovery (*wholeheartedness*), so as to, together with other instruments, further sustain professional understanding and growth through reflective practice' (p. 53).

Resonating with the statements above, Karlsson in Chapter 6 sees self-narrative as an opportunity for teachers (and researchers alike) to 're-story themselves'. She reports a self-narrative study in which a teacher-researcher self-reflects on her experience in a self-access study context. According to her, narrative as a method allows for self-reflexivity because the researcher actively constructs knowledge and uses his/her own life to interpret participants' lives and events. She used narrative as a double narrative: generated by participants in interaction with the voice of the researcher – herself – as a narrator. As such, narratives are dialogical and shaped in the co-telling. This is what Karlsson in Chapter 6 called the cycle of experience – past, present, future and interpretation are constructed in the telling. There is self construction as well as constructions by others. She explained this by presenting the concept of *resonance* by Conle (1993):

> When one story causes us to make metaphorical links with another, i.e., through resonance (Conle 1993), we respond to the memories

and stories of others with memories of our own, and together these stories will open up possibilities for our future. This is how narrative will help teachers/counsellors and learners to meet. Resonance is also the process that carries the inquiry along by producing yet further stories. (in Karlsson, p. 85, Chapter 6)

Thus, we can say that this conclusion represents resonance since it is our way of responding to the different stories of teachers and learners reported here, producing other stories and seeing the possibilities that open up for the future. However, in Chapter 6, Karlsson, based on Ochs and Capp (1996), cautions us that 'Each telling only evokes certain memories or concerns in both partners. We only apprehend our partial selves, and only fragments of experience are accessed on each occasion: it is never complete self-understanding on the part of the narrator or the listener/reader' (p. 91).

3 Methodological issues

Three methodological aspects in using narratives seem to emerge from the different chapters of this collection: the role of the narrator/researcher in writing and analysing the narrative, the role of the participants in the analysis of their own narratives, and the use of multimodal narratives.

The first aspect concerns *the role of the narrator/researcher*. What should be the role of the narrator/researcher in analysing narratives? In two chapters in this volume, 6 and 7, the researcher and the narrator were participants in their own study and were able to adopt what Karlsson in Chapter 6 demonstrated to be a double role of the narrator in an autobiography or self-reflective narrative (p. 84). In other words, as the author explains, while narrating, she is both a narrator and a character in her story. Thus, she is 'as much subject to temporal and contextual changes in the story, as are [her] research participants, which in turn will help [her] to maintain a sense of their agency' (p. 90, Chapter 6). In Chapter 7, Sakui and Cowie also adopted this trend. In our opinion, this is an interesting methodological tendency to contrast with the role of an omniscient narrator, as pointed out by Karlsson (in Chapter 6). She suggests that our writing should reflect both the way we have researched and our understanding of narrative. This means that 'a commitment to a personal and subjective narrative follows the recognition of the close link between our own being in the world and the mode of narrative inquiry' (p. 96, Chapter 6).

Concluding Remarks 227

The second aspect refers to *the role participants* should have in the narratives provided to researchers. A couple of chapters in this collection adopted the procedure of asking participants to read the written account of the narrative written by the researchers. For instance, Chik and Benson in Chapter 11 asked the participant to read the story and then talked about it in the third interview. In Chapter 8, Cotterall also asked the students to check their accounts for accuracy, the further round of analysis. This is something that we suggest future studies should do, to add to the complexity of narrative studies, as Karlsson (in Chapter 6) notes – a narrative inside the narrative. This is necessary because, as pointed out by Dutra and Mello, in Chapter 4:

> We have found through teachers' narratives that many times the analytical categories that researchers define in their studies are not clearly separated in teachers' experience. They are lived as a holistic construct, which only gets pieced as demanded by their remembering and retelling. (p. 56)

In Chapter 12, Nikula and Pitkänen-Huhta suggest an interesting perspective in the analysis of this narrative constructed by researcher and participants. They adopted a broad discursive definition of a *narrative contract* between the narrator and the narratee, following Galasiński and Galasińska (2005). The advantages of using photographs, according to the authors, is that they 'triggered more specific mini-narratives – often collaboratively constructed by the participants (see Coates 2005, pp. 90–2) – relating both to the situations and contexts represented in the photographs and to the values and attitudes attached to them.' (Nikula and Pitkänen-Huhta, 173, Chapter 12). This resonates with the current state of art on narrative research which stresses the co-constructed nature of narratives (Pavlenko 2007, p. 180).

This relates to the third aspect – *the use of photographs, drawings and multimedia narratives*. In Chapter 14, Menezes used images to capture the complexity of stories of prospective English teachers. The author cites Gerard and Goldstein (2005, p. 6) who state that 'words and images are much more than the sum of their parts'. In other words, pictures and sounds make up for a network of meanings. By their very nature, these media suggest already a double narrative or a meta-narrative. In Chapter 13 by Kalaja et al. after having drawn pictures of themselves, the students were asked to comment on them, thus producing another narrative, or a meta-narrative. Photographs, according to Nikula and Pitkänen-Huhta in Chapter 12, are narratives in themselves as they tell a story. But the discussion also gave rise to different kinds of stories – which suggest that methodologically speaking, it may be wise to use visual types of data always followed by written or oral ones.

To sum up, using the framework suggested by Pavlenko (2007), we can say that the narratives presented here focus on *subject reality* and on *text reality*. Most chapters focused on subject reality, that is, most of them tried to find out how respondents experienced events or things, in other words, 'their thoughts and feelings about the language learning process' (Pavlenko 2007, p. 165), whereas three chapters (Kalaja et al. Menezes, and Nikula and Pitkänen-Huhta, or 13, 14 and 12) focused on text reality, that is, how respondents narrated the events by using sounds, pictures and drawings. This was done within several theoretical frameworks as laid out in Chapter 1 of this volume (see Table 1.1).

4 Future directions

In this section, we address implications for the classroom and for research. We first highlight some aspects pointed out in some chapters which can help teachers in their daily classroom activities. Then, we make some suggestions for further research so that we can answer other questions and go on constructing knowledge on language teaching and language learning.

4.1 Implications for the classroom

In Chapter 9, Murray suggests the need for teachers to create the conditions in the classrooms for learners to engage in communities of practice. Murray encourages teachers to plan activities that foster a sense of community (inviting outsiders to the classroom, encouraging online discussion, carrying out project work). Other activities, according to Murray, involve having discussion group work, organising social events, giving a place to pop culture in the classroom, and using narratives as a basis for meta-cognitive discussion with students to excite their imagination, identities, investments and pathways thinking. Murphey and Carpenter in Chapter 2 also suggest that teachers should encourage students to write their language learning histories, develop classroom newsletters, and provide near-peer role modelling opportunities for students.

According to Murphey et al. (2005), having students write their language learning histories helps them reflect on and become more aware of their own experiences. We agree with the authors. However, as pointed out by Karlsson in Chapter 6, we need to be careful in order not to 'give rise to frozen stories that become prisons for those telling them'

(p. 91, Chapter 6). In other words, when using narratives with students and teachers, our goals should be to foster connections and to build pathways thinking, and be cautious about teachers or learners who keep telling the same story without reflecting on them. The stories then may become a vehicle for frozen behaviours and thoughts.

The role of teachers in creating communities of practice and in helping students develop agency is of paramount importance to help them 'recognise their own agency in their learning and engage in such behaviours more robustly, helping them learn more effectively in and out of the classroom', as pointed out by Murphey and Carpenter in Chapter 2. Accordingly, 'teachers should think more in terms of how they are scaffolding the *agency* and *pathways thinking* of their students, and whether they are confirming the agency that students demonstrate' (p. 4, Chapter 2). Thus, the new roles for teachers involve acting as propagators of new discourse, scaffolders of pathways thinking, and confirmers of students' agency, in order to take students to the edge of chaos. And how can teachers help learners move to the edge of chaos in the classrooms? Perhaps by not being predictable and by creating lots of *learning opportunities* (Allwright 2005), agency thinking, pathways of thinking, as well as learning ecologies of linguistic contagion (Murphey 2006, 2007). This would help us to empower learners to become experts in language use and to construct their English mediated and textual identities.

4.2 Implications for research

We have seen in this volume that scholars in three continents, carrying out different research projects and employing different methods, have found striking similarities among learners' experiences and feelings in different contexts. It seems that the results of each chapter can be transferred to most of our own contexts. Nevertheless, we consider multinational projects a promising enterprise not only for the research team we recruited to produce this volume, but for other researchers who teach EFL as well as other foreign languages in different parts of the world and in different contexts and who are interested in narrative research.

Comparative research in EFL/ESL and in other foreign languages could reveal if there are more common patterns among students in different contexts than the ones revealed in this volume and answer other questions which still remain unanswered. How different are the language learning histories of EFL students from those who study other foreign languages? Do different genders present different experiences?

Which aspects are more prevalent in male and female narratives? What do unsuccessful language learners reveal in their narratives? How much does a learner's cultural background influence her experiences? Research could also focus on other aspects such as narrative differences concerning age and social class.

The different narratives presented here were collected in different countries. Future research could collect narratives in both the first language and second language of the students, as suggested by Pavlenko (2007), to see if there is any difference in the telling of the stories, in terms of how the subjects construct themselves and their identities in their first language and in the foreign language.

In the context of Japan more research is needed to deconstruct the myth that Japanese language students are passive learners. In Brazil, contexts other than public schools should be investigated in order to reinforce or challenge the results reported in Chapter 5 by Miccoli that there are no significant differences between English language teaching in public and private schools. Besides, more background information is needed as students in private schools usually attend language classes outside regular school, and that can make all the difference.

Most of our research focuses on winners. We must also give voice to the ones who failed in their learning processes and find out why they gave up learning a foreign language.

Narrative form is another focus which deserves more research. How are experiences organised in this genre? What are the most recurrent events and in which order are they narrated? In the multimedia ones, what are the stories told in texts and images and how are the visual elements interrelated with written text? This would move us closer to a focus on *text reality* of narratives, that is, 'how humans author selves in narratives', as suggested by Pavlenko (2007, p. 170).

The studies in this volume by Kalaja et al. (in Chapter 13) and Menezes (in Chapter 14), the former with drawings and the latter with different kinds of images, provide evidence that students usually depict themselves facing the viewer. There might be other common features in this kind of multimodal texts and joint research could point out to some universal characteristics. Kalaja et al. realised that there are differences between visual and verbal representations, but what are the main differences? Which meanings are there in the visual texts that are not at least inferable from textual narratives?

Sakui and Cowie in Chapter 7 also mention the kinds of emotions which surfaced when facing student resistance. It was an emotional experience for both, which shows the roller-coaster of emotions in teaching and how important it is for teachers to be tuned in with their emotions in teaching through self-narrative. In this self-discovery journey Sakui 'realised that her ultimate goal for [that] class should be to enhance [students'] self-esteem. Teaching English became secondary' (p. 101, Chapter 7). This resonates with a number of recent studies which highlight the emotional dimension and quality of life of the classroom (Allwright 2006; Wright 2006) and of teaching (Zembylas 2006). Chapter 6 by Karlsson also shows how the emotion of shame was crucial to Johanna's, an EFL student's, loss of interest and investment in language learning. Karlsson suggests that we have to understand the role of autobiographical elements and emotions in language learning and how we use them, hide them or act on them, as emotions interfere with our identities. We believe this is an interesting venue that future narrative studies could investigate further.

Finally, an international narrative databank would help to foster integrative research enterprise that allows for social-historical analysis of a large pool of narrative production as suggested by Pavlenko (2007). One international corpus is under construction with the help of several collaborators of this volume and around 500 language learning narratives are already available at the AMFALE project [http://www.veramenezes.com/amfale.htm]. We need to expand that corpus so that collaborative research projects may be planned in the near future.

5 Final remarks

In conclusion, several questions were asked in the course of this volume and attempts made to answer them. We have reflected on EFL interaction experienced by learners and counsellors (Karlsson, Chapter 6); how teachers experience students' resistance (Sakui and Cowie, Chapter 7); how English mediated identity is developed (Block, Chapter 10); what photographs reveal about teenagers' English learning (Nikula and Pitkänen-Huhta, Chapter 12); what visual self-portraits reveal about EFL learners' experiences in Finland (Kalaja et al., Chapter 13); to what factors learners attribute their successes (Murphey and Carpenter, Chapter 2); what learners' learning histories tell us about acquisition as a complex system and what kind of knowledge emerges from the interaction among text, hypertext, images and sounds in multimedia narratives (Menezes, Chapter 14). We also learned about beliefs and prejudices (reported by Murray, Barcelos, Miccoli, Cotterall, Chik and Benson, Dutra and Mello, or in Chapters 9, 3, 5, 8, 11 and 4) in different contexts.

After reading all the chapters we can paraphrase Sakui and Cowie in Chapter 7 who said that by narrating, reflecting and analysing their experiences, they had a better understanding of their own teaching. We think we can say the same after playing with our kaleidoscope of lived experiences: the ones narrated and the ones vicariously lived by reading this volume.

Based on the assumption that narratives and stories provide only a fragmented view and that understanding is always partial (Ochs and Capp 1996), this volume does not provide a conclusive view of narratives, but a glimpse of the unfolding perspectives and alternative views on narrativising learning and teaching EFL.

Note

1. Social capital is defined by the authors according to Portes (1998, p. 6) as 'The ability of actors to secure benefits by virtue of membership in social networks or other social structures' (p. 4).

References

Alanen, R., 2003. A sociocultural approach to young language learners' beliefs about language learning. In P. Kalaja and A.M.F. Barcelos, eds *Beliefs about SLA: New Research Approaches*. Dordrecht: Kluwer, pp. 55–85.

Aljafreeh, A. and Lantolf, J.P., 1994. Negative feedback as regulation and second language learning in the Zone of Proximal Development. *Modern Language Journal*, **78**, pp. 465–83.

Allwright, D., 2005. From teaching points to learning opportunities and beyond. *TESOL Quarterly*, **39** (1), pp. 9–31.

Allwright, D., 2006. Six promising directions in applied linguistics. In S. Gieve and I.K. Miller, eds *Understanding the Language Classroom*. New York: Palgrave, pp. 11–17.

Allwright, R., 1983. Classroom-centered research on language teaching and learning: a brief historical overview. *TESOL Quarterly*, **17** (2), pp. 191–204.

Almeida Filho, J.C.P., ed. 1999. *O Professor de Língua Estrangeira em Formação*. Campinas: Pontes.

Amos Hatch, J. and Wisniewski, R., 1995. Life history and narrative: questions, issues, and exemplary works. In J. Amos Hatch and R. Wisniewski, eds *Life History and Narrative*. London: Falmer Press, pp. 113–36.

Anderson, B., 1983. *Imagined Communities: Reflections on the Origin and Spread of Nationalism*. Rev.ed. London: Verso.

Andersson, S.B., 1995. Social scaling in children's family drawings: a comparative study in three cultures. *Child Language Journal*, **5**, pp. 27–. Available from: http//:sas.epnet.com/Delivery/Print.Save.asp?tb=0&_ug=sid+56D56D90-18B1-4C87-B3 [cited 25 July 2006].

Antón, M., 1999. The discourse of a learner-centered classroom: sociocultural perspectives on teacher-learner interaction in the Zone of Proximal Development. *Modern Language Journal*, **83**, pp. 303–18.

Antón, M. and DiCamilla, F.J., 1999. Socio-cognitive functions of L1 collaborative interaction in the L2 classroom. *Modern Language Journal*, **83**, pp. 233–47.

Arnold, J., ed. 1999. *Affect in Language Learning*. Cambridge: Cambridge University Press.

Aronsson, K. and Andersson, S., 1996. Social scaling in children's drawings of classroom life: a cultural comparative analysis of social scaling in Africa and Sweden. *British Journal of Developmental Psychology*, **14**, pp. 301–14.

Assay, T. and Lambert, M., 1999. The empirical case for the common factors in therapy: quantitative findings. In M. Hubble, B. Duncan and S. Miller, eds *The Heart and Soul of Change: What Works in Therapy*. Washington, DC: American Psychological Association, pp. 23–55. Available from: www.literacy.unisa.edu.au/Papers/JEEPaper6.pdf [cited 20 October 2005].

Atkinson, R., 1998. *The Life Story Interview*. Thousand Oaks, CA: Sage.

Ayano, M., 2006. Japanese students in Britain. In M. Byram and A. Feng, eds *Living and Studying Abroad: Research and Practice*. Clevedon: Multilingual Matters, pp. 11–37.

Bailey, K., 1983. Competitiveness and anxiety in adult second language learning: looking at and through the diary studies. In H. Seliger and M. Long, eds *Classroom-Oriented Research in Second Language Acquisition*. Rowley, MA: Newbury House, pp. 67–103.

Barbara, L. and Ramos, R.C., eds 2003. *Reflexão e Ações no Ensino-Aprendizagem de Línguas*. Campinas: Mercado de Letras.

Barcelos, A.M.F., 1995. A cultura de aprender língua estrangeira (inglês) de alunos de Letras. Unpublished MA thesis. Universidade Estadual de Campinas, Campinas.

Barcelos, A.M.F., 2000. Understanding teachers' and students' language learning beliefs in experience: a Deweyan approach. Unpublished PhD thesis. The University of Alabama, Tuscaloosa, AL, USA.

Barcelos A.M.F., 2001. Metodologia de pesquisa das crenças sobre aprendizagem de línguas: estado da arte. *Revista Brasileira de Lingüística Aplicada*, 1 (1), pp. 71–92.

Barcelos, A.M.F., 2006 (a). Cognição de professores e alunos: tendências recentes na pesquisa de crenças sobre ensino e aprendizagem de línguas. In A.M.F. Barcelos and M. H. Vieira-Abrahão, eds *Crenças e Ensino de Línguas: Foco no Professor, no Aluno e na Formação de Professores*. Campinas: Pontes, pp. 15–41.

Barcelos, A.M.F., 2006 (b). O que dizem as pesquisas sobre cognição de professores de línguas no Brasil? Algumas reflexões. Paper presented at the roundtable on Formação de professores de língua estrangeira. XI SILEL. Uberlândia, Brazil.

Barcelos, A.M.F., 2006 (c). Narrativas, crenças e experiências de aprender inglês. *Linguagem e Ensino*, 9 (2), pp. 145–75.

Barcelos, A.M.F. and Kalaja, P., 2003. Conclusion: exploring possibilities for future research on beliefs about SLA. In P. Kalaja and A. Barcelos eds *Beliefs about SLA: New Research Approaches*. Dordrecht: Kluwer, pp. 231–38.

Bauman, Z., 2004. *Identity: Conversations with Benedetto Vecchi*. Cambridge: Polity Press.

BBC News, 2006. Overseas student numbers double. *BBC News* [internet], 12 September. Available from: http://news.bbc.co.uk/2/hi/uk_news/education/5338024.stm [cited 10 February 2007].

Beattie, M., 2000. Narratives of professional learning: becoming a teacher in learning to teach. *Journal of Education Inquiry*, 1 (2), pp. 1–23.

Bell, J.S., 2002. Narrative inquiry: more than just telling stories. *TESOL Quarterly*, 36 (2), pp. 207–13.

Belz, J., 2002. Second language play as representation of the multicompetent self in foreign language study. *Journal of Language Identity and Education*, 1 (1), pp. 13–39.

Benson, P., 2001. *Teaching and Researching Autonomy in Language Learning*. Harlow: Pearson Education.

Benson, P., 2005 (Auto)biography and learner diversity. In P. Benson and D. Nunan, eds *Learners' Stories: Difference and Diversity in Language Learning*. Cambridge: Cambridge University Press, pp. 4–21.

Benson, P. and Nunan, D., eds 2002. The experience of language learning. Special Issue. *Hong Kong Journal of Applied Linguistics*, 7 (2).

Benson, P. and Nunan, D., eds 2005. *Learners' Stories: Difference and Diversity in Language Learning*. Cambridge: Cambridge University Press.

Benson, P., Chik, A. and Lim, H.Y., 2003. Becoming autonomous in an Asian context: autonomy as a sociocultural process. In D. Palfreyman and R.C. Smith, eds *Learner Autonomy across Cultures: Language Education Perspectives.* Basingstoke: Palgrave Macmillan, pp. 23–40.

Block, D., 1994. A day in the life of a class: teacher/learner perceptions of task purpose in conflict. *System,* 22 (4), pp. 473–86.

Block, D., 1995. Exploring learners worlds: two studies. Unpublished PhD thesis, University of Lancaster.

Block, D., 1996. A window on the classroom: classroom events viewed from different angles. In K. Bailey and D. Nunan, eds *Voices from the Language Classroom.* New York: Cambridge University Press, pp. 168–94.

Block, D., 2000. Learners and their meta-pedagogical awareness. *International Journal of Applied Linguistics,* 10 (1), pp. 97–123.

Block, D., 2002. Destabilized identities and cosmopolitanism across language and cultural borders: two case studies. *Hong Kong Journal of Applied Linguistics,* 7 (2), pp. 1–19.

Block, D., 2003. *The Social Turn in Second Language Acquisition.* Edinburgh: Edinburgh University Press.

Block, D., 2006 (a). *Multilingual Identities in a Global City: London Stories.* London: Palgrave Macmillan.

Block, D., 2006 (b). Identity in applied linguistics: where are we? In T. Omoniyi and G. White, eds *The Sociolinguistics of Identity.* London: Continuum, pp. 34–49.

Block, D., 2007. *Second Language Identities.* London: Continuum.

Blommaert, J., 2005. *Discourse. A Critical Introduction.* Cambridge: Cambridge University Press.

Bohn, H.I., 2003. The educational role and status of English in Brazil. *World Englishes,* 22 (2), pp. 159–72.

Bourdieu, P., 1984. *Distinction.* London: Routledge.

Bourdieu, P., 1985. The forms of social capital. In J.G. Richardson, ed. *Handbook of Theory and Research for the Sociology of Education.* New York: Greenwood, pp. 241–58.

Bourdieu, P., 1991. *Language and Symbolic Power.* Oxford: Polity.

Bourdieu, P., 1998. *Practical Reason.* Stanford, CA: Stanford University Press.

Brazil. 1998. Secretaria de Educação Fundamental. *Parâmetros Curriculares Nacionais 3 e 4 ciclo do Ensino Fundamental.* Brasília: MEC/SEF.

Brazil. 2002. Secretaria de Educação Básica. *Parâmetros Curriculares Nacionais. Ensino Médio.* Brasília: MEC/SEB.

Breen, M., 1986. The social context of language learning – a neglected situation. *Studies in Second Language Acquisition,* 7, pp. 135–58.

Brooks, M., 2005. Drawing as a unique mental development tool for young children: interpersonal and intrapersonal dialogues. *Contemporary Issues in Early Childhood,* 6 (1), pp. 80–91.

Bruner, J., 1986. *Actual Minds, Possible Worlds.* Cambridge, MA: Harvard University Press.

Brutt-Griffler, J., 2002. *World English: A Study of Its Development.* Clevedon: Multilingual Matters.

Budd, R. and Wright, T., 1992. Putting a process syllabus into practice. In D. Nunan, ed. *Collaborative Language Teaching and Learning.* Cambridge: Cambridge University Press. pp. 208–29.

Burkitt, E., Barrett, M. and Davis, A., 2005. Drawings of emotionally characterized figures by children from different educational backgrounds. *The International Journal of Art & Design Education*, **24**, pp. 71–83.

Burnett, C., and Gardner, J., 2006. The one less travelled by ... the experience of Chinese students in a UK university. In M. Byram and A. Feng, eds *Living and Studying Abroad: Research and Practice*. Clevedon: Multilingual Matters, pp. 64–90.

Burns, A., 1999. *Collaborative Action Research for English Language Teachers*. Cambridge: Cambridge University Press.

Canagarajah, S., 2004. Subversive identities, pedagogical safe houses, and critical learning. In B. Norton and K. Toohey, eds *Critical Pedagogies and Language Learning*. Cambridge: Cambridge University Press, pp. 116–221.

Canagarajah, S., 2005. Critical pedagogy in L2 learning and teaching. In E. Hinkel, ed. *Handbook of Research in Second Language and Research*. Mahwah, NJ: Lawrence Erlbaum, pp. 931–49.

Carvalho, V.C.P.S., 2000. A aprendizagem de língua estrangeira sob a ótica de alunos de letras: Crenças e mitos. Unpublished MA thesis. Universidade Federal de Minas Gerais.

Celani, M.A.A., ed. 2002. *Professores e Formadores em Nudança*. Campinas: Mercado de Letras.

Chaiklin, S. and Lave, J., 1996. *Understanding Practice: Perspectives on Activity and Context*. Cambridge: Cambridge University Press.

Cherney, I.D., Seiwert, C.S., Dickey, T.M. and Flichtbell, J.D., 2006. Children's drawings: a mirror to their minds. *Educational Psychology*, **26**, pp. 127–42.

Clandinin, D.J. and Connelly, F.M., 1995. *Teachers' Professional Knowledge Landscapes*. New York: Teachers College Press.

Clandinin, D.J. and Connelly, F.M., 2000. *Narrative Inquiry: Experience and Story in Qualitative Research*. San Francisco, CA: Jossey-Bass.

Coates, J., 2005. Masculinity, collaborative narration and the heterosexual couple. In J. Thornborrow and J. Coates, eds *The Sociolinguistics of Narrative*. Amsterdam: John Benjamins, pp. 89–106.

Coelho, H.S.H., 2005. 'É possível aprender inglês em escolas públicas?' Crenças de professores e alunos sobre o ensino de inglês em escolas públicas. Unpublished MA thesis. Universidade Federal de Minas Gerais, Belo Horizonte.

Cole, A.L. and Knowles, J.G., 2001. *Lives in Context: The Art of Life History Research*. Walnut Creek, CA: Altamira.

Conceição, M.P., 2004. Vocabulário e consulta ao dicionário: analisando as relações entre experiências, crenças e ações na aprendizagem de LE. Unpublished PhD thesis. Universidade Federal de Minas Gerais, Belo Horizonte.

Conle, C., 1993. Learning culture and embracing contraries: narrative inquiry through stories of acculturation. Unpublished PhD thesis. University of Toronto.

Conle, C., 1999. Why narrative? Which narrative? Our struggle with time and place in teacher education. *Curriculum Inquiry*, **29** (1), pp. 7–33.

Conle, C., 2000. Thesis as narrative or 'What is the inquiry in narrative inquiry?'. *Curriculum Inquiry*, **30** (2), pp. 189–214.

Conle, C., ed. 2006. *Teachers' Stories, Teachers' Lives*. New York: Nova Science Publishers.

Connelly, F.M. and Clandinin, D.J., 1990. Stories of experience and narrative inquiry. *Educational Researcher*, **19** (5), pp. 2–14.

Cook, V., 1999. Going beyond the native speaker in language teaching. *TESOL Quarterly*, 33 (2), pp. 185–209.
Cotterall, S., 1995. Readiness for autonomy: investigating learner beliefs. *System*, 23 (2), pp. 195–205.
Cotterall, S., 2005. 'It's just rules ... that's all it is at this stage'. In P. Benson and D. Nunan, eds *Learners' Stories: Difference and Diversity in Language Learning*. Cambridge: Cambridge University Press, pp. 101–12.
Cotterall, S., 2006. Language advising: a problem solution approach. *Leaa Lenguas en Aprendizaje Autodirigido. Revista Electrónica de la Mediateca del CELE-UNAM*. [Online], 1 (1). Available from: http://cad.cele.unam.mx/leaa/ [cited 9 January 2007].
Cotterall, S. and Crabbe, D., (2008). Learners talking: from problem to solution. In T. Lamb and H. Reinders, eds *Learner and Teacher Autonomy: Concepts, Realities and Responses*. Amsterdam: John Benjamins, pp. 125–40.
Coughlan, P. and Duff, P.A., 1994. Same task, different activities: analysis of SLA tasks from an activity theory perspective. In J.P. Lantolf and G. Appel, eds *Vygotskian Approaches to Second Language Research*. Norwood, NJ: Ablex, pp. 173–93.
Cowie, N., 2004. The emotional lives of experienced EFL teachers. In M. Swanson and K. Hill, eds *Keeping Current in Language Education: Proceedings of the JALT 2003 International Conference on Language Teaching and Learning, 21–24 November 2003*. Tokyo: JALT.
Cox, M.W., Koyasu, M., Hiranuma, H. and Perara, J., 2001. Children's human figure drawings in the UK and Japan: the effects of age, sex and culture. *British Journal of Developmental Psychology*, 19, pp. 275–92.
Craig, C.J., 2007. Narrative inquiries of geographically close schools: stories given, lived, and told. *Teachers College Record*, 109 (1), pp. 160–91.
Creswell, J.W., 1998. *Qualitative Inquiry and Research Design: Choosing Among Five Traditions*. Thousand Oaks, CA: Sage.
Cunha, Nara B., 2005. Experiências de aprendizagem: um estudo de caso sobre as experiências de estudo fora da sala de aula de alunos de Letras/Inglês em uma instituição particular de ensino superior. Unpublished MA thesis. Universidade Federal de Minas Gerais. Programa de Pós-Graduação em Estudos Lingüísticos.
Day, C., 1999. *Developing Teachers: The Challenges of Lifelong Learning*. London: Falmer Press.
De Fina, A., 2003. *Identity in Narrative: A Study of Immigrant Discourse*. Amsterdam: John Benjamins.
Deci, E. and Ryan, R., 2002. *Handbook of Self-Determination Research*. Rochester, NY: University of Rochester Press.
Denzin, N., 2005. Indians in the park. *Qualitative Research*, 5 (1), pp. 9–33.
Dewey, J., 1933. *How We Think*. Chicago: Henry Regnery.
Dewey, J., 1938. *Experience and Education*. New York: MacMillan.
Donato, R., 2000. Sociocultural contributions to understanding the foreign and second language classroom. In J. Lantolf, ed. *Sociocultural Theory and Second Language Learning*. Oxford: Oxford University Press, pp. 27–50.
Dörnyei, Z. and Murphey, T., 2003. *Group Dynamics in the Language Classroom*. Cambridge: Cambridge University Press.

Dufva, H., 2003. Beliefs in dialogue: a Bakhtinian view. In P. Kalaja and A.M.F. Barcelos, eds *Beliefs about SLA: New Research Approaches*. Dordrecht: Kluwer, pp. 131–51.

Dufva, H. and Alanen, R., 2005. Metalinguistic awareness in dialogue: Bakhtinian considerations. In J. Kelly-Hall, G. Vitanova and L. Marchenkova, eds *Dialogue with Bakhtin on Second and Foreign Language Learning: New Perspectives*. Mahwah, NJ: Lawrence Erlbaum, pp. 99–118.

Dufva, H., Kalaja, P. and Alanen, R., 2007. Beliefs about language, language learning and teaching: from novice to expert. In A. Koskensalo, J. Smeds, P. Kaikkonen and V. Kohonen, eds *Foreign Languages and Multicultural Perspectives in the EuropeanContext, Fremdsprachen und multikulturelle Perspectives im europäischen Kontext*. Berlin: LIT, pp. 129–38.

Eckert. P. and McConnell-Ginet, S., 1992. Think practically and act locally: language and gender as community-based practice. *Annual Review of Anthropology*, 21, pp. 461–90.

Eiken. n.d. Number of examinees by students. [Internet]. Available from: http://www.eiken.or.jp/advice/situation/student_2005.html [cited 15 January 2007].

Elbaz-Luwisch, F., 2002. Writing as inquiry: storying the teaching self in writing workshops. *Curriculum Inquiry*, 32 (4), pp. 403–28.

Eldridge, M., 1998. *Transforming Experience: John Dewey's Cultural Instrumentalism*. Nashville, TN: Vanderbilt University Press.

Ellis, R., 1994. The *Study of Second Language Acquisition*. Oxford: Oxford University Press.

Ellis, R., 2005. *Instructed Second Language Acquisition: A Literature Review*. Ministry of Education: New Zealand.

Eraut, M., 2000. Non-formal learning, implicit learning and tacit knowledge in professional work. In F. Coffield, ed. *The Necessity of Informal Learning*. Bristol: The Policy Press, pp. 12–32.

Escandon, A., 2004. Education/learning resistance in the foreign language classroom: a case study. *AIS St Helens Centre for Research in International Education, Research Paper Series, Working Paper No. 5*. [online]. Available from: http://www.crie.org.nz/research_ paper/Arturo_WP5.pdf [cited 20 September 2005].

ETS. 2005. TOEFL Test and Score Data Summary: 2004–2005 Test Year Data. [Internet] Available from: http://www.ets.org/portal/site/ets/menuitem.c988ba0e5dd572bada20bc47c3921509/?vgnextoid=7a21a73a360f6010VgnVCM10000022f95190RCRD&vgnextchannel=d3f4be3a864f4010VgnVCM10000022f95190RCRD [cited 15 January 2007].

Falout, J., and Falout, M., 2005. The other side of motivation: learner demotivation. In K. Bradford-Watts, C. Ikeguchi, and M. Swanson, eds *JALT2004 Conference Proceedings*. Tokyo: JALT, pp. 280–9.

Freeman, D. and Johnson, K., 1998. Reconceptualizing the knowledge-base of language teacher education. *TESOL Quarterly*, 32 (3), pp. 397–417.

Freeman, D. and Richards, J., eds 1996. *Teacher Learning in Language Teaching*. New York: Cambridge University Press.

Freire, P., 1970/2000. *Pedagogy of the Oppressed*. New York: Herder and Herder.

Galasiński, D. and Galasińska, A., 2005. Untold stories and the construction of identity in narratives of ethnic conflict on the Polish-German border. *Multilingua*, 24, pp. 101–20.

Garcez, P., 2003. Proficiência lingüística ou autoconhecimento: o modelo dos cursos livres e a educação em língua estrangeira na escola regular. Conference at XVII ENPULI, Florianópolis, SC, Brazil.
Gee, J.P., 2004. *Situated Language and Learning*. New York: Routledge.
Geertz, C., 1973. The *Interpretation of Cultures*. New York: Basic Books.
Gerard, A. and Goldstein, B., 2005. *Going Visual: Using Images to Enhance Productivity, Decision-Making and Profits*. Hoboken, NJ: John Wiley & Sons.
Giddens, A., 1991. *Modernity and Self-Identity: Self and Society in the Late Modern Age*. Cambridge: Polity.
Gilstrap, D.L., 2005. Strange attractors and human interaction: leading complex organizations through the use of metaphors. *Complicity*, 2 (1), 55–69. Available from: http://www.complexityandeducation.ualberta.ca/COMPLICITY2/Complicity2.htm [cited 26 December 2006].
Gimenez, T., ed. 2002. *Trajetórias na Formação de Professores de Línguas*. Londrina: Editora UEL.
Glaser, B. and Strauss, A., 1967. *The Discovery of Grounded Theory*. Chicago: Aldine.
Goldstein, T., 1996. *Two Languages at Work: Bilingual Life on the Production Floor*. New York: Mouton de Gruyter.
Gorsuch, G.J., 1998. Yakudoku EFL instruction in two Japanese high school classrooms: an exploratory study. *JALT Journal*, 20 (1), pp. 6–32.
Gorter, D. ed. 2006. *Linguistic Landscape: A New Approach to Multilingualism*. Clevedon: Multilingual Matters.
Grigoletto, M., 2003. Um dizer entre fronteiras: o discurso de professores e futuros professores sobre a língua inglesa. *Trabalhos em Lingüística Aplicada*, 41, pp. 39–50.
Gudmundsdottir, S., 1995. The narrative nature of pedagogical content knowledge. In H. McEwan, H.and K. Egan, eds *Narrative in Teaching, Learning and Research*. New York: Teachers College, pp. 24–38.
Hamilton, M., 2000. Expanding the new literacy studies: using photographs to explore literacy as social practice. In D. Barton, M. Hamilton and R. Ivanič, eds *Situated Literacies: Reading and Writing in Context*. London: Routledge, pp. 16–34.
Haneda, M., 1997. Second language learning in a 'community of practice': a case study of adult Japanese learners. *The Canadian Modern Language Review*, 54 (1), pp. 11–27.
Haneda, M., 2006. Classrooms as communities of practice: a reevaluation. *TESOL Quarterly*, 40 (1), pp. 807–17.
Hargreaves, A., 2000. Mixed emotions: teachers' perceptions of their interactions with students. *Teaching and Teacher Education*, 16 (8), pp. 811–26.
Harris, D.B., 1963. *Children's Drawings as Measures of Intellectual Maturity*. New York: Harcourt, Brace and World.
Harris, J., 2005. What do free-hand and computer-facilitated drawings tell teachers about the children who drew them? Available from: http://www.iste.org./inhouse/publications/jrte/28/5/harris/artcile/textonly.cfm [cited 15 January 2007].
Harrison, B., 2002. Photographic visions and narrative inquiry. *Narrative Inquiry*, 12 (1), pp. 87–111.

Hatori, R., 2005. A policy on language education in Japan beyond nationalism and linguicism. *Second Language Studies*, 23 (2), pp. 45–69.
Hawkins, M., 2005. Becoming a student: identity work and academic literacies in early schooling. *TESOL Quarterly*, 39 (1) pp. 59–82.
Heath, S.B., 1983. *Ways with Words: Language, Life and Work in Communities and Classrooms*. Cambridge: Cambridge University Press.
Hegel, G.W., 1991. *O sistema da vida ética*. Lisboa: Edições, 70.
Heikkinen, A., 1999. A discourse analysis of success and failure accounts in learning English as a foreign language. Unpublished MA thesis. University of Jyväskylä, Department of English.
Heikkinen, A. and Kalaja, P., 2001. ' "Imin kieltä itseeni kuin pesusieni": selityksiä vieraan kielen oppijoiden menestymiselle ja epäonnistumiselle'. In M. Charles and P. Hiidenmaa, eds *Tietotyön yhteiskunta – kielen valtakunta* [AFinLA Yearbook 59]. Jyväskylä: AFinLA, pp. 197–223.
Hochschild, A., 1983. *The Managed Heart: The Commercialization of Human Feeling*. Berkeley, CA: University of California Press.
Hodge, R. and Jones, K., 2000. Photography in collaborative research on multilingual literacy practices: images and understanding of researcher and researched. In M. Martin-Jones and K. Jones, eds *Multilingual Literacies*. Amsterdam: John Benjamins, pp. 299–318.
Holliday, A., 1994. *Appropriate Methodology and Social Context*. Cambridge: Cambridge University Press.
Holliday, A., 2002. Distinguishing the voice of researchers and the people they research in writing qualitative research. In K.S. Miller and P. Thompson, eds *Unity and Diversity in Language Use* [BAAL Studies in Applied Linguistics 17]. London: BAAL and Continuum, pp. 125–37.
Holliday, A., 2005. *The Struggle to Teach English as an International Language*. New York: Oxford University Press.
Hooker, C., Nakamura, J. and Csikszentmihalyi, M., 2003. The group as mentor: social capital and the systems model of creativity. In P. Paulus and B. Nijstad, eds *Group Creativity: Innovation through Collaboration*. Oxford: Oxford University Press, pp. 225–44.
Horwitz, E.K., 1985. Using student beliefs about language learning and teaching in the foreign language methods course. *Foreign Language Annals*, 18 (4), pp. 333–40.
Hubble, M., Duncan, B. and Miller, S., eds 1999. *The Heart and Soul of Change: What Works in Therapy*. Washington, DC: American Psychological Association.
Hunt, D., 1987. *Beginning with Ourselves*. Cambridge, MA: Borderline Books.
Iddings, A.C.D, Haught, J. and Devlin, R., 2005. Multi-modal representations of self and meaning in English-dominant classroom. In J. Kelly-Hall, G. Vitanova and L. Marchenkova, eds *Dialogue with Bakhtin on Second and Foreign Language Learning: New Perspectives*. Mahwah, NJ: Lawrence Erlbaum, pp. 33–53.
Isomöttönen, A., 2003. A discursive study of hard-of-hearing learners' explanations for failure and success in learning English as a foreign language. Unpublished MA thesis. University of Jyväskylä, Department of Languages.
Ivanič, R., 2004. Discourses of writing and learning to write. *Language and Education*, 18, pp. 220–6.
Jaatinen, R., 2003. *Vieras kieli oman tarinan kieleksi: Autobiografinen refleksiivinen lähestymistapa vieraan kielen oppimisessa ja opettamisessa*. Tampere: Tampere University Press.

Jackson, J., 2006. Ethnographic pedagogy and evaluation in short-term study abroad. In M. Byram and A. Feng, eds *Living and Studying Abroad: Research and Practice*. Clevedon: Multilingual Matters, pp. 134–56.

Janesick, V., 2000. The Choreography of qualitative research design: Minuets, improvisations, and crystallization. In N. Denzin and Y. Lincoln, eds *Handbook of Qualitative Research*. 2nd edn. Thousand Oaks, CA: Sage, pp. 379–99.

Jenkins, J., 2006. Points of view and blind spots: ELF and SLA. *International Journal of Applied Linguistics*, 16, pp. 137–62.

Jenkins, J., 2007. *English as a Lingua Franca: Attitude and Identity*. Oxford: Oxford University Press.

Johnson, K. and Freeman, D., 2001. Teacher learning in second language teacher education: a socially-situated perspective. *Revista Brasileira de Lingüística Aplicada*, 1 (1), pp. 53–69.

Johnson, K.E. and Golombek, P.R., eds 2002. *Teachers' Narrative Inquiry as Professional Development*. Cambridge: Cambridge University Press.

Johnston, P., 2004. *Choice Words: How Our Language Affects Children's Learning*. Portland, ME: Stenhouse Publishers.

Jolley, R.P., Fenn, K. and Jones, L., 2004. The development of children's expressive drawing. *British Journal of Developmental Psychology*, 22, pp. 545–67.

Kalaja, P., 2004. 'So maybe Freddie (Mercury) and his bandmates really are to blame': explaining success (or failure) in learning EFL. In K. Mäkinen, P. Kaikkonen and V. Kohonen, eds *Future Perspectives in Foreign Language Education*. Oulu: Oulu University Press, pp. 123–32.

Kalaja, P. and Barcelos, A.M.F., eds 2003. *Beliefs about SLA: New Research Approaches*. Dordrecht: Kluwer.

Kalaja, P. and Dufva, H., 1997.'Kohtalona koulu': englanninopettajan ammattiurasta ja identiteetistä. In A. Mauranen and T. Puurtinen, eds *Translation – Acquisition – Use* [AFinLA Yearbook 55]. Jyväskylä: AFinLA, pp. 203–18.

Kalaja, P. and Dufva, H., 2005. *Kielten matkassa: Opi oppimaan vieraita kieliä*. Helsinki: Finn Lectura.

Kalaja, P., Dufva, H. and Nordman, L., 1998. Puhutaan kielillä – kielet ja kielivalinnat opettajien elämäkerroissa. In M.-R. Luukka, S. Salla and H. Dufva, eds *Puolin ja toisin: Suomalais-virolaista kielentutkimusta* [AFinLA Yearbook 56]. Jyväskylä: AFinLA, pp. 131–46.

Kanno, Y., 2000. Bilingualism and identity: the stories of Japanese returnees. *International Journal of Bilingual Education and Bilingualism*, 31, pp. 1–18.

Kanno, Y. and Norton, B., 2003. Imagined communities and educational possibilities: introduction. *Journal of Language, Identity, and Education*, 2 (4), pp. 241–9.

Kelly-Hall, J., Vitanova, G. and Marchenkova, L., eds 2005. *Dialogue with Bakhtin on Second and Foreign Language Learning: New Perspectives*. Mahvah, NJ: Lawrence Erlbaum.

Kendrick, M. and McKay, R., 2004. Drawings as an alternative way of understanding young children's constructions of literacy. *Journal of Early Childhood Literacy*, 4 (1), pp. 109–28.

Kouritzin, S., 2000 (a). Bringing life to research: life history research in ESL. *TESL Canada Journal*, 17 (2), pp. 1–35.

Kouritzin, S., 2000 (b). Immigration mothers redefine access to ESL classes: contradiction and ambivalence. *Journal of Multilingual and Multicultural Development*, 21 (1), pp. 14–9.

Kozulin, A., 1998. *Psychological Tools: A Sociocultural Approach to Education.* Cambridge, MA: Harvard University Press.
Kramsch, C. and Lam, W.S.E., 1999. Textual identities: the importance of being non-native. In G. Braine, ed. *Non-native Educators in English Language Teaching.* Mahwah, NJ: Lawrence Erlbaum, pp. 57–75.
Kress, G. and van Leeuwen, T., 1996. *Reading Images: The Grammar of Visual Design.* London: Routledge.
Kress, G., Jewitt, C., Ogborn, J. and Tsatsarelis, C., 2001. *Multimodal Teaching and Learning.* London: Continuum.
Kyratzis, A. and Greene, J., 1997. Jointly constructed narratives in classrooms: co-construction of friendship and community through language. *Teaching and Teacher Education,* 13 (1), pp. 17–37.
La Voy, S.K., Pedersen, W.C., Reitz, J.M., Brauch. A.A., Luxenberg, T.M. and Nofsinger, C.C., 2001. Children's drawings: a cross-cultural analysis from Japan and the United States. *School Psychology International,* 22, pp. 53–63.
Labov, W., 1972. *Sociolinguistic Patterns.* Philadelphia, PA: University of Pennsylvania.
Lakoff, G. and Johnson, M., 1980. *Metaphors We Live by.* Chicago, IL: The University of Chicago Press.
Lantolf, J.P., ed. 2000. *Sociocultural Theory and Second Language Learning.* Oxford: Oxford University Press.
Lantolf, J. P. and Appel, G., eds 1994. *Vygotskyan Approaches to Second Language Acquisition.* Norwood, NJ: Ablex.
Lantolf, J. and Genung, P., 2003. 'I'd rather switch than fight:' an activity theoretic study of power, success, and failure in a foreign language classroom. In C. Kramsch, ed. *Language Acquisition and Language Socialization.* London: Continuum, pp. 175–96.
Lantolf, J. and Pavlenko, A., 2001. (S)econd (l)anguage (a)ctivity theory: understanding second language learners as people. In M. Breen, ed. *Learner Contributions to Language Learning: New Directions in Research.* Harlow: Pearson Education, pp. 141–58.
Lantolf, J.P. and Thorne, S.L., 2006. *Sociocultural Theory and the Genesis of Second Language Development.* Oxford: Oxford University Press.
Larsen-Freeman, D., 1997. Chaos/complexity science and second language acquisition. *Applied Linguistics,* 18, pp. 141–65.
Larsen-Freeman, D., 2000. Second language acquisition and applied linguistics. *Annual Review of Applied Linguistics,* 20, pp. 165–81.
Lasky, S., 2000. The cultural and emotional politics of parent-teacher interaction. *Teaching and Teacher Education,* 16 (8), pp. 843–60.
Lather, P., 1986 (a). Issues of validity in openly ideological research: between a rock and a soft place. *Interchange,* 17 (4), pp. 63–84.
Lather, P., 1986 (b). Research as praxis. *Harvard Educational Review,* 53 (3), pp. 257–77.
Lave, J. and Wenger, E., 1991. *Situated Learning: Legitimate Peripheral Participation.* Cambridge: Cambridge University Press.
Lemke, J., 2001. Discursive technologies and the social organization of meaning. *Folia Linguistica,* 35 (1–2) [Special issue: 'Critical Discourse Analysis and Cognition', R. Wodak, issue editor], pp. 79–96.
Leontiev, A.N., 1978. *Activity, Consciousness, and Personality.* Englewood Cliffs, NJ: Prentice-Hall.

Leontiev, A.N., 1981. *Problems of the Development of the Mind*. Moscow: Progress.
Leppänen, S. and Kalaja, P., 1997. Vieraan kielen oppijoiden elämäkerrat – tarinoita sankarioppijan matkan varrelta. *FINLANCE*, 17, pp. 33–56.
Leppänen, S. and Kalaja, P., 2002. Autobiographies as constructions of EFL learner identities and experiences. In E. Kärkkäinen, J. Haines and T. Lauttamus, eds *Studia Linguistica et Litteraria Septentrionalia: Studies Presented to Heikki Nyyssönen*. Oulu: University of Oulu, pp. 189–203.
Lewin, R., 1992. *Complexity: Life at the Edge of Chaos*. New York: Macmillan.
Li, D.C.S., 2002. Pragmatic dissonance: the ecstasy and agony of speaking *like* a native speaker of English. In D.C.S. Li, ed. *Discourses in Search of Members: In Honor of Ron Scollon*. Lanham, MD: University Press of America, pp. 559–93.
Liberali, F.C., 2004. A constituição da identidade do professor de inglês na avaliação de sua aula. *Revista Brasileira de Lingüística Aplicada*, 4 (2), pp. 45–56.
Lieblich, A., Tuval-Mashiach, R. and Zilber, T., 1998. *Narrative Research: Reading, Analysis and Interpretation*. Thousand Oaks, CA: Sage.
Lim, H-Y., 2002. The interaction of motivation, perception and environment: one EFL learner's experience. *Hong Kong Journal of Applied Linguistics*, 7 (2), pp. 91–106.
Lima, S.S., 2005. Crenças de uma professora e alunos de quinta série e suas influências no processo de ensino e aprendizagem de inglês em escola pública. Unpublished MA Thesis. UNESP, São José de Rio Preto.
Lincoln, Y. and Guba, E., 1985. *Naturalistic Inquiry*. Newbury Park, CA: Sage.
Linell, P., 2005. *The Written Language Bias in Linguistics: Its Nature, Origins and Transformations*. London: Routledge.
Maberly, P., 2004. Personal communication.
Magalhães, M.C.C., ed. 2004. *A Formação do Professor como um Profissional Crítico*. Campinas: Mercado de Letras.
Malcolm, D., 2005. An Arabic-speaking English learner's path to autonomy through reading. In P. Benson and D. Nunan, eds *Learners' Stories: Difference and Diversity in Language Learning*. Cambridge: Cambridge University Press, pp. 69–82.
Marr, T., 2005. Language and the capital: a case study of English 'language shock' among Chinese students in London. *Language Awareness*, 14 (4), pp. 239–53.
Martin, A., 2004. The 'katakana effect' and teaching English in Japan. *English Today*, 20 (1), pp. 50–5.
Martin, K.J., 2000. 'Oh, I have a story': narrative as a teacher's classroom model. *Teaching and Teacher Education*, 16 (3), pp. 349–63.
Maturana, H.R., 2001. *A Árvore do Conhecimento: As Bases Biológicas da Compreensão Humana*. São Paulo: Palas Athena.
McGroarty, M., 1998. Constructive and constructivist challenges for applied linguistics. *Language Learning*, 48 (4), pp. 591–622.
McKay, S. and Wong, S-L., 1996. Multiple discourses, multiple identities: investment and agency in second-language learning among Chinese adolescent immigrant students. *Harvard Educational Review*, 66 (3), pp. 577–608.
McVeigh, B., 2002. *Japanese Higher Education as Myth*. Armonk, NY: M.E. Sharpe.
Measor, L. and Sikes, P., 1992. Visiting lives: ethics and methodology in life history. In I. Goodson, ed. *Studying Teachers' Lives*. New York: Routledge, pp. 209–33.

Meinhof, U. and Galasiński, D., 2000. Photograhpy, memory, and the construction of identities on the former East-West German border. *Discourse Studies*, 2 (3), pp. 323–53.

Mello, H. and Dutra, D., 2004. A construção conceptual do processo de interação na sala de aula de língua estrangeira. *The ESPecialist*, **25** (special issue), pp. 59–80.

Menezes, V. n.d. AMFALE on-going project for the international collection of language learning histories. Available from: http://www.veramenezes.com/amfale.htm.

MEXT (Ministry of Education, Sports, Science and Technology; 2005. School Education. *Japan's Education at a Glance 2005*. Available from: http://www.mext.go.jp/english/statistics/0501019.htm [cited August 14 2007].

Miccoli, L., 1997. Learning English as a foreign language in Brazil: a joint investigation of learners' experiences in a university classroom or going to the depths of learners' classroom experiences. Unpublished PhD thesis. University of Toronto. Graduate Department of Education.

Miccoli, L., 2000. A deeper view of EFL learning: students' classroom experiences. *Claritas*, 6 (3–4), pp. 185–204.

Miccoli, L., 2001. Reflexão crítica no processo de aprendizagem: o ponto de vista do aluno sobre experiências de aprendizagem de língua inglesa. In E.A. de M. Mendes and. P.M. Oliveira. e Benn-Ibler, eds *O Novo Milênio: Interfaces V. Lingüísticas e Literárias*. Belo Horizonte: FALE-UFMG, pp. 123–40.

Miccoli, L., 2003. Individual classroom experiences: a socio-cultural comparison for understanding EFL classroom learning. *Ilha do Desterro*, **41** (1), pp. 61–91.

Miccoli, L., 2004. Collective and individual classroom experiences: a deeper view of EFL learning in a Brazilian university. *Revista Virtual da Linguagem – ReVel*. 2 (2). Available from: http://www.revelhp.cjb.net/ [cited 17 May 2007].

Miccoli, L., 2006. Tapando buracos em um projeto de formação continuada à distância para professores de LE: avanços apesar da dura realidade. *Linguagem e Ensino*, **9** (1), pp. 129–58.

Japanese Ministry of Economy, Trade and Industry, 2005. Survey of selected service industries. [Internet] Available from: http://www.meti.go.jp/statistics/index.html [cited 15 January 2007].

Mohan, B. and Smith, S.M., 1992. Context and cooperation in academic texts. In D. Nunan, ed. *Collaborative Language Teaching*. Cambridge: Cambridge University Press, pp. 81–99.

Moraes, L.M., 2002. Língua estrangeira moderna. In Brasil, *Parâmetros Curriculares Nacionais. Ensino Médio*. Brasília: MEC/SEB, pp. 93–138.

Morita, N., 2004, Negotiating participation and identity in second language academic communities. *TESOL Quarterly*, **38** (4), pp. 573–603.

Murphey, T., ed., 1997 (a). *Forty Language Hungry Students' Language Learning Histories*. Nagoya: South Mountain Press.

Murphey, T., ed., 1997 (b). *Language Learning Histories*. Nagoya: South Mountain Press.

Murphey, T., 1998 (a). Friends and classroom identity formation. *IATEFL Issues*, **145**, pp. 15–6.

Murphey, T., ed. 1998 (b). *Language Learning Histories II*. Nagoya: South Mountain Press.

Murphey, T., 1999. Publishing students' language learning histories: for them, their peers, and their teachers. *Between the Keys* (the Newsletter of the JALT Material Writers SIG) [online], 7 (2), pp. 8–14. Available from: http://www2.dokkyo.ac.jp/%7Eesemi029/pages/LanguageLearningHistories.htm [cited 26 June 2004].

Murphey, T., 2002. From the horse's mouth: advice from students to teachers. *Learning Learning* (JALT Learner Development SIG Newsletter), 9 (1), pp. 2–10.

Murphey, T., 2004. Participation, dis-identification, and Japanese university entrance exams. *TESOL Quarterly*, 38 (4), pp. 700–10.

Murphey, T., 2006. Learning ecologies of linguistic contagion. *Languaging*, 7. Available from: http://www.geocities.com/languaging/2006/L7.html [cited July 31 2007].

Murphey, T., 2007. Learning ecologies of linguistic contagion. Lecture delivered at the International Conference of the Brazilian Association of English University Teachers. Belo Horizonte, Brazil, 3–6 July 2007.

Murphey, T. and Arao, H., 2001. Changing reported beliefs through near peer role modeling. *TESL-EJ*, 5 (3), pp. 1–14. Available from: http://tesl-ej.org/ej19/a1.html [cited September 15 2007].

Murphey, T., Chen, J. and Chen, L-C., 2005. Learners' constructions of identities and imagined communities. In P. Benson and D. Nunan, eds *Learners' Stories: Difference and Diversity in Language Learning*. Cambridge: Cambridge University Press, pp. 83–100.

Murphy, J.J., 1999. Common factors of school-based change. In M. Hubble, B. Duncan, and S. Miller, eds *The Heart and Soul of Change: What Works in Therapy*. Washington, DC: American Psychological Association, pp. 361–86.

Murray, G., 1999. Autonomy and language learning in a simulated environment. *System*, 27, pp. 295–308.

Murray, G., (2008). Pop culture and language learning: learners' stories informing EFL. *Innovation in Language Learning and Teaching*, 2, pp. 1–16.

Murray, G. and Cotterall, S., 2006. *Independent Learning: What's it All About?* Akita: Akita International University.

Neffa, Cláudia. S.A., 2004. A cultura de avaliar de um professor/coordenador de disciplinas de LE: um estudo de caso no ensino médio. Unpublished MA thesis. Universidade Federal de Minas Gerais. Programa de Pós-Graduação em Estudos Lingüísticos.

Nelson, C.P., 2004. The role of networks in learning to write. *Proceedings of the 2004 Complexity Science and Educational Research Conference*, September 30 –October 3, Chaffey's Locks, Ontario, Canada, pp. 91–105. Available from: http://www.complexityandeducation.ualberta.ca/conferences/2004/proceedings.htm [cited 19 January 2007].

Nikula, T., 2000. Kielioppi kiehtovaksi – piirrostöitä käyttäen. In E. Kallio, ed. *Itsensä näköinen yliopisto-opettaja*. Jyväskylä: Institution for Educational Research, pp. 129–40.

Nikula, T. and Pitkänen-Huhta, A., 2005. The role of English in the everyday lives of Finnish teenagers: a multi-method approach. A paper given at BAAL 38th Annual Meeting, Bristol, UK, September 2005.

Norton, B., 2000. *Identity and Language Learning: Gender, Ethnicity and Educational Change*. Harlow: Longman.

Norton, B., 2001. Non-participation, imagined communities and the language classroom. In M. Breen, ed. *Learner Contributions to Language Learning: New Directions in Research*. Harlow: Longman/Pearson Education, pp. 159–71.

Norton, B. and Toohey, K., eds 2004. *Critical Pedagogies and Language Learning*. Cambridge: Cambridge University Press.

Nuñez, R.E., 1995. What brain for god's eye? biological naturalism, ontological objectivism and searle. *Journal of Consciousness Studies*, 2 (2), pp. 149–66.

Ochs, E. and Capp, L., 1996. Narrating the self. *Annual Review of Anthropology*, 25, pp. 19–43.

Ockerman, C., 1997. Facilitating and learning at the edge of chaos: expanding the context of experiential education. *AEE International Conference Proceedings*. Available from: http://eric.ed.gov/ERICDocs/data/ericdocs2/content_storage_01/0000000b/80/23/71/61.pdf. [cited 19 December 2006].

Ohta, A., 2000. Rethinking interaction in SLA: developmentally appropriate assistance in the zone of proximal development and the acquisition of L2 grammar. In J. Lantolf, ed. *Sociocultural Theory and Second Language Learning*. Oxford: Oxford University Press, pp. 51–78.

Oliveira, E. and Mota, I.O., 2003. Ensino de língua inglesa na educação básica: entre a 'qualidade' dos cursos de idiomas de iniciativa privada e o silenciamento das escolas públicas estaduais paulistas. *Trabalhos em Lingüística Aplicada*, 42, pp. 125–34.

Omoniyi, T. and White, G. eds 2006. *The Sociolinguistics of Identity*. London: Continuum.

Oxford, R.L. and Green, J., 1996. Language learning histories: learners and teachers helping each other understand learning styles and strategies. *TESOL Journal*, 5 (1), pp. 20–3.

Paiva, V.L.M.O., 2003. A LDB e a legislação vigente sobre o ensino e a formação de professor de língua inglesa. In C.M.T. Stevens and M.J.C. Cunha, eds *Caminhos e Colheita: Ensino e Pesquisa na Área de Inglês no Brasil*. Brasília: Editora da UnB, pp. 53–84.

Paiva, V.L.M.O., 2005. Autonomia e complexidade: uma análise de narrativas de aprendizagem. In M.M. Freire, M.H.V. Abrahão and A.M.F. Barcelos, eds *Lingüística Aplicada e Contemporaneidade*. Campinas and São Paulo: Pontes and ALAB, pp. 135–53.

Paiva, V.L.M.O., 2006 (a). Memórias de aprendizagem de professores de língua inglesa. *Contexturas*, 9, pp. 63–78.

Paiva, V.L.M.O., 2006 (b). Autonomia e complexidade. *Linguagem e Ensino*, 9 (1), pp. 77–127.

Paiva, V.L.M.O., 2006 (c). Online teacher training and multimedia narratives. *Essential Teacher*, 3 (4), pp. 34–7.

Palfreyman, D. and Smith, R., 2005. *Learner Autonomy across Cultures*. London: Palgrave Macmillan.

Papastergiadis, N., 2000. *The Turbulence of Migration*. Cambridge: Polity.

Patton, M. Q., 1990. *Qualitative Evaluation and Research Methods* (2nd edn) Newbury Park, CA: Sage.

Pavlenko, A., 2001. Language learning memoirs as a gendered genre. *Applied Linguistics*, 22 (2), pp. 213–40.

Pavlenko, A., 2002 (a). Narrative study: whose story is it anyway? *TESOL Quarterly*, 36, pp. 213–18.

Pavlenko, A., 2002 (b). Poststructuralist approaches to the study of social factors in second language learning and use. In V. Cook, ed. *Portraits of the Language User*. New York: Multilingual Matters, pp. 277–302.

Pavlenko, A., 2004. 'The making of an American': negotiation of identities at the turn of the twentieth century. In A. Pavlenko and A. Blackledge, eds *Negotiation of Identities in Multilingual Contexts*. Clevedon: Multilingual Matters, pp. 34–67.

Pavlenko, A., ed. 2006. *Bilingual Minds: Emotional Experience, Expression and Representation*. Clevedon: Multilingual Matters.

Pavlenko, A., 2007. Autobiographic narratives as data in Applied Linguistics. *Applied Linguistics*, **28** (2), pp. 163–88.

Pavlenko, A. and Blackledge, A., eds 2004. *Negotiation of Identities in Multilingual Settings*. Clevedon: Multilingual Matters.

Pavlenko, A. and Lantolf, J.P., 2000. Second language learning as participation and the (re)construction of selves. In J. Lantolf, ed. *Sociocultural Theory and Second Language Learning*. Oxford: Oxford University Press, pp. 155–77.

Pavlenko, A., Blackledge, A., Piller, I. and Teutsch-Dwyer, M., eds 2001. *Multilingualism, Second Language Learning, and Gender*. New York: Mouton de Gruyter.

Pawlikowska-Smith, G., 2000. *Canadian Language Benchmarks 2000: English as a Second Language for Adults*. Ottawa: Centre for Canadian Language Benchmarks.

Pietikäinen, S., 2006. Narrating indigenous identity, negotiating language practices: the case of multilingual Sami community. A paper given at the 16th Sociolinguistic Symposium, Limerick, Ireland, September 2006.

Pitkänen-Huhta, A. and Nikula, T., 2006. English in the everyday practices of Finnish teenagers – Photographs as a methodological tool. A paper given at BAAL/IRAAL Annual Meeting, Cork, Ireland, September 2006.

Platt, E. and Brooks, F., 2002. Task engagement: a turning point in foreign language development. *Language Learning*, **52**, pp. 365–400.

Polkinghorne, D.E., 1995. Narrative configuration in qualitative analysis. *International Journal of Qualitative Studies in Education*, **8** (1), pp. 8–25.

Portes, A., 1998. Social capital: its origins and applications in modern sociology. *Annual Review of Sociology*, **24**, pp. 1–24.

Porto, Cristina., 2003. Percepções de professoras de Letras/Inglês sobre avaliação de aprendizagem: um estudo de caso. Unpublished MA thesis. Universidade Federal de Minas Gerais. Programa de Pós-Graduação em Estudos Lingüísticos.

Prosser, J., ed. 1998. *Image-Based Research*. London: Falmer Press.

Prosser, J. and Schwartz, D., 1998. Photographs within the sociological research process. In J. Prosser, ed. *Image-Based Research*. London: Falmer Press, pp. 115–30.

Radley, A. and Taylor, D., 2003. Remembering ones' stay in hospital: a study in photography, recovery and forgetting. *Health: An Interdisciplinary Journal for the Social Study of Health, Illness and Medicine*, **7** (2), pp. 129–59.

Radley, A., Hodgetts, D. and Cullen, A., 2005. Visualizing homelessness: a study in photography and estrangement. *Journal of Community & Applied Social Psychology*, **15**, pp. 273–95.

Richards, J., 1998. *Beyond Training*. Cambridge: Cambridge University Press.

Richards, J.C. and Lockhart, C., 1994. *Reflective Teaching in Second Language Classroom*. Cambridge: Cambridge University Press.

Ricoeur, P., 1984. *Time and Narrative I*. Chicago, IL: The University of Chicago Press.

Riessman, C., 1993. *Narrative Analysis*. Newbury Park, CA: Sage.

Roebuck, R., 2000. Subjects speak out: how learners position themselves in a psycholinguistic task. In J. Lantolf, ed. *Sociocultural Theory and Second Language Learning*. Oxford: Oxford University Press, pp. 79–95.

Saito, H. and Eisenstein Ebsworth, M., 2004. Seeing English language teaching and learning through the eyes of Japanese EFL and ESL students. *Foreign Language Annals*, 37 (1), pp. 111–24.

Sakui, K., 2002. Swiss cheese syndrome: knowing myself as a learner and teacher. *Hong Kong Journal of Applied Linguistics*, 7 (2), pp. 136–51.

Salo, U., 2005. *Ankarat silkkaa hyvyyttään: Suomalainen opettajuus*. Helsinki: WSOY.

Schmidt, M., 2000. Role theory, emotions and identity in the department leadership of secondary schooling. *Teaching and Teacher Education*, 16 (8), pp. 827–42.

Schmidt, R., 1983. Interaction, acculturation and the acquisition of communicative competence: a case study of an adult. In N. Wolfson and E. Judd, eds *Sociolinguistics and Language Acquisition*. Rowley, MA: Newbury House, pp. 137–74.

Schmidt, R. and Frota, S., 1985. Developing basic conversational ability in a second language: a case study of an adult learner of Portuguese. In R. Day, ed. *Talking to Learn*. Rowley, MA: Newbury House, pp. 237–326.

Shoaib, A. and Dörnyei, Z., 2005. Affect in lifelong learning: exploring L2 motivation as a dynamic process. In P. Benson and D. Nunan, eds *Learners' Stories: Difference and Diversity in Language Learning*. Cambridge: Cambridge University Press, pp. 22–41.

Slimani, A., 1989. The role of topicalisation in classroom language learning. *System*, 17 (2), pp. 223–34.

Snyder, C., Michael, S. and Cheavens, J., 1999 Hope as a psychotherapeutic foundation of common factors, placebos, and expectations. In M. Hubble, B. Duncan, and S. Miller, eds *The Heart and Soul of Change: What Works in Therapy*. Washington, DC: American Psychological Association, pp. 179–200.

So, S. and Dominguez, R., 2005. Emotion processes in second language acquisition. In P. Benson and D. Nunan, eds *Learners' Stories: Difference and Diversity in Language Learning*. Cambridge: Cambridge University Press, pp. 83–100.

Sparkes, A., 1996. *Writing the Social in Qualitative Inquiry*. Exeter University Monograph. Exeter: RSU, Exeter University.

Stake, R.E., 1995. *The Art of Case Study Research*. Thousand Oaks, CA: Sage.

Stanley, L., 1992. *The Auto/biographical I. The Theory and Practice of Feminist Auto/biography*. Manchester: Manchester University Press.

Stanley, L., 1993. On auto/biography in sociology. *Sociology*, 27 (1), pp. 41–52.

Straub, J., Zielke, B. and Werbik, H., 2005. Autonomy, narrative identity, and their critics. In W. Greve, K. Rothermund and D. Wentura, eds *The Adaptive Self: Personal Continuity and Intentional Self–development*. Cambridge, MA: Hogrefer and Huber, pp. 323–50.

Swain, M. and Miccoli, L.S., 1994. Learning in a content-based, collaboratively-structured course: the experience of an adult ESL learner. *TESL Canada Journal*, 12 (1), pp. 15–8.

Swales, S. 1994. From metaphor to metalanguage. *English Teaching Forum*, 32, 8– Available from: http://exchanges.state.gov/forum/vols/vol32/no3/p8.htm [cited 30 March 2007].

Taylor, C., 1994. *Multiculturalism: Examining the Politics of Recognition*. Princeton, NJ: Princeton University Press.

Taylor, M., 1994. 'The pit as pendulum Chaos, models, experiments and attractors in Poe's "A Descent into the Maelstrom"' *Kutjo Gakum Daugaku Ronsyu*. Treatises and Studies by the Faculty of Kinjo Gakuin University: Studies in English Language and Literature 35, pp. 177–209.

Telles, J.A., 2000. Biographical connections: experiences as sources of legitimate knowledge. *International Journal of Qualitative Studies in Education*, 13 (3), pp. 162–251.

Telles, J.A., 2002. A trajetória narrativa. In T. Gimenez, ed. *Trajetórias na Formação do Professor de Línguas*. Londrina: Editora da Universidade Estadual de Londrina, pp. 15–38.

Telles, J.A., 2004. Reflexão e identidade profissional do professor de LE: Que histórias contam os futuros professores? *Revista Brasileira de Lingüística Aplicada*, 4 (2), pp. 57–83.

Teutsch-Dwyer, M., 2001 (Re)constructing masculinity in a new linguistic reality. In A. Pavlenko, A. Blackledge, I. Piller and M. Teutsch-Dwyer, eds *Multingualism, Second Language Learning, and Gender*. Berlin: Mouton de Gruyter, pp. 175–98.

Thiessen, D., 2006. Student knowledge, engagement, and voice in educational reform. *Curriculum Inquiry*, 36 (4), pp. 345–58.

Thornborrow, J. and Coates, J., eds 2005. *The Sociolinguistics of Narrative*. Amsterdam: John Benjamins.

TOEIC. 2005. Report on test takers worldwide 2005. [Internet] Available from: http://www.ets.org/portal/site/ets/menuitem.c988ba0e5dd572bada20bc47c39 21509/?vgnextoid=8d8106e3631df010VgnVCM10000022f95190RCRD&vgnex tchannel=41b7d898c84f4010VgnVCM10000022f95190RCRD [cited 15 January 2007].

Toohey, K., 1996. Learning English as a second language in kindergarten: a community of practice perspective. *The Canadian Modern Languages Review*, 52 (2), pp. 549–76.

Turunen, P., 2003.'Taloni huojuu vielä pahasti': metaphorical expressions used by university students about themselves as learners of English and about their teachers. Unpublished MA thesis. University of Jyväskylä, Department of Languages.

Turunen, P. and Kalaja, P., 2004. Kieltenoppijat ja – opettajat – metaforisesti. In P. Muikku-Werner and H. Stotesbury, eds *Minä ja kielitiede – soveltajan arki* [AFinLA Yearbook 62]. Jyväskylä: AFinLA, pp. 73–88.

Tusting, K., 2003. A review of theories of informal learning. *Working Paper No 2*. Lancaster: Lancaster Literacy Research Centre.

UKCOSA: The Council for International Education. 2007. Higher education statistics. [online]. Available from: http://www.ukcosa.org.uk/pages/hestats.htm [cited 10 February 2007].

van Lier, L., 1988. *The Classroom and the Language Learner*. New York: Longman.

Varto, J., 2005. Koulun syytä etsimässä: tiedon ja taidon erilaiset tehtävät kasvatuksessa. In T. Kiilakoski, T. Tomperi and M. Vuorikoski, eds *Kenen kasvatus?*

Kriittinen pedagogiikka ja toisinkasvatuksen mahdollisuus. Tampere: Vastapaino, pp. 197–217.

Velve, B., Greer, A., Deirdre, L. and Escott-Stum, S., 2002. Chaos theory as a planning tool for community-based educational experiences for health students. *Journal of Allied Health*, 31 (3), pp. 147–152. Available from: http://www.findarticles.com/p/articles/mi_qa4040/is_200210/ai_n9123126 [cited 19 December 2006].

Ventola, E., Charles, C. and Kaltenbacher, M., eds 2004. *Perspectives on Multimodality*. Amsterdam: John Benjamins.

Vieira-Abrahão, M.H., 2002. A importância relativa de fatores contextuais na construção da abordagem de ensinar do professor. *Contexturas*, 6, pp. 59–77.

Vieira-Abrahão, M.H. ed. 2004. *Prática de Ensino de Língua Estrangeira: Experiências e Reflexões*. Campinas: Pontes, ArteLíngua.

Vygotsky, L.S., 1978. *Mind in Society*. Cambridge, MA: Harvard University Press.

Vygotsky, L.S., 1987. *The Collected Works of L.S. Vygotsky. Volume 1. Problems of General Psychology, Including the Volume Thinking and Speech*. Edited by R.W. Rieber and A.S. Carton. Translation by N. Minick. New York: Plenum Press.

Walker, S., 2003. Uma visão geral do ensino de inglês no Brasil. In C.M.T. Stevens and M.J.C. Cunha, eds *Caminhos e Colheita: Ensino e Pesquisa na Área de Inglês no Brasil*. Brasília: Editora da UnB, pp. 35–52.

Wallace, M., 1998. *Action Research for Language Teachers*. Cambridge: Cambridge University Press.

Wenger, E., 1998. *Communities of Practice: Learning, Meaning, and Identity*. Cambridge, MA: Cambridge University Press.

Wenger, E., McDermott, R. and Snyder W.M., 2002. *Cultivating Communities of Pracitice: A Guide to Managing Knowledge*. Boston: Harvard Business School Press.

Willis, P., 1977. *Learning to Labour*. Farnborough: Saxon House.

Winograd, K., 2005. *Good Days and Bad Days: Teaching as a High-wire Act*. Lanham, MD: ScarecrowEducation.

Woods, D., 1996. *Teacher Cognition in Language Teaching*. Cambridge: Cambridge University Press.

Wright, T., 2006. Managing the classroom life. In S. Gieve and I.K. Miller, eds *Understanding the Language Classroom*. New York: Palgrave, pp. 64–87.

Zeichner, K.M., 2003. Educating reflective teachers for learner-centered education: possibilities and contradictions. In T. Gimenez, ed. *Ensinando e Aprendendo Inglês na Universidade: Formação de Professores em Tempos de Mudança*. Londrina: ABRAPUI, 2003, pp. 3–19.

Zeichner, K.M. and Liston, D.P., 1996. *Reflective Teaching: An Introduction*. Mahwah, NJ: Lawrence Erlbaum.

Zembylas, M., 2006. Beyond teacher cognition and teacher beliefs: the value of the ethnography of emotions in teaching. *International Journal of Qualitative Studies in Education*, 18 (4), pp. 465–87.

Index

accent(s)
 British accent, 164
 differences, 160
 English accents, 160, 212
 Manchester accent, 164
 native accent, 162
 unfamiliar accents, 155
acculturation, 155
acquisition metaphor, 3
advising sessions, 119, 120, 122, 125, 127
affinity spaces, 33
agency, 17, 20, 21, 22, 31, 33, 212, 220, 221, 223, 229
 attribution, 18
 emergent agency, 30
 individual agency, 143, 222
 outside school, 224
 student agency, 33
 thinking, 18, 28, 30
ambivalence, 147, 149
AMFALE project, 230
anxiety, 211
Asian backgrounds/cultures, 165
attitudes, 52, 54, 55, 62, 98, 114, 144, 167, 190, 227
attractors
 chaotic attractors, 202
 definition of, 202
 periodic attractors, 206
 strange attractors, 202
attributions, 21
 agency attribution, 18
 discourse of, 19
 theory, 6, 17
autobiographical (elements, events), 86, 88, 92, 95, 98, 231
autobiographies, 52, 83, 84, 85, 86, 87, 88, 89, 201, 226
autonomous learning, 108
autonomy, 38, 44, 46, 57, 62, 84, 86, 100, 105, 107, 110, 203
 degree of, 203
 importance of, 57
 learner autonomy, 32, 87, 106, 107, 110, 127, 212

belief(s), 5, 6, 8, 10, 17, 35, 36, 38, 46, 64, 190, 198, 199, 203, 225, 230
 authentic beliefs, 198
 definition of, 37
 about language, 190
 teachers', 62
belonging, 156, 160
 sense of, 129, 137
bilingual(s), 156, 157, 167
Brazilian education, 64
Brazilian educational laws, 10
Brazilian EFL classrooms, 79
Brazilian EFL teachers, 10, 64, 65, 74, 78
 experiences, 65, 67
Brazilian schools, 47, 75
Brazilian society, 39, 47
Brazilian students, 41, 64, 65, 72
Brazilian TV programs, 210
Brazilians, 10, 36, 73

chaos
 edge of, 203, 220, 229
 theory, 200
classrooms, 142, 144, 151, 152, 153, 228
collaborative action research, 60
collaborative session, 50
communities, 18
 Japanese community, 118
 of learners, 126
 as a motivating force, 128
 of practice, 19, 128, 129, 131, 132, 133, 134, 135, 136, 137, 138, 139, 140, 143, 152, 219, 221, 223, 229
complex systems, 206
 characteristics of, 202, 212, 213

251

complexity, 201
connaissance and *reconnaissance*, 151
contexts, 3, 4, 5, 13, 21, 22, 24, 29, 30, 32, 33, 35, 36, 38, 39, 49, 50, 52, 53, 64, 71, 74, 77, 88, 89, 114, 190, 203, 218, 219, 224, 229
  authentic contexts, 199
  Brazilian contexts, 39, 224, 230
  constraints, 46
  EFL/ESL contexts, 5, 8, 13, 17, 20, 144, 171, 186, 219
  of experience, 66
  factors, 23, 24, 27, 28
  of Finland, 186, 187, 191
  of Japan, 230
  immersion context, 10
  in-school context, 23, 29
  learning contexts, 138, 213, 218, 219, 220, 221
  naturalistic context, 141, 142, 151
  non-English-speaking context, 200
  out-of-school contexts, 23, 29, 171, 223, 224
  of photographs, 172
  school context, 78, 183, 206, 209, 210
  social contexts, 18
  of study, 13
  teaching context, 68, 70, 100
  work context, 211
contextual approach, 53
contextual domain, 67
counselling, 84
  learner-counselling dialogues, 84
counsellor, 89
critical incidents, 158
critical pedagogy, 98, 106, 107

data, 118, 119
  analysis of, 119, 130
  autobiographical data, 127
  coding, 119, 131
  data collection, 130
discourse representation, 49
discrimination, 155, 162, 163, 166
diversity, 4, 5, 68, 203, 208

drawings, 187–97
  analysis of, 188
  drawing books, 193
  drawing other media, 195
  human figure drawings, 187
  interpretation of, 195
  as a means of collecting data, 191
  subset of, 192, 193

education
  educational abuse, 21
  formal education, 175, 179
educational environment
  formal, 179
EFL
  classrooms, 142, 144, 151, 152, 153
  classroom experiences, 149
  contexts, 5
  learners/students, 142, 144, 153
  learning and teaching experiences, 4
  narratives, 4, 141
  teachers, 147
ethnography, 66
  methods, 174
emic, 20
  definition of, 200
  theories, 66
emotionality of teaching, 106
emotions, 4, 88, 99, 100, 106, 110, 224, 225, 230, 231
  emotional demands, 106
  emotional dimension, 230
  emotional dynamics, 66
  emotional experience, 99, 105
  emotional impact, 100, 104, 105
  emotional labour, 106
  emotional response, 105
  emotional state(s), 105, 106
  emotional support, 110
  how to deal with, 110
  intertwining of, 95
emplotment, 85
empowerment, 18, 108, 109, 184
English language
  English language proficiency, 157, 163, 166
  as a lingua franca, 9
English teaching in Brazil, 36

Index

entertainment, 225
Etic
  definition of, 200
expectancy, 18, 19
experience(s), 13, 36, 43, 47, 66, 84, 85, 87, 90, 91, 92, 96, 156, 157, 158, 160, 164, 166, 167, 168, 206, 218, 225
  affective experiences, 73
  of border crossing, 167
  classroom experiences, 65, 66, 67
  concept of, 224
  contextual experiences, 74, 75
  critical experiences, 152, 153, 219, 220
  definition of, 224
  Dewey's concept of, 37
  direct classroom experiences, 68
  direct experiences, 66, 67, 77
  disappointing experience, 165
  of/with discrimination, 163, 165, 167
  emotional experience, 99
  fragments of, 226
  indirect experiences, 66, 67, 74, 76, 77
  inside the classroom, 206, 207, 208
  language learning experiences, 43, 55
  language learning experiences and beliefs, 46
  learning experiences, 201
  of linguistic and cultural transplantation, 157
  lived experiences, 217
  outside the classroom, 206, 209, 211, 212
  overseas experience, 156, 157, 158, 165, 167, 168
  pedagogical, 68, 70
  social experiences, 71, 72
  teachers' experiences, 65, 67, 68, 78, 224
  vicarious, 85
evaluation, 70
experientialism, 200
expertise, 176, 183
  expertise through learning English, 182
  kind of, 182

feeling of inferiority, 43
Finland, 5, 7, 8, 9, 14, 91, 171, 186, 187, 190, 191, 198, 231
Finnish, 9, 180, 181, 182, 190
Finnish society, 175, 176, 184
foreigner(s), 161, 162, 164

globalisation, 5
goals, 118, 119, 120, 121, 122, 123, 127

hopefulness, 18
human behavior
  definition of, 222

identities, 18, 107, 109, 128, 135, 141, 143, 144, 151, 152, 156, 157, 158, 166, 167, 218
  aspect of, 175
  change, 159
  construction of, 171, 172, 173, 221
  definition of, 143
  developing of, 157
  English mediated identities, 144, 152, 153, 154, 219
  ethnic, 166
  language learner identities, 225
  of language users, 222
  notion of, 167
  poststructuralist approach to, 142
  research, 142
  social construction of, 130
  teachers', 84, 220
  textual identity, 149, 152, 154
imagination
  concept of, 129
  as a mode of belonging, 129
imagined communities, 20, 109, 129, 130, 133, 134, 135, 138, 139, 140, 223, 225
  definition of, 129
independent language learning, 114, 115, 126, 127
independent language learning facility, 114
index, 175
indexing, 174, 175, 184
Input-Interaction-Output model, the, 3

interaction and continuity, principles of, 37
interviews, 6, 158, 159, 162, 164
  analysis of, 131
  coding, 131, 158, 159
  data, 168
  life history interview, 130
investment(s), 20, 100, 105, 106, 107, 108, 110
  lack of, 109

Japan, 5, 11, 114, 115, 118, 122, 125
  English language learning in, 114
Japanese, 114, 117, 120, 122, 123
Japanese Ministry of Education, 115
Japanese universities, 98

kaleidoscope, 4, 13, 86, 88, 217, 218, 221, 232

language advisers, 115
language advising sessions, 115, 118
language learning, 126, 128
  formal language learning, 118, 176, 178, 179
  formal learning, 171, 175, 176, 180, 184, 185
  incidental learning, 176, 180, 181
  independent language learning, 114
  informal learning, 171, 172, 175, 176, 177, 178, 184, 185
  language learning histories, 4, 13, 17, 20, 47, 119, 152, 153, 154, 199, 201, 213, 224, 228
  language learning strategies, 116
  learning Japanese as a foreign language, 129
language shock, 155
learners
  Japanese learners, 113, 117, 127
  Spanish learner, 219
learning ecologies, 30, 229
learning environment, 30
life history, 128
life history research, 130

mediational means, 188, 189, 191, 195
memoirs, 201
memory, 90, 92
metaphor, 86

participation metaphor, 3
methodology
  methodological aspects, 226
  methodological issues, 226
motivation, 114, 121, 125, 134, 139
  earlier motivation, 124
  impact of the curriculum on, 113
  lack of, 123
  motivating force, 139
  nature of, 127
multimedia language learning histories, 119, 199, 201, 213
multimedia narratives, 227
music, 224
  role of, 210
myth, 200, 221, 230
  double narrative, 225
  lessons learned from the, 218

narrative(s), 6, 36, 37, 39, 40, 43, 46, 52, 156, 225, 228
narrative analysis of, 4, 5, 6, 7, 8, 14, 158, 167, 227
narrative approach, 156, 157, 167
  autobiographical narrative, 83, 84, 87
narrative contract, 173, 227
narrative databank, 231
  definition of, 227
  EFL narratives, 141
  experiential narrative, 85
narrative form, 230
narrative inquiry, 50, 52, 62, 88, 96, 97, 130, 158, 176, 226
  meta-narrative, 227
  multimodal narratives, 8, 13
  oral narratives, 13
  power of, 223
  research, 35, 37, 47, 50, 51, 52, 90, 126, 127, 200, 217, 218, 225, 227
  self narratives, 13
  threads, 167
  visual narrative(s), 187, 188, 189, 191, 195
  written narratives, 6, 13
narrator
  omniscient narrator, 226
  role of, 226
native speaker(s), 116, 117, 120, 136, 160, 161, 162, 166, 167, 210, 211

naturalistic context, 141, 142, 151
near peer role model, 31
negotiation of difference, 143
non-native speakers, 163

objectivism, 200
ontological security, 142, 149

participants
  peripheral participant(s), 129, 135, 137
  role of, 226, 227
pathways thinking, 18, 223, 229
peripheral participation, 133, 134, 137, 139, 221
photographs, 171–6, 181–4, 222, 227
  advantage of, 227
  taking photographs, 174
pop culture, 139
practice, 76, 77
pre- and in-service education, 49
private courses, 10
private English courses, 36, 41
private language courses, 36
private language teaching institutions, 115
private schools, 10
professional development, 50
public or private schools, 36
public schools, 39, 40, 42, 43, 45, 46, 48

reconceptualisation, 49
reflective practice, 49
reflective research, 51
reflective teaching, 50
regular schools, 10, 36
relationships
  with students, 145
  with teachers, 145
research, 4, 13, 20, 22, 31, 37, 230
  attribution research, 32
  comparative research, 229
  definition of, 217
  future research, 32, 36, 228, 230
  implications for, 228, 229
  on narratives, 4
research projects, 14, 53, 68, 116, 119, 130, 186, 190, 198, 229, 231
  psychotherapy research, 17, 22

research questions, 38, 67, 188
  research context, 4
  research methodology, 86
  ways of doing, 4
resistance, 104, 105, 108, 109, 110, 220
resonance, 85, 225, 226

school English, 64, 65, 67, 78
second language acquisition, 38, 52, 113, 155, 156, 199, 201, 202, 206, 212
  as a complex system, 231
  and identity, 156
second language acquisition process, 213
  research on, 64
second language learner
  as bilinguals, 156
self-access centres, 139
self-esteem, 108, 230
self-observation, 49
self-portrait(s), 186, 188, 191, 196, 197
self-reflexivity, 84
senpais, 137
senpai system, 137
social capital, 18, 19, 20, 21, 30, 31, 32, 144, 148, 222, 231
social class, 143, 144, 147
social cultural approach, 186, 188
social cultural framework, 191
sociocultural idea, 188
sociocultural theory, 18, 128
Spain, 7, 152, 219, 220
Spanish, 113, 144, 145, 154, 219
speaking proficiency, 163
stories of language learning, 176
strategies, 119, 120, 122, 123, 125, 127
student(s)
  Asian students, 129, 163
  Chinese students, 163, 164
  Finnish students, 186
  Hong Kong students, 155, 157, 163, 164, 167, 168
  international students, 155
  Japanese students, 114
  student resistance, 98, 105, 107, 110, 230

subject reality, 228
subjectivism, 200
symbolic capital (economic, cultural, social), 144

teacher(s), 49, 51, 55, 77, 106, 145, 161, 197, 228, 229
  education, 51
  emotion, 98, 99, 110
  development, 49, 51
  images of, 207
  in-service, 49, 55, 59
  pre-service, 49, 53, 55, 58, 59, 61
  role of, 229
teachers' discourse, 54, 56
teachers' frustration, 73
teaching theories, 56
technology, 115
text reality, 228
theory, 76, 77
  theory effectiveness, 54, 59
  and practice, 49
  theory reconceptualisation, 59

visual methods, 173
visual narrative(s), 187, 188, 189, 191, 195
voice
  give voice to, 230
  learners', 83